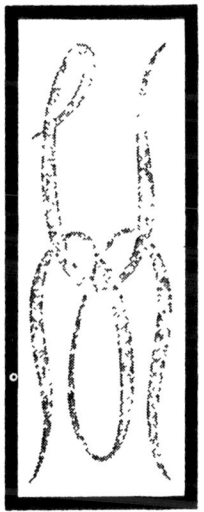

THE FINANCIAL MANAGEMENT OF AGRIBUSINESS FIRMS

FRANK J. SMITH, JR. and KEN COOPER

Books for Business
New York-Hong Kong

The Financial Management of Agribusiness Firms

by
Frank J. Smith
Ken Cooper

ISBN: 0-89499-094-2

Copyright © 2001 by Books for Business

Reprinted from the 1977 edition

Books for Business
New York - Hong Kong
http://www.BusinessBooksInternational.com

All rights reserved, including the right to reproduce this book, or portions thereof, in any form.

In order to make original editions of historical works available to scholars at an economical price, this facsimile of the original edition of 1977 is reproduced from the best available copy and has been digitally enhanced to improve legibility, but the text remains unaltered to retain historical authenticity.

Acknowledgments

The authors wish to express their thanks to Jarvis Cain, Fletcher Dickinson, Gerald Emmer, Arvid Knudtson, Maxey Love, David Volkin, and Robert A. Willson, who served on an advisory committee for this project. Their assistance in helping us formulate various ideas as well as their constructive criticism at various stages is gratefully acknowledged. The authors also wish to express their appreciation to colleagues at the University of Minnesota, Professors Martin K. Christiansen, O. B. Jesness, E. Fred Koller, and Harold Stevenson who provided critical and helpful reviews of this manuscript. The authors, of course, accept the final responsibility for the material published herein.

Thanks are also due Lewis Norwood and Paul O. Mohn of the Federal Extension Service who represented the U.S. Department of Agriculture in developing and coordinating the contract under which this work was done.

Finally, we are immensely grateful to members of our secretarial staff — Mrs. Jane Francen, Mrs. Patricia O'Brien, and Miss Regina Slama for their competent and cheerful assistance in developing various drafts of this manuscript.

CONTENTS

	Page
Chapter 1 Introduction	1
The Firm, Its Objectives and Financial Management	1
The Profit Objective in Focus	3
The Organization of This Text	4
Suggested Readings	6
Chapter 2 The Concept of Sources and Uses of Funds	7
Fund Flows	7
The Balance Sheet Approach to Source and Use Analysis	9
Identifying Changes in Balance Sheet Composition	10
Projecting Financial Needs	13
Identifying Working Capital Position	16
Some Modifications	18
Practicality and Pitfalls	18
A Note on Depreciation as a Source of Funds	19
Suggested Readings	20
Problem Set	21
Chapter 3 Managing Short-Term Funds	23
Elements of Efficient Liquidity	23
Optimizing Working Capital Sectors	28
Accrued Liabilities	28
Trade Accounts Payable	29
Inventory Management	31
Receivables	33
Cash	34
Short-Term Uses from Long-Term Sources	36
Summary	37
Appendix — Analyzing Trade Credit Problems	39
How Much Credit Should There Be in a Firm's Total Sales Package?	39
To Whom Should a Firm Make Credit Terms Available	42
How Does a Firm Establish Collection Procedures?	44
Summary	45
Suggested Readings	45
Problem Set	47

viii   The Financial Management of Agribusiness Firms

Chapter 4   Management of Long-Term Funds — Maximizing Returns 49
   Analyzing Investment Proposals 50
   The Relation of Economic Value and Time 52
      Background and Mechanics 52
      Some Applications 61
      Other Measures 69
   Dealing With the Uncertainty Problem 71
      Estimating Cash Flows 72
      Present-Value Discount Factors 75
      Application to Discounted Rate of Return 75
      How Much Risk? 76
   Ranking Proposals 76
   Two Other Considerations in Capital Usage 78
   Suggested Readings 80
   Problem Set 81

Chapter 5   Managing Long-Term Funds — Minimizing the Cost of Capital 83
   Quality Aspects 84
      Security Features 84
      Summary and Appraisal of Quality Factors 88
   Measuring the Cost of Capital 89
      Fixed-Payment Obligations 89
      Residual Equity 91
         Proprietary Corporations 92
         Cooperative Corporations 97
   Overall Cost of Capital 100
   The Concept of Financial Leverage 101
   Other Sources of Long-Term Funds 105
      Noncash Expenses 105
      Leasing 105
   Suggested Readings 107
   Problem Set 109

Chapter 6   Profit Planning 111
   Benefits from Planning 112
   Profit Analysis 113
      Sales Volume Forecasting 113

Cost Analysis	117
Product Mix Considerations	120
Profit Forecast	122
Break-Even Analysis	128
Cash Budget	137
Pro Forma Balance Sheet	140
Suggested Readings	143
Problem Set	145

Chapter 7 Financial Analysis and Control 147

Ratio Analysis	148
Profitability	149
Liquidity Ratios	155
Solvency Ratios	157
Efficiency Ratios	158
Common Size Statements	160
Summary of Ratio Analysis	161

Appendix — An Example Financial Control System for a Farm Supply Firm 163

Essentials of a Control System	163
Developing Associated Materials	164
Problems of Implementation	165
Instructions for the Bookkeeper	166
Forms and Charts for the Control System	173
Suggested Readings	182
Problem Set	183

Chapter 8 Financial Problems in the Growing Firm . . . 185

Why Grow?	185
Methods and Problems of Growth	188
Financial Problems	190
Emblem Dairy Corporation Case	197
Suggested Readings	204

Additional Suggested Readings 205

Index 207

THE FINANCIAL MANAGEMENT OF
AGRIBUSINESS FIRMS

CHAPTER 1
Introduction

This text examines the financial management function from a general management point of view. It is intended primarily for use by extension educators in their programs to improve financial management skills and capacities of owners, managers, and manager trainees of agricultural marketing and farm supply firms.

The objective of this text is to provide a reasonably detailed outline of basic financial management principles on which extension educators may build programs suitable to the needs of their special clientele. Where possible, the examples employed to illustrate principles are drawn from "real world" experiences. In general, however, the text remains a step away from offering solutions to the financial management problems confronting specific commodity marketing and farm supply firms. It is assumed that extension educators, working in environmental situations with which they are familiar, can make the appropriate adaptations of principles to particular problem situations.

The Firm, Its Objectives, and Financial Management

All firms, whether they be proprietorships, partnerships, or proprietary or cooperative corporations, are organized to achieve certain objectives.[1] Some of these objectives or purposes are common to all firms. To justify its existence, any firm must offer some worthwhile product or service. Moreover, it must fulfill the needs of its owners and employees in terms of generating income and providing a satisfactory outlet for their creativeness. Finally, the firm has certain obligations to the community in which it resides, in much the same sense as individual citizens do. At the very least, if it hopes to survive, it must avoid antisocial activities.

In addition to these general objectives the firm must have others which are quite specific and which are designed to achieve or complement the former. Among these, one would typically find objectives with respect to profitability, company size, the public image of the company

---

[1] Strictly speaking, a cooperative is also a "proprietary" organization. We use the term in this text to distinguish between cooperatives and other types of corporations only because alternative designations are unsatisfactory.
 For an excellent discussion of company objectives, goals, and policies see Leon Garoian and Arnold F. Haseley "The Board of Directors in Agricultural Marketing Firms," Oregon State University, 1964, p. 31–48.

with respect to the quality of products or services it renders, innovation and risk taking, and personnel relations. Others could be listed. It must be emphasized that objectives are not mutually exclusive and, indeed, recognizing their interdependence and insuring their consistency are of prime importance to the successful operation of the firm.

To achieve their objectives, firms typically organize their activities along functional lines — procurement, production, marketing, personnel, and finance. In large companies each of these functions may be supervised by a senior manager. In small companies the general manager may be responsible for all these areas. Since our focus in this text is on financial management, we will not place much emphasis on the other management functions. This lack of emphasis neither reflects on their importance nor is intended to imply that these functions are independent. It would be folly, for example, to undertake a market expansion program without giving due regard to the impact it would have on the location and capacity of production facilities or the availability of funds to carry out such an expansion. Thus, while our major concern here is with finance, we wish to stress at the outset its interdependence with other functions, all of which are oriented to achieving the firm's objectives.

What specifically does financial management contribute to the business team? Traditionally, the finance function has included two responsibilities — raising capital and maintaining control programs. In the past, except in those cases where he was also the general manager, the financial manager was usually not involved directly in the investment process. Typically, the decision to invest was made and then the steps to procure the necessary funds were taken. The early control function was primarily concerned with protecting certain of the firm's assets from loss. Cash control methods were set up to make sure that different individuals handled cash receipts, disbursements, and accounting. Similarly, systems were developed to control inventory, accounts receivable, and fixed assets — particularly those that could be easily removed from the firm's premises.

The two traditional responsibilities are still an important part of the finance function. But as the demands for more complete information for the decision process grew, the responsibilities typically encompassed by this function were enlarged. Now the function includes the estimation of cash receipts and disbursements, the analysis of the probable impacts of various project proposals on the firm's profits as well as on its financial position, the forecasting of future economic developments and their likely influence on the sources and uses of funds, and sources and uses post mortems in which explanations of the differences between projected results and those realized are sought. These major tasks performed in the finance area clearly cut across functional lines and make financial management the economic "conscience" of the firm.

The activities performed in the finance function are guided by two major concerns — the firm's liquidity (its ability to meet its obligations on time) and the profitability of the firm as a whole as well as that of individual projects. As Johnson points out, these twin concerns can be in conflict.[2] Since every dollar the company owes or borrows costs it money, idle dollars placed in zero or low return uses for purposes of liquidity reduce the profitability of the firm. And yet, because no one can predict with certainty how well the flow of income will match the outflow of cash, some idle balances or very liquid accounts must be maintained so that obligations can be met on time. The major problem confronting those charged with managing the finance function is striking a happy balance between profitability and liquidity.

The above is not intended to suggest that all firms have or should have an individual who specializes in financial management. Large firms frequently do; small firms usually do not. In some firms the duties are spread over a number of individuals and departments. But whether the firm has a specialist in this area or not, the duties implied by the finance function must be executed. The twin objectives of liquidity and profitability are as important to the survival of the one-man firm as they are to the corporate giant; they differ among companies only in their complexity. In later chapters, therefore, when we speak of the financial manager we are not necessarily thinking of an individual but rather of the functions implied by this title.

The Profit Objective in Focus

In this text, the profitability of alternative courses of action will receive major emphasis. Since profitability can mean different things to different people, we will attempt to clarify our use of the term. We see profits as a flow of net incomes accruing to a business organization as the result of its business activities. The "flow" concept makes time an explicit factor in profit considerations. Since a dollar received today is worth more than one received next year, projects that yield high returns in the early years and low returns later are more profitable than projects

[2] Robert W. Johnson, *Financial Management*, second edition, Allyn and Bacon Company, Inc., Boston, 1963, p. 10.

in which the reverse is true, even though the total dollar amounts may be identical. Thus, for example, a project that yields $2 the first year and $1 the next has a higher present value than one that yields $1 the first and $2 the next — assuming that the risks associated with each are identical. We will discuss this concept in greater detail in chapter 4.

Risk is the second factor which must be taken into account in the assessment of profitability. Since attitudes toward risk are subjective, different firms would probably place different risk discounts on identical projects. This need not concern us here, however, since a given firm knows its own risk preferences and can discount among alternative projects accordingly. More will be said on risk evaluation later.

Taking time and risk into account, a business firm will seek those projects that yield the greatest present value of future income. Thus, with an identical investment of $10,000, if the present value of the future income flow created by project A is $15,000 and that of project B is $14,000, project A would be chosen.

It must be recognized that decisions are not made solely on the basis of profitability criteria. Other objectives of the firm must be considered. For example, if project A would require considerable reshuffling or replacement of employees, it could be rejected because it conflicts with the firm's objectives with respect to personnel relations or to the community in which it resides.

Profit, as it is generally defined, may be adapted to cooperative forms of organizations even though the latter may not seek profit in the usual sense. Cooperatives are organized to benefit the member-patrons who are also the owners of the organization. It would be perfectly reasonable for a cooperative to choose those alternatives that tend to maximize the future incomes of its members. This income could be reflected in the net margins generated by the organization, or in the very real income contribution of higher prices for farm products than would otherwise be received, or in lower prices for farm inputs. Thus, in the case of cooperatives, there are the added dimensions of prices of products or inputs to be considered in the estimation of income flows.

The Organization of This Text

In the chapters that follow, we will emphasize fundamental concepts of financial management and the development of tools useful in financial analysis.

Chapters 2 through 5 focus on the sources and uses of funds. Chapter 2 is devoted to the development of the underlying conceptual frame of reference and introduces the reader to the balance sheet approach to source and use analysis. Chapter 3 is devoted to a discussion of the management of short-term funds. Its emphasis is on cash, inventory, and trade credit problems. Trade credit is given extensive analytical treatment in a special appendix to chapter 3.

Chapters 4 and 5 bring the reader to grips with the processes associated with "capital budgeting." Chapter 4 is devoted to the development of a framework for the analysis and selection of alternative long-term investment opportunities. It deals at length with economic value in relation to time, and demonstrates how the concepts of net present value and discounted internal rate of return can be applied in the analysis of new investment opportunities or replacement and cost saving proposals. It also discusses some cruder measures commonly used in evaluating investments.

Chapter 5 discusses the conceptual and measurement problems associated with minimizing the cost of capital. The two major factors affecting the cost of capital — quality considerations and capital structure composition — are treated extensively. Particular attention is paid to the applications and limitations of the concept of financial leverage.

In chapter 6, the discussion turns to profit planning. Techniques for sales volume forecasting, cost analysis, product mix selection, and profit budgeting are developed. Applications of break-even analysis to profit forecasting and the concept of "operating leverage" are explored. Procedures for the development of cash budgets and pro forma balance sheets are also presented.

The focus of chapter 7 is on financial analysis and control. It briefly outlines basic information needs for the management decision process and deals extensively with ratio analysis as one method of reading the financial health of the business. In an appendix to the chapter, an example control system for a farm supply business is developed.

Chapter 8 is devoted to a discussion of the financial problems in the growing firm. It examines the economic justification for growth; the means by which firms grow, with particular emphasis on the merger process; and the associated financial problems, with special reference to asset valuation problems of firms involved in merger negotiations. Finally, a case study of a rapidly growing agricultural marketing firm is presented.

Suggested readings are presented at the end of each chapter and additional readings are listed on page 205. Chapters 2-7 also have problem sets.

Suggested Readings

American Management Association. *The Financial Manager's Job.* New York: American Management Association, 1964.

Archer, Stephen H., and Charles A. D'Ambrosio. *Business Finance: Theory and Management.* New York: Macmillan Company, 1966, p. 177–196, 313–320.

Beranek, William. *Analysis for Financial Decisions.* Homewood, Ill.: Richard D. Irwin, Inc., 1963, p. 1–15.

Dauten, Carl A., et al. "Toward a Theory of Business Finance," *The Journal of Finance.* 10 (May 1955), p. 107–143.

Garoian, Leon and Arnold F. Haseley, *The Board of Directors in Agricultural Marketing Firms.* Oregon State University, 1964.

Johnson, Robert W. *Financial Management*, third edition. Boston: Allyn and Bacon, Inc., 1966, p. 3–16.

Lindsay, Robert, and Arnold W. Sametz. *Financial Management.* Homewood, Ill.: Richard D. Irwin, Inc., 1963, p. 31–36.

Solomon, Ezra. *The Theory of Financial Management.* New York: Columbia University Press, 1963, p. 1–25.

Weston, J. Fred. "The Finance Function," *The Journal of Finance.* 9 (September 1954), p. 265–82.

Weston, J. Fred. *The Scope and Methodology of Finance.* Englewood Cliffs, N.J.: Prentice-Hall, Inc., 1966.

Weston, J. Fred, and Eugene F. Brigham. *Managerial Finance*, revised edition. New York: Holt, Rinehart, and Winston, Inc., 1966, p. 3–16.

CHAPTER 2
The Concept of Sources and Uses of Funds

This and the following three chapters focus on the sources and uses of funds. This chapter develops the general conceptual frame of reference and outlines the balance sheet approach to source and use analysis; chapter 3 focuses on the management of short-term funds, while chapters 4 and 5 consider these problems in relation to long-term funds.

Fund Flows

Figure 1 is a simple but useful way of looking at the flow of funds through a firm. Initially, and from time to time thereafter, owners and creditors pump funds — investments and loans (including trade credit) — into the cash balance tank of the firm. Product sales for cash, sales of fixed assets, and the collection of accounts receivable further "recharge" the cash balance. On the other hand, investment in fixed assets, material and product inventories, and labor and overhead costs all draw on the cash balance. Repayment of debt, interest, taxes, and paid-out profits make further demands on it. Over time, the inflows from operations must exceed the outflows if the business is to be justified.

Herein, of course, lies the challenge to management. There is nothing in the system that assures that the income flow will exceed the outflow. In fact, one might look at the various components of the flow diagram as elements in an obstacle course, all of which must be overcome if indeed there is to be any income flow at all. It is not uncommon, for example, for firms to have money tied up in fixed assets that they really don't need, or to have their money tied up in fixed assets that are obsolete by any standard and, therefore, incapable of producing as much output per dollar of input as similar but technically modern assets would. Thus, less than attainable dollar flows are achieved. Similarly, when labor productivity is low, whether because of lack of training, low morale, or because more labor is employed than is needed, the income flow is impeded.

The obstacles that raw materials and finished products inventories pose to the flow of funds are reasonably self-evident. Firms performing any sort of manufacturing function need stocks of raw material to transform into finished products. The accumulation of stocks that exceed manufacturing needs and reasonable contingency reserves ties up money. Finished product inventories present a major hurdle. Indeed, in more than one company it was precisely in this area where the flow of funds came to an end. Having made a wrong estimate of the public taste or its willingness to part with large sums of money to acquire a firm's particular product, the potential seller is left with the alternatives of incurring large warehousing costs or dumping the product. At a less dramatic level, virtually all firms are confronted with the problem of striking a happy balance between excessive stocks in inventory and being out of stock.

Accounts receivable are another major obstacle that can clog the income flow. Accounts not collected obviously reduce the flow. Those that are collected when past due likewise reduce the flow because they result in higher credit service costs. Further, funds "locked in" on receivable accounts may preclude higher returns from alternative investment opportunities.

Management can and should develop well-defined policies in all of

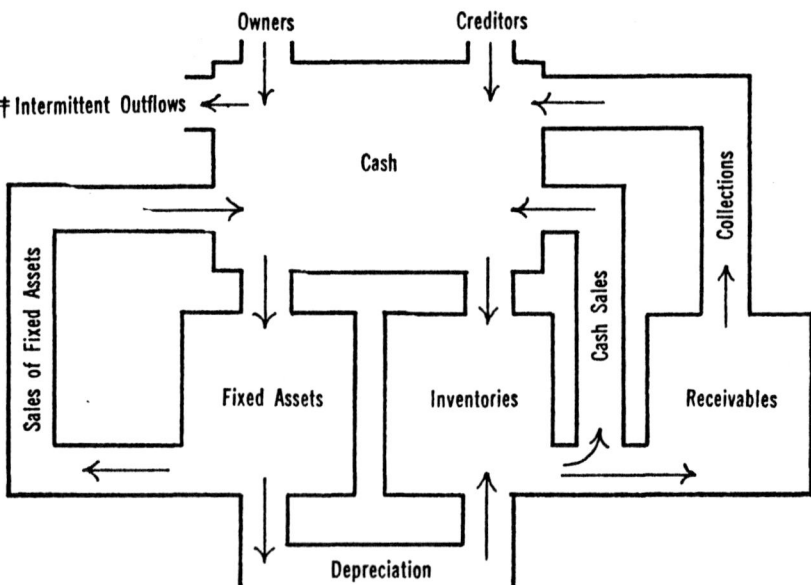

Figure 1. Flow of funds through a business. * †

‡Intermittent Outflows: Interest, Income Taxes, Withdrawals by Owners, Repayment of Debt Retirement of Other Securities

* The "pipelines" are shown to be the same size merely for ease of illustration.
† From Robert W. Johnson, *Financial Management*, third edition, p. 36. Copyright 1966 by Allyn and Bacon, Inc., Boston. Reprinted with permission.

the areas discussed above. It must be kept in mind, however, that the flow of funds is not entirely controllable by the firm. For example, as the level of general economic activity in the country rises and falls, consumer incomes are affected. Demands for consumer or producer goods can fall, affecting the price and/or quantities sold. Buyers may hold off purchases in expectation of a price decline and the firm can experience a slowdown in movement of stock out of inventories. A "tight money" situation may result in a slowdown in the collection of accounts receivable as customers seek to finance their own operations by taking advantage of trade credit. New competition can enter the scene forcing a reduction in price or a slowdown of sales. A technological breakthrough could result in accelerated obsolescence of the firm's fixed assets.

Finally, action by owners and creditors can have tremendous impact on fund flows. In part, their willingness to support the firm is based on their assessment of its internal operation and in part on their assessment of the firm in relation to its external environment. Owners who take out inordinately high "dividends" from operations can reduce the flow of money into operations, which in turn may ultimately reduce the flow of product and income. Creditors who are unwilling to support the business at reasonable rates of interest or who are unwilling to support it at times of critical need can have a similar impact.

The problems described above are common to all firms whether single proprietorships, partnerships, proprietary corporations, or cooperative organizations. Rational management seeks to control as many of the factors that could have an impact on the firm's profitability and longevity as it can. For those events over which it has no control, it tries to provide sufficient reserve strength so the firm does not topple when the first unexpected event occurs.

The conceptual scheme presented above brings into focus the major areas of management concern in the finance function. Coming to grips with these problems demands an analytical framework. This chapter begins the translation of this conceptual scheme into something operationally useful in the analysis of sources and uses of funds.

The Balance Sheet Approach to Source and Use Analysis

One way of looking at the sources and uses of funds in a firm is through changes in its balance sheet. Over time, the financial structure of a firm changes as physical assets wear out or become obsolete and new assets are purchased. Accounts receivable may fluctuate in response to the general changes in the business environment or as a result of changes in credit policies. The inventory account may increase in response to a rising tempo of activity, while the demands for cash may increase for the same reason. As these asset accounts expand or contract, as the case may be, the needs for supporting debt and equity capital change also. Source and use analysis is helpful in pinpointing these changes and the associated capital requirements. In what follows we discuss the mechanics and applications of this tool.

Identifying Changes in Balance Sheet Composition

Changes in the composition of balance sheet items can be highlighted by the preparation of a sources and uses of funds statement. It has become standard financial terminology to refer to asset increases, liability decreases, and equity decreases as uses of funds. Similarly, asset decreases and liability and equity increases are referred to as sources of funds. While it is true that at any point in time assets represent a use, and liabilities and equity a source of funds, the focus of source and use analysis is on period-to-period changes. A useful way of classifying balance sheet changes into sources and uses is as follows:

Sources	Uses
Equity increases	Asset increases
Liability increases	Liability decreases
Asset decreases	Equity decreases

Typically, the construction of the sources and uses of funds statement begins with the selection of two balance sheets. The most recent balance sheet, for example, may be compared with one from the preceding month, quarter, or year. The focus is on the change in each of the accounts in the asset, liability, and equity sections of the balance sheet. More elaborate analyses might focus on the month-to-month or year-to-year changes over a considerable time period.

Table 1 illustrates a commonly used approach to source and use analysis. It compares year-end balance sheets for a hypothetical firm for the years 1974 and 1975. By focusing on the between-year changes, it becomes apparent that creditors increased their support of the firm moderately through respective changes of $8,000 and $2,000 in accounts payable and taxes payable. Likewise, the owners increased their support by $40,000, which we will assume derived in large part from the previous year's profits. Current notes payable increased by $58,000, just canceling out the decline of $58,000 in long-term notes payable. For all practical purposes, this simply reflected an accounting transfer from one classification to another — the result of a $58,000 long-term note which matured in 1975. The net increase in capital available to the firm, therefore, is $50,000, the sum of the net changes in the equity and liability sections of the balance sheet.

How was this $50,000 increase in capital used? Looking at changes in assets, it can be seen that part of it was used to establish a marketable securities account of $30,000. Other portions were used to increase accounts receivable by $10,000 and net equipment (equipment minus accumulated depreciation on equipment) by $15,000. The sum of these positive changes is $55,000, $5,000 more than the net change in total assets. This is accounted for by a $5,000 decrease in the cash account. The negative change in cash made it a source supporting an increase in the other asset — in effect, simply a transformation of one form of asset into another.

Another way of summarizing sources and uses is presented in table 2, which derives from table 1. It shows the between-year changes in

Table 1. Roseville Marketing and Supply Company, comparative balance sheets

	December 31 1974	December 31 1975	Net changes
Current assets			
Cash	$50,000	$45,000	− $5,000
Marketable securities	0	30,000	+ 30,000
Accounts receivable	110,000	120,000	+ 10,000
Inventory	125,000	125,000	0
Supplies	15,000	15,000	0
Total current assets	$300,000	$335,000	
Fixed assets			
Equipment	400,000	435,000	+ 35,000
Less: Accumulated depreciation	(110,000)	(130,000)	+ (20,000)
Buildings	485,000	515,000	+ 30,000
Less: Accumulated depreciation	(170,000)	(200,000)	+ (30,000)
Land	95,000	95,000	0
Total fixed assets	$ 700,000	$ 715,000	
Total assets	1,000,000	1,050,000	
Current liabilities			
Accounts payable	80,000	88,000	+ 8,000
Taxes payable	12,000	14,000	+ 2,000
Notes payable	0	58,000	+ 58,000
Total current liabilities	$92,000	$160,000	
Long-term debt			
Notes payable	158,000	100,000	− 58,000
Equity	750,000	790,000	+ 40,000
Total liabilities and equity	$1,000,000	$1,050,000	

Table 2. Roseville Marketing and Supply Company, sources and uses of funds statement (company year-end balance sheets for 1974 and 1975)

Sources:	
Cash (asset decrease)	$5,000
Accumulated depreciation, buildings (asset decrease)	30,000
Accumulated depreciation, equipment (asset decrease)	20,000
Accounts payable (liability increase)	8,000
Taxes payable (liability increase)	2,000
Equity (equity increase)	40,000
Total sources*	$105,000
Uses:	
Marketable securities (asset increase)	$30,000
Accounts receivable (asset increase)	10,000
Equipment (asset increase)	35,000
Buildings (asset increase)	30,000
Total uses *	$105,000

*The $58,000 shift from long-term debt to short-term liabilities shown in table 1 is basically a bookkeeping entry and does not represent a change in financial structure from a sources and uses standpoint. If included, it would artificially increase both total sources and total uses by $58,000.

each of the several accounts and identifies each account as to whether it is a source or a use of funds. Note that sources include three asset accounts, decreases in cash, accumulated building depreciation, and accumulated equipment depreciation; two liability accounts, increases in accounts and taxes payable; and an increase in the equity account. On the other hand, uses are made up of increases in four asset accounts—marketable securities, accounts receivable, equipment, and buildings.

It must be emphasized that it is not uncommon for a particular account to shift from a source to a use between time periods. Whether it is classified a source or a use depends entirely on whether the change between accounting periods was positive or negative. Thus, in the example above, if the equity account had decreased instead of increased, it would have been classified as a use of funds rather than a source. Similarly, if the marketable securities account had decreased rather than increased, it would have been classified as a source rather than a use. In any case, since we are dealing with balance sheet items, for each change in uses there must be an offsetting change in sources so that, finally, total uses exactly equal total sources.

On balance, our hypothetical firm seems to have done well during the period under consideration, but on the basis of the evidence we have before us we don't know whether or not it did as well as it might have. For example, is the $30,000 purchase of marketable securities a better use of funds than, say, an increase in inventory or the purchase of some fixed asset, or combination of assets, that would absorb that sum?

Similarly, while it is clear that total assets increased by $50,000, we neither know whether this increase was in keeping with the general growth objectives of the company nor can we tell from the statement whether the firm would be better off carrying more or less debt. Questions such as these will be treated in the next three chapters. While source and use statements can't answer such questions, they do help us determine what previous changes in balance sheet composition led to the current financial condition and how they did so; thus they pave the way for us to ask why and whether or not the best possible results are being achieved.

Projecting Financial Needs

A source and use approach can provide a framework for projecting future financial needs. Assume that an examination of 1976 asset requirements indicates that the following additions to asset accounts are necessary:

Cash	$ 5,000
Accounts receivable	5,000
Inventory	10,000
Buildings	30,000
Equipment	10,000
Total	$60,000

Adding these proposed increases to the 1975 year-end asset position of the firm, a projected year-end 1976 asset position can be developed. This is illustrated in table 3. Take particular note of the fact that total assets at the end of December 1976 are precisely the same as they were

Table 3. Proposed assets of the Roseville Marketing and Supply Company, December 31, 1976

	December 31, 1975	Proposed changes	December 31, 1976
Cash	$45,000	+ $5,000	$50,000
Marketable securities	30,000	0	30,000
Accounts receivable	120,000	+ 5,000	125,000
Inventory	125,000	+ 10,000	135,000
Supplies	15,000	0	15,000
Equipment	435,000	+ 10,000	445,000
Less: Accumulated depreciation	(130,000)	+ (30,000)	(160,000)
Buildings	515,000	+ 30,000	545,000
Less: Accumulated depreciation	(200,000)	+ (30,000)	(230,000)
Land	95,000	0	95,000
	$1,050,000	0	$1,050,000

14   *The Financial Management of Agribusiness Firms*

at the end of December 1975. Is it possible to plan for a $60,000 increase in some asset accounts without increasing overall capital requirements? Clearly it is, if there are offsetting changes in other accounts.

In table 3 it was assumed that normal depreciation for buildings and equipment was $30,000 for each account. At the end of 1975, net buildings equaled $315,000. As can be seen below, the projected $30,000 increase in buildings was exactly offset by the $30,000 increase in accumulated depreciation. Thus, net buildings at the end of 1976 remain at $315,000.

	December 31, 1975	Projected changes	December 31, 1976
Buildings	$515,000	$30,000	$545,000
Less: Accumulated depreciation	(200,000)	(30,000)	(230,000)
Net buildings	$315,000	0	$315,000

Applying this analysis to the equipment accounts, we have the following results:

	December 31, 1975	Projected changes	December 31, 1976
Equipment	$435,000	$10,000	$445,000
Less: Accumulated depreciation	(130,000)	(30,000)	(160,000)
Net equipment	$305,000	($20,000)	$285,000

In this case, only $10,000 of the $30,000 depreciation was applied to new equipment. Net equipment declined by $20,000. Assuming that the total liability and equity accounts remain unchanged, other asset accounts would absorb the difference — $5,000 to cash, $5,000 to accounts receivable, and $10,000 to inventory.

Depreciation changes are not the only way to reduce an asset account to provide capital for use somewhere else in the business. For instance, if the firm wanted to purchase additional new equipment and wished to keep its cash account unchanged, it could sell marketable securities and use the cash thus derived to buy equipment. This method is illustrated below. Assume the following three asset account balances:

Cash	$ 30,000
Marketable securities	50,000
Equipment	100,000

The firm wishes to keep cash at $30,000 while purchasing $30,000 of new equipment, but does not want to increase the total amount of capital in the business by borrowing or by adding to equity. A simple, two-step shifting of assets will bring about the desired result. First, $30,000 of marketable securities could be sold and the three accounts would appear as follows:

Cash	$ 60,000
Marketable securities	20,000
Equipment	100,000
	$180,000

After the equipment is purchased they would be as follows:

Cash	$ 30,000
Marketable securities	20,000
Equipment	130,000
	$180,000

The above examples demonstrate that the composition of a firm's financial structure can change without increasing or decreasing the total amount of capital being employed. Similar illustrations could have been developed for shifts in the liability and equity sections of the balance sheet.

Of course, a firm need not rely solely on shifting funds from one account to another to change its financial structure. By borrowing or by issuing preferred or common stock, or other securities, a firm's total capital can be increased. It can be allocated among the several accounts as management sees fit. Table 4 contains a comprehensive summary of the ways a firm can change the composition of its balance sheet.

Identifying Working Capital Position

Source and use statements are frequently developed to place focus on the net working capital position of the firm (net working capital is defined as current assets minus current liabilities). For this purpose, the source and use statement is developed by identifying the changes in fixed assets, long-term debt, and equity as is illustrated in table 5-A. Because current accounts have been excluded from the statement, sources and uses are not equal. This inequality reflects the change in net working capital. In the illustration, total sources exceed total uses by $25,000. This is precisely the amount by which net working capital has increased over the period.

Table 5-B details the changes in the several current accounts. The newly created $30,000 marketable securities account and the increase of $10,000 in accounts receivable offset the $5,000 decrease in cash and the increases of $8,000 in accounts payable and $2,000 in taxes payable, to explain the $25,000 net increase in working capital.

Table 4. Alternative ways of changing balance sheet composition

I. Asset accounts may be changed by:
  A. Shifts between asset accounts.
     Example: Cash may be increased by collecting receivables.
     Example: Cash may be decreased by purchasing new equipment.
  B. Changes in the total amount of assets.
     1. Increasing or decreasing borrowing.
        Example: A short-term bank loan increases both notes payable and cash.
        Example: Purchasing merchandise on account increases inventory and accounts payable.
        Example: Repaying a bank loan or paying accounts payable reduces both cash and total borrowings.
     2. Increasing or decreasing equity.
        Example: A new issue of stock could be sold for cash, increasing both equity and assets.
        Example: A cash dividend could be paid, reducing both equity and assets.
II. Liability accounts may be changed by:
  A. Shifts between liability accounts.
     Example: A bank loan is taken out to pay accounts payable.
  B. Changes in the total amounts of liabilities.
     1. Increasing or decreasing total assets.
        Example: (As in section I-B-1 above.)
     2. Increasing or decreasing total equity.
        Example: Long-term debt is retired by proceeds from a new preferred stock issue.
III. Equity accounts may be changed by:
  A. Shifts between equity accounts.
  B. Changes in the amount of equity.
     1. Increasing or decreasing assets.
     2. Increasing or decreasing liabilities.

Some Modifications

Since the sources and uses of funds statement is summary information, it will not reflect all of the transactions that took place during the period under consideration. It is frequently useful to identify the individual items that make up the change in the several accounts. For example, in examining changes in a firm's equity position, making net profit a distinguishable element in the source and use statement can make an important contribution to an analyst's understanding of what is taking place. Likewise, when depreciation expense (an operating statement item) differs from the net change in accumulated depreciation (balance sheet item), a more detailed breakdown may be in order.[3]

---
[3] On the operating statement, depreciation appears as a "noncash" expense for the period covered. On the balance sheet, it appears as a cumulative total of these operating expense charges. If no assets have been fully depreciated or if none has been sold, the between-year change in accumulated depreciation will equal the depreciation expense shown on the operating statement. If assets have been scrapped or sold, there will be a discrepancy.

Table 5. Roseville Marketing and Supply Company, sources and uses of funds statement for year ended December 31, 1975

	Change from last period	Source	Use
— A —			
Fixed assets			
Equipment	+ $35,000		$35,000
Less: Accumulated depreciation. . . .	+ (20,000)	$20,000	
Buildings	+ 30,000		30,000
Less: Accumulated depreciation . . .	+ (30,000)	30,000	
Land			
Equity	+ 40,000	40,000	
Totals		$90,000	$65,000
Net sources (sources minus uses).		$25,000	

	— B —	Changes in net working capital	
		increase	decrease
Current accounts			
Cash			$5,000
Marketable securities		$30,000	
Accounts receivable		10,000	
Inventory			
Supplies			
Accounts payable			8,000
Taxes payable			2,000
Totals *		$40,000	$15,000
Increase in net working capital.		$25,000	

* Again, the changes in notes payable have been omitted. For an explanation see the note in table 1.

Table 6, which is a modified version of table 5-A, illustrates how this might be done. It shows that our hypothetical company had a net profit of $30,000, had paid-in equity of $10,000, and had total depreciation expenses of $30,000 for equipment and $30,000 for buildings. Additional information indicates that the firm retired a piece of equipment that was fully depreciated and originally cost $10,000. Since the net change in the equipment account was $35,000 (table 5-A), this means that $45,000 of new equipment was purchased during the year.

Through similar procedures, additional detail could be added to the source and use statement. It must be emphasized that detail has no value in and of itself. Only insofar as it leads to insights that will assist in the decision-making process is it useful.

Table 6. Summarized sources and uses of funds statement for year ended December 31, 1975

Sources derived from:	
Depreciation of equipment	$30,000*
Depreciation of buildings	30,000
Net profit	30,000
Paid-in equity	10,000
Total sources	$100,000
Were used to:	
Increase in net working capital	$25,000
Purchase of new equipment	45,000*
Purchase of building	30,000
Total uses	$100,000

*Because the firm retired a fully depreciated piece of equipment originally worth $10,000, the equipment depreciation account and the new-equipment-purchased account are both larger by this amount than the difference shown for these accounts in table 5-A.

Practicality and Pitfalls

The sources and uses of funds statement, like many other tools of analysis, must be used with care. Since it compares changes in the firm's financial structure between any two selected points in time, which may be separated by a month, 3 months, 6 months, or a year, one must guard against making inferences about balance sheet composition at some interim point in the period. Because many firms prepare balance sheets just once a year, one could get a very distorted picture by simply making year-end comparisons. Such distortions can be minimized by developing and analyzing monthly balance sheet statements.

Furthermore, if one is interested in examining trends in various source and use accounts, he would be well advised not to limit himself to considering two points in time for essentially the same reasons as above. Looking at month-to-month changes and perhaps comparing these to similar changes in other years will provide a more reliable base for projection.

Finally, it must be emphasized that the balance sheet approach to source and use analysis really has nothing to say about whether or not the firm is being operated in the most profitable fashion. While this kind of analysis identifies the sources of funds, it gives no indication of the associated capital costs. Similarly, while it can pinpoint how funds are being used, it gives no indication as to whether or not these uses represent the highest return proposals available.

It is essential that those who employ source and use analysis realize that it is a summary device for examining changes in financial structure. Additional information and analysis is required to determine whether or not the changes observed were in harmony with the long-run objectives of the firm. The three chapters that follow are intended to provide some tools that will round out the analytical process.

A Note on Depreciation as a Source of Funds

Before closing this chapter it will be useful to clarify the concept of depreciation as a source of funds. Recall that through depreciation the firm attempts to recoup outlays made on assets whose use-life may extend over a number of years. It does this by charging a portion of the initial cost of the fixed asset to current operations. These current charges to operations are generally based on an estimate of the asset's use-life. It appears on the operating statement as a noncash expense item. Thus, for example, if a firm had a net after-tax operating profit of $100,000 and depreciation charges of $25,000, it would find itself with $125,000 of total additional funds to manage. This is so because depreciation expense is not a cash expense. The $25,000 was not paid out to anyone, as is true in the case of other expenses. Thus, it is still available to the firm to use as it sees fit.

It must be emphasized that depreciation as a source of funds is contingent on the firm's generating a level of sales revenue sufficient to cover cash costs plus noncash costs. If the firm has revenues which only cover cash costs, for example, depreciation as a source "dries up." Or if revenues are such that only part of noncash costs are covered, then only that portion that is covered can be truly regarded as a source.

It is true, of course, that even if a firm sustains a loss, the between-period change in accumulated depreciation on its balance sheet will normally appear as a source. But depreciation as a source in this case is illusory. An example will serve to demonstrate why.

Assume that in a particular year a firm has revenues of $100,000, cash expenses of $100,000, and allowable depreciation charges of $25,000. In short, it has lost $25,000. Further, assume that no fixed assets were fully depreciated or sold during the year. A source and use analysis would indicate that the accumulated depreciation account on the balance sheet had increased by $25,000. Following the rules we discussed earlier in this chapter for identifying sources and uses, this increase would constitute a source. How would the $25,000 be "used"? If the firm had produced a profit it could be used to increase cash, inventory, buildings, or some other asset account. But this firm produced a loss and an examination of the balance sheet would show that an equity account (retained earnings) had decreased by exactly this amount. A decrease in an equity account is a "use" of funds. Did the change in accumulated depreciation really constitute a source in this case? Clearly not. The equity holders simply absorbed a $25,000 decrease in their net worth. Unless the firm borrowed or raised additional equity capital it would have $25,000 less funds to use than it had in the preceding period.

Suggested Readings

Federal Reserve Bank of San Francisco. "Cash Flows and Corporate Investment," *The Monthly Review*. (February 1963), p. 2–7.

Helfert, Erich. *Techniques of Financial Analysis*, revised edition. Homewood, Ill.: Richard D. Irwin, Inc., 1967, p. 3–29.

Lindsay, Robert, and Arnold W. Sametz. *Financial Management*. Homewood, Ill.: Richard D. Irwin, Inc., 1963, p. 3–30.

Mason, Perry. *Cash Flow and the Funds Statement*. The American Institute of Certified Public Accountants, 1961, Research Study No. 2.

U.S. Department of Agriculture, Economic Research Service. *Rising Depreciation of Assets in Agricultural Marketing Firms*. U.S. Department of Agriculture, Agricultural Economic Report No. 47, 1963.

Weston, J. Fred, and Eugene F. Brigham. *Managerial Finance*, revised edition. New York: Holt, Rinehart, and Winston, Inc., 1966, p. 89–92.

PROBLEM SET

I Francen Farm Supply Company

Assume that for the Francen Farm Supply Company there was no direct cash investment by the owners during the year. The firm reported a net operating margin of $12,500 for the year ended December 31, 1975. It finds it more difficult on December 31, 1975, to pay its merchandise suppliers when due than it did on December 31, 1974. Below are year-end balance sheets for 1974 and 1975.

	December 31, 1974	December 31, 1975
Assets		
Cash	$10,000	$500
Accounts receivable	30,000	49,500
Inventories	60,000	60,000
Total current assets	$100,000	$110,000
Fixed assets, net	60,000	60,000
Other assets	40,000	40,000
Total assets	$200,000	$210,000
Liabilities		
Total current liabilities	$25,000	$25,000
Long-term debt	0	0
Total liabilities	$25,000	$25,000
Capital equities		
Total capital equities	175,000	185,000
Total liabilities and capital equities	$200,000	$210,000

Questions

1. Prepare and comment on a source and use statement for the period.
2. How much net working capital did the firm have on December 31, 1974, and December 31, 1975?
3. How much of the year's net margin was retained in the business?
4. Why is the firm finding it more difficult to stay current with suppliers?
5. What action would you recommend to correct the situation?

II Christiansen Dairy Plant

Operations for the Christiansen Dairy Plant for the year ended December 31, 1975, were satisfactory — $25,000 of the year's net margins were retained in the business, as evidenced by the $25,000 increase in total capital equities.

During the year, the plant's net working capital decreased by a substantial amount, and on December 31, 1975, the association was finding it difficult to make current payments to producers for milk.

	December 31, 1974	December 31, 1975
Assets		
Cash	$40,000	$10,000
Accounts and notes receivable	100,000	60,000
Inventories	60,000	55,000
Total current assets	$200,000	$125,000
Fixed assets, net	250,000	325,000
Other assets	50,000	50,000
Total assets	$500,000	$500,000
Liabilities		
Accounts payable	$125,000	$125,000
Other current liabilities	25,000	25,000
Total current liabilities	$150,000	$150,000
Long-term debt	50,000	25,000
Total liabilities	$200,000	$175,000
Capital equities		
Total capital equities	300,000	325,000
Total liabilities and capital equities	$500,000	$500,000

Questions

1. Prepare and comment on a source and use statement for the period.
2. What are the two factors which caused the decrease in net working capital?
3. What action will you recommend to relieve the "tight" working capital situation on December 31, 1975?

CHAPTER 3
Managing Short-Term Funds

The length of the "cash-to-cash" cycle for funds varies significantly, depending on the use to which funds are put. The stream of returns from an investment in a building or machine may continue for a number of years. On the other hand, raw material may be transformed into finished product and sold for cash in a very short time period. It is useful to make a distinction between short-term and long-term funds even though the firm's objective in both cases is to minimize the costs and maximize the returns from them.

In this chapter the focus is on the management of short-term funds — the working capital sectors of the balance sheet. A firm's working capital is reflected in its current asset accounts — typically, cash, accounts receivable, inventories, or any other asset readily convertible into cash. To determine a firm's net working capital position, which is the major measure of its liquidity (its ability to pay its bills on time), we subtract current liabilities — accounts payable, taxes payable, accrued payables, short-term notes payable, and long-term debt which will mature within the year. As we suggested in chapter 1, here is where the manager's dilemma of choosing between profitability and liquidity is sharpest. Funds held in idle balances produce no revenues but maximize liquidity, on the one hand, while funds completely tied up in investments may produce maximum profits and zero liquidity. Somehow or other, the manager must strike a happy balance.

Elements of Efficient Liquidity

Suppose that a firm's working capital transactions were known with certainty. For example, assume that on the 5th of each month Eintag Grain Company purchases $30,000 worth of wheat on track to be resold in its original form to a cash customer for $32,000. The firm has no fixed assets, but rents a room for 2 days each month for a total cost of $100, which is paid on checkout day. This is also the same day that the grain payment is made. After the bills are paid the president of the company (its only employee) turns the $1,900 profit over to his wife and relaxes until the 5th of the next month when exactly the same routine will be followed. The balance sheet of Eintag after a month's business is completed reads as follows:

24   The Financial Management of Agribusiness Firms

Eintag Grain Company
Balance sheet (1)
January 7, 1975

Current assets	0	Current liabilities	0
Long-term assets	0	Long-term debt	0
		Equity	0
Total	0	Total	0

The fact is that Eintag has no need for assets because the business operates smoothly in their absence for all but 2 days of the month. The firm can rent all physical assets for the exact period they are needed. Since proceeds from sales are collected before the supplier and landlord demand payment, there is no cash problem. The president withdraws the monthly profit from the firm because there is no internal investment need.

Even though the example is a gross simplification, it does point out some key issues of working capital management. First, Eintag had a fortunate relationship between cash inflow and cash outflows. It was able to sell the merchandise it acquired for cash before payment for the merchandise was due. What if the supplier also demanded cash payment? Then Eintag would be forced to borrow $30,000 for one day. While the expense wouldn't be great, there would be a cost associated with providing working capital on a short-term basis.[4]

The relationship between cash inflows and outflows could be distorted in many ways. For example, assume that the firm purchases grain for cash and that its customer is given a month to pay. In this situation, Eintag would have a different balance sheet on January 7.

Eintag Grain Company
Balance sheet (2)
January 7, 1975

Current assets		Current liabilities	
Accounts receivable ...	$32,000	Notes payable	$30,100*
Fixed assets	0	Long-term debt	0
		Equity	1,900
Total	$32,000	Total	$32,000

* Assume that Eintag must borrow $30,000 to pay the supplier and $100 to pay office rent.

The complexion of the business has changed somewhat. Now, instead of having $1,900 in cash immediately after sale, the cash comes in 1 month later. The profit is no longer $1,900, since it was necessary for the firm to borrow $30,100 at 6 percent, resulting in an interest

[4] For example, at 6 percent, total interest charges would be $5 ($30,000 x $\frac{1}{360}$ x $\frac{6}{100}$ = $5).

expense of slightly over $150. Profits are reduced to $1,750. Therefore, the firm's balance sheet early after collecting the receivables and paying off the note, would read as follows at the close of business on February 4:

Eintag Grain Company
Balance sheet (3)
Late on February 4, 1975

Current assets		Current liabilities	0
Cash	$1,750	Long-term debt	0
Fixed assets	0	Equity	$1,750
Total	$1,750	Total	$1,750

Because Eintag granted 30-day credit terms to customers, its profit was reduced; further, the profit was "tied up" in accounts receivable for a full month after the sale. Perhaps this was necessary. Competitive pressures may have been such that the firm had to offer liberal credit terms. But the point made here is that, because cash inflows lagged outflows, working capital needs changed.

This problem can be magnified by assuming that Eintag decides to move from a once-per-month to a continuous operation. Now it purchases $30,000 worth of merchandise per day for cash and sells it for $32,000 but must wait 1 month to collect. Just prior to the collection of the first sale, the balance sheet would appear as follows:

Eintag Grain Company
Balance sheet (4)
February 4, 1975

Current assets	
Accounts receivable ($32,000 × 31)	$992,000
Fixed assets	0
Total	$992,000
Current liabilities	
Notes payable ($30,000 × 31)	$930,000
Rent payable * ($50 × 31)	1,550
Interest payable † (496 × $5)	2,480
Total	$934,030
Long-term debt	0
Equity	57,970
Total	$992,000

* Assume that rent is paid at the end of the month so that Eintag is just borrowing to cover its purchases.

† Calculation of interest was based on a 6 percent rate. The daily interest on a $30,000 loan closely approximates $5 ($30,000 x 0.06/360 = $5). If the company borrows $30,000 each day for 31 days and repays nothing during the period, by the end of the month the cash borrowed on the first day will have interest payable of $155 (31 x $5); the second day $150 (30 x $5); the third day $145 (29 x $5); ... the 31st day $5 (1 x $5). A shortcut to determining the total interest payable for the month would be to sum the days in the period (1 + 2 + 3 + 4 ... + 29 + 30 + 31 = 496) and multiply by the interest cost per day per $30,000 borrowing unit (496 x $5 = $2,480).

After collecting $32,000 from the January 5 sale and making payments of $155 for interest, $30,000 for retirement of a note (both part of the original January 5 transaction), and $1,550 for the first month's rent, the February 5 balance sheet would be as follows:

Eintag Grain Company
Balance sheet (5)
February 5, 1975

Current assets	
Cash	$295
Accounts receivable *	992,000
Fixed assets	0
Total	$992,295
Current liabilities	
Notes payable *	$930,000
Rent payable *	50
Interest payable *	2,480
Long-term debt	0
Equity	59,765
Total	$992,295

* Includes February 5 transactions.

Several examples relating to the preceding balance sheet illustrate the cost impact when cash inflows and outflows do not match. Assume that:

(a) Everything remains the same except that the supplier also grants 1-month terms. The net effect would be to increase the cash and equity accounts by the amount of the interest expense, $155, and increase the equity account again by the amount of accrued interest, $2,480. As this example suggests, if cash inflows and outflows had matched, the firm could have saved nearly $2,500 per month or close to $30,000 annually! This is illustrated in modified balance sheet (5A).

(b) Everything remains the same as in (a) except that all sales are cash sales. Here the cash inflows from each sale lead the outflows (which are noninterest open-account transactions) by 1 month. Now the firm has cash in advance of payments that can be held as cash or used for any other purpose in the business. The cash could be used to retire the accounts payable, but this is wasting available resources because the supplier made it clear that the firm need not pay for 30 days. There must be a better use for the asset.

Eintag could use the cash to purchase more inventory but this is wasteful too, since the company operates with certainty in all business transactions. The firm needs $30,000 of merchandise per day. Assuming that there is no possibility of delivery delays, why have more? There is no profit in unneeded inventory.

Why not purchase a fixed asset? Now that Eintag operates every day of the month, the annual rental is $18,250 (365 × $50). It might be cheaper to purchase the space needed than to continue to pay rent. To keep our focus on working capital, we will assume that an investment in a building or other fixed asset is not the best alternative.

Perhaps it would be best to hold the collections in cash form. This deserves a fast veto because cash is a nonearning asset. Eintag operates in a certainty situation, and management knows exactly what its cash requirements are. Since cash is not an investment, it should be transformed into some current asset such as marketable securities.

Assume for a moment that the firm did invest the cash not needed to meet current expenditures in 4 percent Treasury bills. Balance sheet (5B) shows the impact of this assumption.

Eintag Grain Company
Balance sheet (5) modified
February 5, 1975

Current assets	(5)	(5A)	(5B)
Cash	$295	$450	0
Marketable securities	0	0	$992,450
Accounts receivable	992,000	992,000	0
Accrued interest receivable *	0	0	1,736
Fixed assets	0	0	0
Totals	$992,295	$992,450	$994,186
Current liabilities			
Accounts payable	0	$930,000	$930,000
Notes payable	$930,000	0	0
Rent payable	50	50	50
Interest payable	2,480	0	0
Long-term debt	0	0	0
Equity	59,765	62,400	64,136
Totals	$992,295	$992,450	$994,186

* This figure assumes a daily return of $3.50 ($32,000 x 0.04 x 1/360) per interest day up to that time.

As with assumption (*a*), $2,480 per month in interest is saved. In addition, $1,736 in interest is earned. Over the period of a year the combined total would be over $50,000! As the statement indicates, difference in the cash flow patterns can have a substantial influence on the profit performance of a firm.

The illustration of the Eintag Grain Company was, of course, a gross simplification in many aspects. The firm handled only one product, had only one supplier, and had no fixed assets, labor costs, maintenance costs, or overhead charges. The cash flow pattern in most firms is much more complicated.

Even though many agriculturally related firms are highly specialized, most of them produce more than one product. They sell to a variety of customers; some pay their bills on time, others do not, and credit losses occur. Furthermore, most of these firms have a substantial investment in buildings and equipment that are subject to the vagaries of obsolescence as well as natural hazards. Typically, they purchase raw products and other production inputs from a large number of suppliers whose willingness and capacity to grant credit vary greatly. They, as other firms, are vulnerable to the inroads of competition as well as to the impacts of the ebb and flow of general economic activity on their business fortunes. In short, the "real world" firm operates in a very uncertain environment.

To be sure, the degree of uncertainty varies from firm to firm. As it increases, the amount of assets needed to meet the liquidity requirement increases. Whatever its environment, the firm must determine its liquidity needs and then proceed to structure the working capital sector at least cost. Least-cost working capital implies that, given the firm's liquidity needs, there is some combination of cash, accounts receivable, inventory, marketable securities, and short-term accounts payable which is optimal. It is to this problem that we now turn.

Optimizing Working Capital Sectors

The previous discussion has suggested that all working capital sectors should be managed to achieve least-cost liquidity. The next step is to look at these sectors to determine how this might be accomplished.

Accrued Liabilities

Accrued liabilities are obligations that the firm has acquired and will be paying off in cash in the near future. Included are taxes payable, salaries and wages payable, interest payable, etc. They all imply that a cash outflow will occur at some future date.

Some accrued liabilities are dependent on factors other than liquidity. For example, the amount of income tax payable is based on net profits. When a firm improves its profit position it also increases taxes payable. From a liquidity standpoint, the financial manager has little opportunity to influence the impact of taxes payable on working capital. He can make sure that the tax bill isn't paid until due, so that the firm can conserve its cash for other purposes in the interim period.

There are other accrued liabilities over which the firm does have more liquidity discretion. A good example is accrued payrolls. A firm can choose among paying employees weekly, every 2 weeks, or monthly. Assuming a weekly payroll of $1,000, the firm could conserve $1,000 cash for an additional week if it paid employees every 2 weeks. Likewise, if employees are paid monthly, the cash conserved would increase accordingly. A similar example would be a firm that meets its payroll weekly but with a 1-week lag. Wages earned during the week of July 11-15 would be paid to the employees on July 22. On July 29 the employees would receive wages earned during July 18-22, etc. In effect, the employees are providing the firm with financing equivalent to 1 week's wages. The careful planning of accrual payment dates can be financially advantageous.

Trade Accounts Payable

While it is part of the liquidity function to be able to pay bills when due, it is advantageous *not to pay them until due*. As pointed out earlier, when a supplier provides credit he is offering it as part of his product package. The purchaser is paying for credit in the total price because the supplier has to more than cover all costs if his operations are to be profitable. Rule number one is to fulfill the obligation of paying bills on time, but to retain the resources in the business until payment is due.

A separate trade credit problem arises when discount terms are granted. For instance, suppose that a supplier offers terms of 2/10, n/30. If the customer pays within 10 days he may deduct 2 percent from the price in submitting his payment; if he decides against it, he is obligated to pay the entire bill in 30 days. From a financial viewpoint, it is usually quite attractive to take the discount. For example, if on February 1 a firm purchased $5,000 worth of merchandise under the terms 2/10, n/30, it may send a check for $4,900 ($5,000 − $5,000 × 0.02 = $4,900) for payment in full any time through February 11. From February 12 through March 3, it must pay the full $5,000. What's the difference? By comparing the two offers it can be seen that under the second method the firm has the use of the $4,900 for 20 additional days, for a charge of $100.

Is the $100 a reasonable amount to pay for a 20-day extension of credit? The answer for most firms is "No!" As shown below, the effective interest rate is almost 37 percent.

$$\text{principal} \times \text{rate} \times \text{time} = \text{interest charge}$$
$$\$4,900 \times \text{rate} \times 20/360 = \$100$$
$$272.2 \text{ rate} = \$100$$
$$\text{rate} = 0.367 \text{ or } 36.7\%$$

Most firms can find a cheaper rate than this. For example, assume that the firm did not have the cash to pay in 10 days, but knew it would be available at the end of the 30-day period. The manager borrows $4,900 from the bank for 20 days at 6 percent on February 2 and repays the loan plus interest on March 3, the same date that the $5,000 is due. This is illustrated as follows:

30-day payment to supplier		$5,000.00
10-day payment to supplier	$4,900.00	
Bank interest ($4,900 × 0.06 × 20/360) ...	16.34	
		4,916.34
Total net savings		$ 83.66

By borrowing and taking the discount offered, the firm could save $83.66.

With few exceptions, firms make a special effort to take discounts of this type even if they must borrow to do it. As a matter of fact, failure to do so is often a sign of weakness. It implies that either short-term credit is unavailable or that management is ignorant of the true costs involved.

This discussion of trade credit points out the advantages of (*a*) paying bills on the date they are due and (*b*) taking discounts whenever possible. This assumes that a choice of supplier has been made. It might be wise to discuss some of the factors involved in making this selection.

Given everything else equal, a firm will usually purchase from a supplier offering the lowest price. But seldom is everything else equal. Suppliers have different attributes, such as special delivery service, good repair service, free advice, etc., and the final choice may depend on these things as well as price. For example, two companies may both sell the same product for cash, one charging $10,000 per carload and the other $9,950. Assume that the purchaser uses one carload per week throughout the year. A little quick arithmetic shows that if he buys from the low-priced supplier he saves $2,600 in costs annually. However, the high-priced supplier has a staff of technicians who are available to provide expert advice to its steady customers. The question that must be answered is whether or not it is worth $2,600 per year to have access to the team of experts. While this decision is not solely a financial one, the example shows that the financial manager must be so informed that he does not base his decisions solely on the money cost of the package without being aware of what is included.

Inventory Management

For many firms the largest working capital account is inventory. As with other assets, the firm attempts to get a high return on the funds invested in inventory. Enough resources should be committed to make certain that customer orders can be filled. Being out of stock not only reduces sales but may lose customers. On the other hand, care must be taken that unneeded stocks are not maintained. Since they "tie up" capital that might better be used elsewhere, determining optimum inventory size is a delicate problem for many firms. If kept relatively small, those responsible for selling may believe it to be inadequate. If large, those responsible for efficient use of capital resources may believe it to be wasteful.

A first step in inventory optimization is to identify the factors that influence its size. There are five: sales volume, item cost, order cost, storage and handling costs, and out-of-stock costs.[5]

A projection of sales is important in inventory planning because it provides an estimate of the number of units that will be needed in a designated time period. Dollar size of the inventory sector will be influenced greatly by the stock's cost per unit. If a firm holds 10,000 units, the inventory value will be dependent on the cost per unit times the number of units on hand.

It may not be necessary to purchase an entire period's supply of inventory at one time. For instance, if the time period is a month, a firm might purchase goods weekly or daily. Since inventory size multiplied by the cost per unit equals total inventory, the resources tied up in inventory can be reduced by frequent orders.

With a fixed quantity of inventory needed during a period, there is an inverse relationship between the size of order and the number of orders placed. Frequent ordering may reduce the investment of resources in inventory, but may increase the cost of ordering. On the other hand, a large order often costs less per unit for the supplier to ship. Part of this saving may be passed along in the form of lower per unit prices. But when inventory increases there are often increased handling and storage expenses.

Taking these factors into account, a commonly used formula for determining optimum order size is as follows:[6]

---

[5] There is an additional factor of item value decline in special situations where spoilage, styling, etc., add uncertainty to item values.

[6] A derivation of the formula can be found in many finance and quantitative management texts. One such source is R. I. Levin and C. A. Kirkpatrick, *Quantitative Approaches to Management*, 1965, McGraw-Hill Book Company, New York, chapter 5.

32 The Financial Management of Agribusiness Firms

$$EOQ = \sqrt{\frac{2 \times A \times C}{P \times I}}$$

Where: EOQ = economic order quantity
A = units of item needed during period
C = cost of processing an order
P = price per unit of goods being purchased
I = annual inventory carrying charge as a percent of annual inventory value

For illustrative purposes, assume that the projected needs of a product are 14,400 units for the coming year. Considering the time spent by clerks, paperwork, etc., it is estimated that each order costs $5 to process. Purchase price per unit is $1 and the ratio between annual inventory carrying charges as a percentage of annual inventory value is 0.1. Placing these figures in the formula and solving indicates that the economic order quantity is 1,200 units per lot.

$$EOQ = \sqrt{\frac{2 \times 14{,}400 \times 5}{1 \times 0.1}}$$

$$= \sqrt{\frac{144{,}000}{0.1}}$$

$$= 1{,}200$$

It follows that 12 orders (14,400 ÷ 1,200 = 12) will be scheduled throughout the year. At a cost of $1 per unit, the cost of a purchase would be $1,200. There is a good chance that maximum inventory will be around $1,200, depending on the ability to predict sales and the possible out-of-stock cost or profit lost due to a shortage of merchandise. For example, if inventory needs were known with certainty, the firm would purchase one 1,200-unit shipment and would not buy again until these were gone. However, suppose it was difficult to predict purchase patterns. Perhaps a firm would average sales of 1,200 units per month, with a range from 900 to 1,400. If the firm only had 1,200 to sell and it needed 1,400, it would need a supplier offering prompt service to avoid the loss of 200 units in sales. If the service is not fast and a substantial loss would be incurred by being out of stock, it would be wise to establish a reorder point related to inventory level and delivery service rather than observe strict adherence to a time schedule.

As in the previous illustration, suppose an average of 40 units (40 × 30 days = 1,200) are sold each day but that sales may vary from as much as 100 to as few as 5 units. Out-of-stock costs are high. If they are to be avoided, an order must be placed at a point where delivery can be made before current inventory supplies are exhausted. For example, if delivery takes 2 days, a reorder point might be 200 or 220 units. If 1-day service is available, the reorder point would be somewhere around 100, etc.

The key factors in inventory management are knowing (a) the economic order quantity and the various factors necessary in calculating it, (b) the out-of-stock costs, and (c) the period of time from reorder signal to arrival of the goods. If an inventory is made up of several different products, an analysis of this type should be made on each product. This is often feasible when data processing is available. When it becames too expensive to examine each product in this way, a firm might select a few representative items and make estimates over the entire line.

Receivables [7]

Trade receivables are often considered a necessary evil by firms. They would rather have cash sales because they eliminate the credit paperwork and the need to invest resources in receivables. Accounts receivable must be evaluated in terms of their effectiveness as a sales promotion device and/or their convenience to the offering firm.

There are many examples of convenience usage of receivables. Certain public utilities provide continuous service but collect only once a month. Daily billings would not only be a nuisance but would cost the firm more than the benefit received from having the cash sooner.

A more complex aspect of trade credit is its use as a selling device. In this case, it functions in the same way as do cash discounts, special offers, and advertising. All are offered in the hope of attracting customers. For example, suppose two firms were offering the same fertilizer at the same price but one offered cash-only terms and the other allowed payment as much as 30 days later. If the other terms of trade are the same the customer would buy from the latter. But usually what one firm can do, so can another. A short-term advantage can be lost as other firms respond with perhaps more generous credit programs of their own. As with advertising and discounts, trade credit must be used with care. Getting the sale may have a negative impact if the firm must give up too much.

Trade receivables are expensive. A dollar tied up in accounts receivable isn't available to buy merchandise, pay bills, or invest in any other way. In effect, the firm has elected to finance its customers. As with any other investment, credit should be granted only after ex-

[7] See appendix to this chapter for a detailed treatment of the analysis of trade credit programs.

amining the credit worthiness of the other party and making sure it is a profitable investment.

How can it be determined if trade credit is a profitable investment? A prerequisite is determining the credit worthiness of the customer. Losses through uncollectible accounts can quickly consume profits earned on other sales. A second factor concerns the credit period granted. As part of the sales function of trade credit, longer credit terms may lead to more sales.

Table 7 is a hypothetical illustration of how different credit terms might influence sales and profits. Starting with the cash-only sales figure

Table 7. Estimated monthly sales and profits under varying credit terms

	Cash only	30 Days	45 Days	60 Days	90 Days
Sales	$100,000	$125,000	$130,000	$132,000	$132,000
Marginal increases	100,000	25,000	5,000	2,000	0
Profits	10,000	12,500	12,800	13,000	12,900
Marginal increases	10,000	2,500	300	200	(100)

and comparing it with 30-day terms, the firm increases profits by $2,500 by offering 30-day terms. Is it worth $2,500 to tie up funds in receivables for 30 days? Unless the firm had a better alternative use for them, it would be. The 45- and 60-day terms generate additional dollar profits, but at a declining rate. Without question, 90-day terms wouldn't be offered because dollar profits decline. In determining the proper length of credit period, the firm must determine if the marginal increases in profits are large enough to offset the disadvantages of delay in cash receipts which could be used in other investment alternatives.

Cash

Cash is the core of working capital analysis. The financial manager must insure that the cash reservoir is maintained at a level high enough so that bills may be paid, on the one hand, while on the other hand he must guard against excessive idle balances. If he fails to pay the bills, the business risks stringent action by creditors; if he maintains excessive idle cash balances, he is foregoing alternative investment opportunities or denying the owners the use of their funds for their private purposes.

If inflows and outflows of cash occurred simultaneously, there would be little need to maintain a cash balance. Except in the most unusual cases, however, there is a lag between the time a business makes outlays and the time income begins to flow. A cycle begins with the purchase of raw material or merchandise, equipment, supplies, services, etc. These all involve cash outlays. Merchandise is held in inventory for varying lengths of time. When the merchandise is sold, there is a lag between the date of sale and the date of collection — the receivables gap.

In large degree, the discrepancy between the inflow and outflow of cash is predictable. The most commonly used tool for this purpose is the cash budget, which estimates the magnitude and timing of cash inflows and cash outflows (see chapter 6). Net differences between inflows and outflows, positive or negative, indicate the amount of cash available for other uses or the amount required to close the gap.

As with other predictive devices, cash budget estimates are subject to error. Sales may be higher or lower than predicted. Cash outlays may also vary from the levels expected. To account for this, the financial manager "builds in" an allowance for uncertainty when estimating net cash flows. The magnitude of this allowance is dependent primarily on the nature of the business and on past experience. In those businesses where incomes and costs are relatively stable, allowances for contingencies need not be large. In those where incomes and costs are volatile, the opposite is true.

Given estimates of the gaps between cash inflows and outflows, what sources of funds may be used to fill them? Where these gaps are short-lived or involve small dollar amounts, the use of idle cash balances is probably the most appropriate device because of the inconvenience and expense of negotiating very short-term or very small loans. On the other hand, where seasonal outflows are likely to exceed inflows for extended periods or by large amounts, the costs of holding idle cash (what it could earn elsewhere in the business) must be compared to the cost of borrowing short-term funds. For example, a vegetable processor whose major outlays occur on a highly seasonal basis but whose income tends to be spread over the year might find it economical to borrow from such organizations as commercial banks, the bank for cooperatives, and other credit-granting agencies rather than to hold idle cash. The willingness of the lending organization to provide such funds is dependent in large degree on the soundness with which the business is being conducted and the kinds of collateral the firm can offer. Businesses whose credit worthiness is limited will be required to maintain larger cash balances than those with excellent credit reputations.

Of course, other sources of funds within the business may be tapped to meet cash needs. The prudent financial manager invests cash that is not immediately needed in such assets as marketable securities, debt instruments of other firms, short-term government bonds, or certificates of deposit. Such investments generate a return on what might otherwise be idle cash, while at the same time offering a high degree of liquidity. The maturing of such investments can frequently be timed to coincide with some particular cash outlay.

Cash management, of course, is part and parcel of inventory and accounts receivable management, discussed earlier. Optimizing inventory levels and using reasonably sound collection methods of receivables reduce cash needs. Similarly, timing outlays to pay bills when due, but not before, as well as taking full advantage of available discounts, reduces total cash requirements.

Short-Term Uses from Long-Term Sources

Earlier in the chapter it was suggested that two key factors in determining liquidity needs were the degree of predictability of future transactions and the relation of cash inflows to outflows on each transaction. Usually, outflows precede inflows in marketing and farm supply firms. The grain elevator purchases the grain from the farmer before selling it. The feed manufacturer buys his ingredients before selling his final product, etc.

An examination of the balance sheet of most firms indicates that current assets sometimes exceed current liabilities by a sizable amount. In such cases some current assets are supported by long-term debt and equity. This is illustrated in the balance sheet below, where current assets are two times current liabilities and 20 percent of the permanent capital structure is supporting current assets:

Balance sheet

Current assets	40%	Current liabilities	20%
		Capital structure *	
Fixed assets	60%	Supporting current assets.	20%
		Supporting fixed assets..	60%
Totals.............	100%		100%

* Long-term debt and equity accounts.

This support is necessary because internal generation of cash — cash inflows from operation — follows the outflows. If payments must be made before proceeds from sales are collected, some source must be providing the cash. The portion of the working capital assets provided by long-term debt and equity accounts (capital structure) will be referred to hereafter as permanent working capital.

How large should the permanent working capital be? It should be at least as large as the aggregate difference between cash inflows and outflows in a slack season — a time when receivables and inventories are at their lowest. From this point on, the actual amount will be dependent on (*a*) the predictability of transactions and (*b*) the short-term borrowing ability of the firm.

Consider the permanent working capital needs of the Roseville Vegetable Processing Company, which cans sweet corn and peas. In its part of the country the canning season lasts 3 months — June, July, and August. Throughout the rest of the year Roseville sells products out of storage, overhauls equipment, and carries on other routine maintenance functions. A careful study of a typical year's activity indicates minimum balances in the following accounts:

Receivables	$ 1,200	(CA)
Inventory (supplies)	3,800	(CA)
Inventory (product)	12,000	(CA)
Accounts payable	4,600	(CL)
Taxes payable	400	(CL)

Dividing these accounts into current assets (CA) and current liabilities (CL), the total difference is $17,000–$5,000, or $12,000. To provide for contingencies, assume that a cash balance is maintained equal to the minimum current liabilities, or $5,000. Therefore, the minimum permanent working capital to be supported by the capital structure is $17,000. Assuming that Roseville does have ample borrowing strength, during the packing season it may use its inventory as collateral to borrow from commercial banks, the bank for cooperatives, or other sources to cover short-term capital needs. Later, when the product is sold and collections made, the short-term loan is repaid and the company returns to its minimum situation.

Summary

In summary, the financial manager attempts to minimize the cost and maximize the returns on short-term funds uses. In the case of uses, primarily current assets, this means optimizing the quantity held. If current assets are larger than necessary, the firm or its stockholders are missing alternative investment opportunities. If understated, the firm may find it difficult to pay its bills.

As far as external sources are concerned, the firm tries to identify those which can supply its needs at least cost. Suppliers of short-term capital may be looked at in much the same light as other organizations who sell to firms. Individuals, banks, and other organizations offer money and other services for a price. The "package" offered by the supplier—the money, the repayment and penalty conditions provided for in the loan agreement, plus whatever advisory or other services are made available—must be examined in relation to the interest rate and other charges (if any) being asked. Choosing from among lenders simply on the basis of which one offers the lowest interest rate may be as "costly" as buying other "inputs" without regard to qualitative differences among them. Judicious comparison of alternative external sources is a must if the firm is to minimize the cost of short-term funds.

APPENDIX—Chapter 3
Analyzing Trade Credit Problems

The granting of credit is common practice in many agricultural marketing and farm supply firms. Transactions are sometimes automatic. The customer's desire to charge his purchase is assumed by the firm.

When a firm grants credit it is, in effect, helping to finance its customers. The customer has use of the merchandise or service being purchased for a number of days, and sometimes months, before being required to pay. Interbusiness charge sales, often referred to as trade credit, represent one of the most important types of financing in our economy. At the end of 1962, trade credit outstanding was estimated at $111 billion.[8]

From the selling firm's standpoint, trade credit can be viewed as part of a total package being sold to customers. This package includes everything the customer receives including merchandise, services, and credit. Logically, the customer will purchase from the seller offering the most attractive package. For example, assume that two firms, A and B, sell exactly the same merchandise for $10. Firm A offers 30-day credit terms while B sells on a cash-only basis. If A and B are direct competitors, most likely A will get the majority of the business because of the 30-day credit terms it offers. If B wishes to be competitive, it may consider granting similar credit terms, lowering its selling price, or offering some other service or product as part of its total package.

Granting trade credit can prove to be an effective sales tool when used properly. When improperly employed, it can be very expensive, and at times disastrous. Questions concerning trade credit constantly confront firm managers. Should credit be granted? To whom? How much? How do you collect a delinquent account from a customer? There are no easy answers to these questions, but there are several factors a manager should consider. The following pages will briefly touch on topics that will be helpful to managers, as follows:

- How much credit should there be in a firm's total sales package?
- To whom should a firm make credit terms available?
- How does a firm establish collection procedures?

How Much Credit Should There Be In a Firm's Total Sales Package?

Whether we are discussing a cooperative or proprietary firm, management is assigned the task of operating the business in a way that will promote the firm's objectives. In the case of the proprietary firm, this usually means making a profit for the owners. For the cooperative, it means generating cost savings for patrons. The credit in a firm's total sales package, therefore, should first be evaluated on its ability to advance the firm's profit or cost-saving objective.

More specifically, a manager attempts to determine exactly what credit terms should be offered to customers. Here, consideration is given to the impact that certain credit terms will have on sales and costs. Some firms find it to their advantage

---

[8] Martin H. Seiden, *The Quality of Trade Credit*, New York National Bureau of Economic Research (1964), p. 1.

to sell on a cash-only basis. Other companies allow payment delays of 30, 60, or 90 days, or more. It is common practice to charge interest for longer payment periods.

Another popular approach is to allow the customer a discount — the right to reduce his total bill by a certain amount, usually stated as a percentage of the total sales price, if the bill is paid before a certain date. Terms similar to 2/10, n/30 are often offered. This means that if the customer pays within 10 days he may reduce his total bill by 2 percent. He is obligated to pay the full amount if he pays after the 10th day. Payment is to be made no later than 30 days after the sale date.

Determining what credit terms to offer is a difficult task. There are usually some guidelines available, however. Terms become standardized throughout an industry for certain product lines. Standardization is logical because it is usually necessary to offer terms equal to those of direct competitors. As pointed out earlier, a firm's package of merchandise, credit, and service should be competitive if it is to attract customers. If a firm's credit terms are less than the industry standard, customers will demand additional services or a lower price. Unless there are other differences in the total sales package, it is usually to the firm's advantage to use the industry terms.

Suppose a firm is considering the possibility of offering credit terms that differ from the industry standard. For illustrative purposes, assume that industry terms are n/30, i.e., payment in full should be received no later than 30 days following the sale. The firm is considering four alternative terms — cash only; 2/10, n/40; n/60; and n/90. A study of the market indicates the following estimated monthly sales, expense, and profit figures associated with each alternative. In each case, it is assumed that all competitors will continue to grant net 30-day terms regardless of what the firm in question does.

Monthly estimates of sales, expenses, and profit for a hypothetical firm under varying credit terms assuming that competitors continue to offer net 30-day terms

			Terms		
Estimated	Cash only	n/30 (current plan)	2/10, n/40	n/60	n/90
Sales	$10,000	$12,500	$16,000	$14,000	$14,300
Expenses *	8,000	9,750	11,500	10,800	11,010
Credit expenses †	0	500	1,200	900	2,190
Discounts granted	0	0	300	0	0
Profit	$2,000	$2,250	$3,000	$2,300	$1,100

* Regular operating expenses excluding credit expenses.
† Includes all clerical expenses, bad debt losses, etc., associated with granting credit.

Based on these estimates, it appears that two proposals will provide a larger profit than the current n/30 terms. The discount approach, 2/10, n/40, appears to be the most profitable. It is estimated that profit would increase by $750 per month over that earned under the n/30 terms. The n/60 terms also appear to be more profitable by $50 per month. It is expected that the cash-only and n/90 terms would result in a lower profit than with n/30 and therefore be dropped from consideration.

Before making any changes in credit terms, a firm had better consider some other factors not included in the analysis so far. The above illustration assumed that competitors would continue to offer n/30 terms. If one firm can increase its profit by changing credit terms, this may be done at the expense of others. Should this be the case, it is likely that the competitors will retaliate with a change in credit terms. When the dust finally settles, the firm making the original change may be worse off than it was originally. Consider the following example in which competitors are assumed to retaliate:

Monthly estimates of sales, expense, and profit for a hypothetical firm under varying credit terms assuming that competitors offer identical terms and that sales remain at $12,500

Estimated	Cash only	n/30 (current plan)	2/10, n/40	n/60	n/90
Sales	$12,500	$12,500	$12,500	$12,500	$12,500
Expenses *	9,750	9,750	9,750	9,750	9,750
Credit expenses †	0	500	1,000	600	1,000
Discounts granted	0	0	250	0	0
Profit	$2,750	$2,250	$1,500	$2,150	$1,750

* Regular operating expenes excluding credit expenses.
† Includes clerical expenses, bad debt losses, etc., associated with granting credit.

As before, profits with n/90 terms appear unfavorable. But the 2/10, n/40 and n/60 terms, which were more profitable than n/30 in the first illustration, are not more profitable when it is assumed that all competitors will match any credit term change the hypothetical company makes. Only the cash-only terms will increase profits above current levels under the "competitors follow suit" assumption.

What changes, if any, should the company make in its credit terms? This depends on what actions competitors could be expected to make. Under the first assumption that competitors would continue to grant n/30 terms, it was estimated that sales would decline by $2,500 if cash-only terms were adopted. Since the cash-only approach is only advantageous if competitors follow suit, it can be eliminated. The 2/10, n/40 terms and the n/60 terms produce a larger profit only if competitors do not follow suit. In this instance, the hypothetical firm is taking $1,500 to $3,500 worth of business away from its competitors. The question is how they will react to this loss in revenue. If they retaliate, the firm would be better off with the n/30 terms now being used, as indicated by the lower profit estimates for the 2/10, n/40 and n/60 terms in this case.

Assuming competitors do not follow suit, a question concerning the profitability of the n/60 terms might still be raised. Under the current 30-day terms, the firm has an accounts receivable balance equal to or closely approximating 1 month's sales, $12,500, since it takes a month to convert a sale into cash. If n/60 terms were adopted, there would be a 2-month period between sales and collection. Accounts receivable would approximate 2 month's sales of $14,000 per month (assuming competitors don't follow suit on changes in credit terms), or $28,000.

Under n/30 terms, the cash from 1 month's sales is received and ready for investment the following month. For example, the cash from January sales is available for investment in inventory or other assets in February. Under n/60 terms, the cash from January sales would not be available until March. This means that the cash necessary for February's inventory purchases must come from some other source.

When considering longer credit terms, the asset needs of the firm must be considered. In the example, the additional $15,500 ($14,000 $\times$ 2 less $12,500) needed to switch from n/30 to n/60 terms must be available without creating too great a strain on other capital needs. The firm might elect to delay or forego the use of some other asset. For example, plans to build a $15,000 storage shed might be set aside. Alternatively, the firm might borrow the $15,500; but a careful examination of costs would indicate that unless the interest rate was less than 4 percent, it would be more profitable to continue the n/30 terms.[9] Or if the firm had $15,500 in cash on hand, it would be better off investing it in any asset yielding a return of 4 percent or better.

Trade credit, while often necessary in maintaining a competitive position, can be expensive. This is true whether establishing credit terms or adjusting those in use for the benefit of a few or all customers. Sometimes, firms offer specific terms but fail to enforce them. Under these circumstances, competitive and profitable n/30 terms can become as costly as n/60 or n/90 terms.

This dilemma between presenting a competitive sales package to customers and avoiding a costly tie-up of funds in accounts receivable is familiar to many firm managers (and to many ex-managers of defunct firms). Trade credit is a sales promotion method that has a major impact on the allocation of firm funds. A sound credit policy should be able to increase profits enough to justify the investment of the firm's capital in accounts receivable.

To Whom Should a Firm Make Credit Terms Available?

An overwhelming percentage of individuals and firms want to pay their bills promptly. To do otherwise can affect the purchaser's ability to obtain credit in the future and tends to suggest a weakness in management. In addition to these factors that might influence later operations, it is embarrassing to some managers to have overdue bills on the books.

If these characteristics were universal among all customers using trade credit, there would be no need to raise the question, *to whom should a firm make credit terms available?* While only a small percentage of firms and individuals fail to meet their obligations, this small group can be enough to wipe out the profit earned on other business. If a firm has 5 percent profits on $30,000 of sales, $1,500 of bad debts can reduce the profit to zero. The successful credit program

---

[9] If the accounts receivable balance was permanently increased by $15,500 and this amount was to be borrowed on an annual basis, the total interest charge at a 4 percent rate would be $620. This is $20 more than the difference in annual profit between the n/30 terms ($2,500 per month $\times$ 12 = $30,000) and the n/60 terms ($2,300 $\times$ 12 = $30,600). This assumes that competitors did not also change to a n/60 basis.

should attempt to pinpoint those few accounts that can turn a sound credit program into disaster.

A good starting point in credit evaluation is to review each customer in terms of the customary 4 C's of credit — character, capacity, capital, and conditions.

Character centers around the integrity and trustworthiness of a customer. The best customers are those who build their businesses on a sound reputation. Public confidence is an important part of any success they might enjoy. A firm of this type is not out to "make a quick buck." Its management realizes that public confidence will lead to greater profits in the long run. One word of caution, however: It takes more than character to pay bills.

The second C, capacity, refers to a firm's ability to pay bills as due. Too often, credit is granted to individuals with high moral standards and low bank accounts. Regardless of a customer's character, bills are paid with cash. A good credit program should include an inquiry into the customer's ability to pay bills.

The third and fourth C's, capital and conditions, are usually less significant than character and capacity when the review is primarily for trade credit. Capital refers to a firm's real worth, the assets that could be claimed by the general creditors should the business fail. In analyzing capital, it is necessary to determine (a) if there are any mortgages on specific assets, (b) what the sale value of the nonmortgaged assets is, and (c) how much net worth the owners have invested. When these questions are answered, the firm can make intelligent estimates concerning the prospects of a customer failing and what portion of the credit granted could be recovered if a failure did occur.

Conditions refer to the dependency of a particular customer's successful operation on factors external to his business. Farmers are particularly vulnerable to weather and fluctuations in the general economy. A bad year can cut deeply into a farm customer's capacity. Several bad years will soon affect the capital position. As the customer's dependence on factors external to his control increases, so does the credit risk involved.

A good credit evaluation program should contain some method of translating the 4 C's of credit into an operational framework. This calls for two things. First, sources of information on potential customers must be located. Second, this information must be evaluated in a meaningful way.

Sources of information may not be as difficult to locate as it might at first appear. A prime source is past experience. After years of dealing with particular types of customers, a firm gains valuable insights. Too often, however, a firm will use past experience as the sole criterion. Time changes many things, including a customer's credit status. As valuable as it is, past experience should be supplemented with other information. Customers might be asked to submit income statements and balance sheets on a periodic basis. From this data, inferences can be drawn concerning both capacity and capital.

Additional information can sometimes be obtained from other firms, banks, community leaders, public records, board members, and professional credit-rating organizations. The value of each of these possible sources will vary depending on local conditions, but the point is that there are various ways of learning about the credit risks associated with individual customers.

Armed with information, a firm may find it useful to establish a set of criteria to help management reach decisions as to a customer's credit worthiness. Using the 4 C's as an example, perhaps a firm would set up a point system similar to the following:

Valley-Vue Farms, R.R. #2, Smithville, December 1, 1975

Category	High	Average	Below average	Poor	Valley-Vue score
Character	30	23	10	0	30
Capacity	45	30	10	0	30
Capital	10	7	5	0	10
Conditions	15	10	5	0	5
Total	100	70	30	0	75

Valley-Vue Farms' credit position, and that of every other customer, would be reviewed periodically and scored. In the above illustration, Valley-Vue received high ratings for character and capital — 30 and 10 points, respectively. An average rating, 30 points, was received on capacity, and it was judged below average, 5 points, on conditions. The total score was the sum of these categories, or 75. Since the total for average overall performance was 70, Valley-Vue would be considered an above-average credit risk.

After a system of this type has been in operation for a period of time, it might be determined that customers scoring below a certain level were not, as a general rule, profitable. Further development of the system might indicate that customers scoring below another point should be allowed credit only up to some dollar limit.

Regardless of the approach used, it is important that credit management be approached in a systematic way. This means that sources of information should be periodically tapped for fresh information, new and better methods of evaluattion should be sought, and standards should be revised to keep the system current and pertinent. This or a similar system can be an aid to decision makers if it is realized that the resulting product can be no better than the effort which preceded it.

How Does a Firm Establish Collection Procedures?

The most important collection procedures have already been discussed. Avoiding bad risks can eliminate practically all collection problems. Two other important "preventive" guides to collection procedures are clear terms and firm action.

Misunderstandings can be avoided by a clear statement of the terms of the agreement. If there is a danger that 2/10, n/30 will be misunderstood, the terms must be carefully written out, explaining the option involved.

Word soon gets around if there is a "soft touch" offering credit. A customer might discover that n/30 can be stretched to n/45 or n/50 without a major complaint from a credit granter. Weak credit enforcement is a bad reputation to acquire and a difficult one to shake without alienating a few customers. A firm has little to gain and quite a bit to lose by being a "soft touch." The same holds true when selected customers get special consideration to help them out of a jam. Before long, the kind-hearted credit-granting firm will be overrun with special requests. The time to avoid this problem is at the outset. Customers must be treated courteously but firmly.

Even with a thorough checking system, clearly stated terms, and consistent treatment of customers, problem accounts do occur. A fairly standard system for collecting delinquent accounts is as follows: A prompt and courteous letter suggesting an oversight is sent a few days after an account becomes overdue. If this letter fails to bring a response, a second letter may be sent in 10-14 days. It should be courteous, but should emphasize the advantages of maintaining a good credit rating. If the customer responds to either of the first two letters saying he is temporarily short of cash, the firm might wish to reply by offering the opportunity to sign a note. If possible, this should be an interest-bearing note, since it costs the granting firm money when there is a collection delay. The delinquent customer should bear at least a part of that cost.[10]

What if the second letter fails to bring results? Depending on the account, some firms might resort to a personal contact or a third letter similar to the second. General procedure is to send a third letter which clearly states that failure to respond promptly will lead to drastic measures that will undoubtedly mean refusing further credit (if this has not already been done) and may mean notification of delinquency to a credit rating service and/or turning the account over to a collection agency. At this stage, the customer's lack of action reduces the value of his goodwill below the value of getting back part of the investment made in his operations.

Summary

The discussion has briefly centered on three problems of credit management — credit terms, evaluation, and collection procedures. Emphasis has been on pointing out the advantages of a strong credit management program and identifying key factors in building and operating it.

In the final analysis, an effective credit program depends on establishing a credit policy and enforcing it. For those interested in additional reading, the suggested reading list that follows should prove to be a good starting point.

Suggested Readings

Beranek, William. *Working Capital Management*. Belmont, Calif.: Wadsworth Publishing Company, Inc., 1966.

Bogen, Jules I., editor. *Financial Handbook*, fourth edition. New York: Ronald Press, 1964.

Dun and Bradstreet, Inc. *Growth in Importance of the Credit Function*. New York, 1959.

———. *How to Control Accounts Receivable for Greater Profits*. New York, 1963.

Ettinger, Richard P., and David Golieb. *Credits and Collections*, fifth edition. Englewood Cliffs, N.J.: Prentice-Hall, 1962.

Gavett, J. William, and John M. Allderidge. *Operational Analysis in Small Manu-*

---

[10] One approach to this problem allows the customer to select a longer pay period at the time of sale. In the terms, it is clearly stated that a carrying charge will be added if the customer wishes to delay payment for an abnormally long period. This approach can alleviate possible diplomatic and financial problems. Firms have been known to make modest profits by providing this type of service.

facturing Companies. Small Business Administration Research Report, 1962, sections II and III.

Hooker, Raymond W. *Attitudes of Wisconsin Bankers Toward Small Business Financing.* Small Business Administration Research Report, 1961.

Hunt, Pearson, Charles M. Williams, and Gordon Donaldson. *Basic Business Finance,* revised edition. Homewood, Ill.: Richard D. Irwin, Inc., 1961, p. 68–84.

Johnson, Robert W. *Financial Management,* third edition. Boston: Allyn and Bacon, Inc., 1966, p. 34–45, 98–157, 120–137.

Kaplan, Robert M. "Credit Risks and Opportunities," *Harvard Business Review.* March-April 1967, p. 83–88.

Levin, Richard I., and C. A. Kirkpatrick. *Quantitative Approaches to Management.* New York: McGraw-Hill Book Company, 1965, p. 113-141.

Lindsay, Robert, and Arnold W. Sametz. *Financial Management.* Homewood, Ill.: Richard D. Irwin, Inc., 1963, p. 267–313.

National Association of Credit Men. *Credit Management Handbook,* second edition. Homewood, Ill.: Richard D. Irwin, Inc., 1965.

Schabacker, Joseph C. *Cash Planning in Small Manufacturing Companies.* Small Business Administration, 1960.

Schultz, William J., and Hedwig Reinhardt. *Credit and Collection Management,* third edition. Englewood Cliffs, N.J.: Prentice-Hall, 1962.

Seiden, Martin H. *The Quality of Trade Credit.* New York: National Bureau of Economic Research Occasional Paper 87, 1964.

Weston, J. Fred, and Eugene F. Brigham. *Managerial Finance,* revised edition. New York: Holt, Rinehart, and Winston, Inc., 1966, p. 117–135, 327–341.

PROBLEM SET

I. Inventory

The manager of Harrod Farm Supply receives orders for 100,000 prefabricated cartons each year. In the past he has purchased the entire lot in late summer and sold from stock throughout the year. The cost per carton is $0.35. The estimated cost of preparing the order is $5. If the relationship between annual inventory carrying charge to annual inventory value is $0.01, what is the most economical order size Harrod can make on cartons?

II. Cash Management

Once each year the Chase County Elevator borrows around $200,000 to see it through the busy grain-purchasing season. A typical borrowing schedule is as follows:

September 1	borrow	$200,000
September 15	repay	100,000
September 30	repay	50,000
October 31	repay	25,000
November 30	repay	25,000

Chase borrows at a rate of 6 percent. Total borrowing costs are $1,125. A member of the board determined that if the permanent cash was increased by $50,000 the debt could be completely repaid in September and total interest costs would be reduced by more than 50 percent to $500. Should Chase permanently increase the size of the cash account by $50,000?

III. Receivables

This year Elkins Feed Manufacturing had sales of $210,000 and a net operating income of $20,000 or slightly less than a 10 percent operating profit. The company is currently operating at 70 percent of capacity. The manager is considering a change in credit policy that offers net 30-day terms to customers that were previously denied any credit arrangements. It is believed that if the proposal is adopted, sales would be increased by $15,000. It is estimated that collection costs would increase from $1,000 to $1,500 and that bad debts on the new accounts would be around 6 percent compared to the 2 percent rate on existing credit sales. Would you recommend adoption of the new proposal?

IV. Payables

The Cansell Canning Works has decided to reexamine its payables policy. Many of the supplies the company purchases are offered on a 1/10, n/30 basis. Total purchases under these terms usually run about $85,000 a year. In the past, the manager has felt that it is better to have the use of the money for an additional 20 days rather than take the 1 percent discount. His argument has been that "This is the only place we can borrow 1 percent money." A member of his staff has questioned this line of thought.

1. Do you believe Cansell should be taking the 1 percent discount?
2. Would you be willing to borrow working capital at an 8 percent interest rate in order to take the discount?

V. O'Brien Grain Elevator

The O'Brien Grain Elevator is able to operate satisfactorily with its present working-capital position. It is planning to construct a building to handle a line of miscellaneous farm supplies to supplement the present grain-marketing operation. It is estimated that the building will cost $30,000, and necessary equipment another $10,000. With these facilities, it is estimated that the yearly *merchandise* sales volume will be about $150,000. It is expected that 40 percent of merchandise sales will be for cash, with the balance sold on n/30-day terms. The firm plans to carry a $20,000 inventory at all times, one-half of which will be financed by accounts payable.

Assets	December 31, 1975
Cash	$4,000
Accounts and notes receivable	30,000
Grain inventory	216,000
Total current assets	$250,000
Fixed assets, net	90,000
Other assets	20,000
Total assets	$360,000
Liabilities	
Storage liability	$190,000
Other current liabilities	40,000
Total current liabilities	$230,000
Long-term debt	0
Total liabilities	$230,000
Capital equities	
Total capital equities	130,000
Total liabilities and capital equities	$360,000

Questions

1. About how much capital will have to be raised to finance the farm supply venture?
2. What action would you recommend to secure the required capital?

CHAPTER 4
Management of Long-Term Funds—Maximizing Returns

This chapter focuses on the analysis and selection of alternative long-term investment opportunities facing the firm. In chapter 5 we will deal with the problem of minimizing the costs of long-term funds. In combination, these two chapters cover what is commonly referred to as capital budgeting.

The importance of decisions relating to long-term investments cannot be overstated. Unlike working capital, which is normally self-liquidating within a year, the decision to invest in fixed assets such as buildings, machinery, and equipment will have impacts on a firm's operations for a long time. Furthermore, the capacity to pay for these long-term assets is dependent on their profitability and not on their liquidation as is true in the case of working capital.

The "cash-to-cash" cycle of long-term investments involves a considerable number of years. The decision process is complicated by increasing uncertainty as the length of the time period in which the asset is expected to be used increases. It is the lot of the decision maker to exist in an uncertain world. Fortunately, there are degrees of uncertainty. We are less uncertain of our expectations about tomorrow than we are of those relating to next week. Similarly, we are likely to be less uncertain of our expectations about next year than we are about those 5 or 10 years from now.

Managers handle the uncertainty problem in a variety of ways. Some have argued that, since we know very little about the future with certainty, there is little point in trying to predict future outcomes; they live in the here-and-now, and they tend to give heavy weight to the present situation and their intuition when making long-term investment decisions. Those whose intuition is "right," or those who are fortunate enough to have "today's" conditions continue to exist for some time in the future (at least as far as their firm is concerned) may succeed — in some cases brilliantly. But many who follow this procedure fail.

On the other hand, more and more managers are making conscious efforts to project future outcomes on a systematic basis. True, in part these projections rely on past and present conditions since this is the base from which the future evolves. But in addition, these managers attempt to determine how trends in factors that have direct effect on their business outcomes are related and to what degree a change in one may be a precursor of a change in another. They also attempt to analyze how their own alternative strategies as well as those of their competitors, will affect future outcomes. Of course, they recognize that such estimates are subject to error and, indeed, they may feel less certain about some projected outcomes than others. But, as we shall see later in the chapter, these "feelings" can be translated into a useful part of the decision process.

Of the two methods of approaching the long-term decision process, we are strongly biased in favor of the latter. We don't view the economic process as a series of random events. By and large, what happens in the economic arena is caused by "good" and "bad" decisions made by the participants in the economic game. Given reasonable objectives, a rational manager can devise strategies which insure high probabilities of achieving them. The random catastrophe, of course, can destroy the effect of the best-laid plans. On the other hand, less than catastrophic events can derail the firm that avoids anticipatory thinking and concerns itself only with the here-and-now.

Analyzing Investment Proposals

The prime function of the financial manager in the capital investment process is the identification of those investment alternatives which will yield the highest profits. His primary focus is on new project proposals, replacement decisions, and cost-saving projects. In addition, he may be charged with evaluating investment in service projects undertaken to strengthen employee morale, or to improve the firm's image and the like.

Where does the analysis start? Assuming that one has identified the feasible alternatives confronting the firm, the first step is to calculate the net investment requirements for each of the proposals. By net investment we mean the sum of the positive and negative changes in total investment associated with the particular project. For example, an investment in a machine may require that a wall in the building in which it is to be used be torn out for its installation. Additional electric power may be required which calls for a rewiring job. Or it may even be necessary to shut down the plant for a few days while modifications are being made. The cash costs of these associated activities must be included in the calculation of net investment. On the other hand, the sale of old assets which the new investment replaces is deductible. In this connection, as we shall see later in this chapter, losses incurred because of the early obsolescence of plant or equipment are not chargeable to the new investment and if they are will lead to erroneous decisions. Finally, although not properly classified as a long-term investment, we remind the reader that working capital requirements are usually closely tied to long-term investment projects and, therefore, must be provided for as part of the overall investment plan.

The second element that must be considered in the analyses of investment proposals is their net impact on cash flows. In the case of new projects, this requires the estimation of cash revenues and the associated cash outlays for the proposals in question so that net cash flow generated by the project in its economic lifetime can be determined. In estimating cash outlays, depreciation and other noncash expenses are not included. Likewise, financing costs, which consist primarily of interest expense and dividends, are excluded for this purpose. The latter constitute the cost of capital, to be treated in chapter 5, and help to determine minimum acceptable returns on investment. Insofar as the new activity will impinge on the "cash flows" of other activities in the firm, positively or negatively, these side effects must be taken into account in estimating the net impact of the proposal. In the case of cost-saving projects, the same consideration applies except that the emphasis is on determining net cost differences resulting from adopting the project.

We wish to emphasize that for the purpose of such estimates, the focus must be on anticipated or future revenues and/or costs. Accounting data, useful as they are in describing the overall asset position of the firm, as well as the sources and uses of funds from some past time period, have distinct limitations as far as the projection process is concerned. To be useful, they must be modified to take into account the likely future changes in product prices, wage rates, material costs, and methods of operation. Furthermore, the distortions created by the arbitrary allocation of certain overhead costs to new investment proposals on the basis of accounting conventions must be avoided. We will deal with some of these forecasting problems later. But it is important for the reader to know now what we have in mind when we talk of income flows in this chapter.

With this general background on the investment process we can now undertake to develop the basic analytical framework for investment decisions. As we have suggested earlier, time and uncertainty play major roles in the identification and selection of profitable investment alternatives. In the remainder of this chapter we will focus first on the relation of economic value to time. We shall consider the background and mechanics for analyses in this area and then we shall look at some applications of these tools to new, replacement, and cost-reducing proposals. In the second major part we will deal with the problems associated with uncertainty in the investment process. We shall suggest some ways by which subjective estimates of risk can be built into estimates of future outcomes. In the final section of the chapter we shall consider the problems associated with ranking alternative investment proposals.

The Relation of Economic Value and Time

Since we shall be dealing extensively with the "time value" of money in this chapter, it will be fruitful for some to examine the mechanics of the evaluation process at an early stage. For the reader who is familiar with the "discounting process" and the use of present value tables, we suggest that he skip to the section entitled "Some Applications" unless he feels he would benefit from a review.

Background and Mechanics

We are all familiar with the concept of bank interest. To induce us to part with our money, banks offer us a "reward" — an interest payment. Why is this reward necessary? Because by allowing the bank to hold our money we are foregoing its use in immediate spending or in other uses. In a sense, what we give up can be thought of as the "opportunity cost" to us of letting the bank use our money. This concept of "opportunity cost" is important in the analyses of alternative investment proposals. The cost of selecting project A may be thought of as the returns foregone by not selecting project B. This idea is at the heart of all that follows.

The Concept of Present Value. If we put $1 into our account at simple 4 percent interest for 1 year, today's dollar at the end of the year is worth $1.04. The computational procedure is simple and straightforward, as follows:

value today	+	4% interest	=	value at end of year
$1.00	+	$1.00(0.04)	=	$1.04

The above formulation can be restated in a simple general equation:
Let:

A_0 = present value
r = interest rate
A_1 = value a year from now

Management of Long-Term Funds—Maximizing Returns

Then:
$$A_1 = A_0 + A_0 r$$
or
$$A_1 = A_0(1 + r)$$

And, as in our example:
$$A_1 = \$1.00(1 + 0.04) = \$1.04$$

Now suppose that we want to know what the present value of $1 received a year from now is — again assuming a simple interest rate of 4 percent. Some minor manipulations of the above equation will help us solve for A_0 (present value) instead of A_1 (value a year from now).

If:
$$A_1 = A_0(1 + r)$$

Then:
$$A_0 = \frac{A_1}{(1 + r)}$$
$$= \frac{1.00}{1 + 0.04}$$
$$= \$0.961$$

In this simple example, to arrive at the present value of a dollar received a year from now we have "discounted" that dollar by the interest foregone in the intervening year. In short, we are discounting that dollar received a year from now by its owner's opportunity cost.

The simple interest problem is a rarity as far as financial analysis is concerned, but it does establish the underlying mechanics of present or future value computation. Typically, we are concerned with projects which extend over a number of years and for this purpose the compound interest idea is relevant. The same fundamental ideas apply. Suppose we are interested in the value of $1 at the end of 2 years which draws 4 percent interest compounded annually. At the end of the first year we have:

$$\$1.00 + \$1.00(0.04) = \$1.04$$

At the end of the second year we have:
$$\$1.04 + \$1.04(0.04) = \$1.082$$

We could carry this process out for any number of years. A general formula, which derives from the simple interest formula shown above, but which is applicable to the compound interest problem for any number of years, is as follows:

Let:
A_0 = present value
r = interest rate
A_n = value after n years

54   The Financial Management of Agribusiness Firms

Then:
$$A_n = A_0(1+r)^n$$

In the problem above:
$$A_n = \$1.00(1+0.04)^2$$
$$= \$1.00(1.082)$$
$$= \$1.082$$

Now suppose we are interested in the present value of $1 received at the end of 2 years, again assuming a 4 percent discount rate. Manipulating the formula we have: [11]

$$A_0 = \frac{A_n}{(1+r)^n}$$
$$= \frac{1.00}{(1+0.04)^2}$$
$$= \frac{1.00}{1.082}$$
$$= \$0.925$$

We could plug any value and any interest rate into the formula and determine the present value at the end of the year selected. But this can be extremely time-consuming, especially for those who do not have access to a calculator or, better still, a computer. Fortunately, tables have been developed which greatly simplify the discounting process. Table 8 is a present-value table. Note that alternative rates of interest (discount rates) are shown in a row along the top. Years are indicated in the left-hand column. Suppose, pursuing our earlier example, we were interested in knowing the present value of $1 received in 10 years, assuming an interest rate of 4 percent compounded annually. We would simply move over to the 4 percent column and down 10 years and read off $0.676. At the end of 20 years the present value would be $0.456.

If instead of simply being interested in the present value of $1, we wanted to know how much the unlikely sum of $243.89 received in 10 years is worth today, again assuming a 4 percent discount rate, how would we use the table? We would multiply $243.89 × $0.676 (the

[11] If we are interested in the present value of a stream of income, the formula becomes:

$$V = \frac{A_1}{(1+r)} + \frac{A_2}{(1+r)^2} + \frac{A_3}{(1+r)^3} + \cdots + \frac{A_n}{(1+r)^n}$$

where:
V = present value of an income stream
A_i = income flows in respective years
r = discount rate

Table 8. Present value of $1

Year hence	1%	2%	4%	6%	8%	10%	11%	12%	13%	14%	15%	16%	17%	18%	20%	22%	24%	25%	30%	35%	40%	45%	50%
1	0.990	0.980	0.962	0.943	0.926	0.909	0.901	0.893	0.885	0.877	0.870	0.862	0.855	0.847	0.833	0.820	0.806	0.800	0.769	0.741	0.714	0.670	0.667
2	0.980	0.961	0.925	0.890	0.857	0.826	0.812	0.797	0.783	0.769	0.756	0.743	0.731	0.718	0.694	0.672	0.650	0.640	0.592	0.549	0.510	0.476	0.444
3	0.971	0.942	0.889	0.840	0.794	0.751	0.731	0.712	0.693	0.675	0.658	0.641	0.624	0.609	0.579	0.551	0.524	0.512	0.455	0.406	0.364	0.328	0.296
4	0.961	0.924	0.855	0.792	0.735	0.683	0.659	0.636	0.613	0.592	0.572	0.552	0.534	0.516	0.482	0.451	0.423	0.410	0.350	0.301	0.260	0.226	0.198
5	0.951	0.906	0.822	0.747	0.681	0.621	0.593	0.567	0.543	0.519	0.497	0.476	0.456	0.437	0.402	0.370	0.341	0.328	0.269	0.223	0.186	0.156	0.132
6	0.942	0.888	0.790	0.705	0.630	0.564	0.535	0.507	0.480	0.456	0.432	0.410	0.390	0.370	0.335	0.303	0.275	0.262	0.207	0.165	0.133	0.108	0.088
7	0.933	0.871	0.760	0.665	0.583	0.513	0.482	0.452	0.425	0.400	0.376	0.354	0.333	0.314	0.279	0.249	0.222	0.210	0.159	0.122	0.095	0.074	0.059
8	0.923	0.853	0.731	0.627	0.540	0.467	0.434	0.404	0.376	0.351	0.327	0.305	0.285	0.266	0.233	0.204	0.179	0.168	0.123	0.091	0.068	0.051	0.039
9	0.914	0.837	0.703	0.592	0.500	0.424	0.391	0.361	0.333	0.308	0.284	0.263	0.243	0.225	0.194	0.167	0.144	0.134	0.094	0.067	0.048	0.035	0.026
10	0.905	0.820	0.676	0.558	0.463	0.386	0.352	0.322	0.295	0.270	0.247	0.227	0.208	0.191	0.162	0.137	0.116	0.107	0.073	0.050	0.035	0.024	0.017
11	0.896	0.804	0.650	0.527	0.429	0.350	0.317	0.287	0.261	0.237	0.215	0.195	0.178	0.162	0.135	0.112	0.094	0.086	0.056	0.037	0.025	0.017	0.012
12	0.887	0.788	0.625	0.497	0.397	0.319	0.286	0.257	0.231	0.208	0.187	0.168	0.152	0.137	0.112	0.092	0.076	0.069	0.043	0.027	0.018	0.012	0.008
13	0.879	0.773	0.601	0.469	0.368	0.290	0.258	0.229	0.204	0.182	0.163	0.145	0.130	0.116	0.093	0.075	0.061	0.055	0.033	0.020	0.013	0.008	0.005
14	0.870	0.758	0.577	0.442	0.340	0.263	0.232	0.205	0.181	0.160	0.141	0.125	0.111	0.099	0.078	0.062	0.049	0.044	0.025	0.015	0.009	0.006	0.003
15	0.861	0.743	0.555	0.417	0.315	0.239	0.209	0.183	0.160	0.140	0.123	0.108	0.095	0.084	0.065	0.051	0.040	0.035	0.020	0.011	0.006	0.004	0.002
16	0.853	0.728	0.534	0.394	0.292	0.218	0.188	0.163	0.141	0.123	0.107	0.093	0.081	0.071	0.054	0.042	0.032	0.028	0.015	0.008	0.005	0.003	0.002
17	0.844	0.714	0.513	0.371	0.270	0.198	0.170	0.146	0.125	0.108	0.093	0.080	0.069	0.060	0.045	0.034	0.026	0.023	0.012	0.006	0.003	0.002	0.001
18	0.836	0.700	0.494	0.350	0.250	0.180	0.153	0.130	0.111	0.095	0.081	0.069	0.059	0.051	0.038	0.028	0.021	0.018	0.009	0.005	0.002	0.001	0.001
19	0.828	0.686	0.475	0.331	0.232	0.164	0.138	0.116	0.098	0.083	0.070	0.060	0.051	0.043	0.031	0.023	0.017	0.014	0.007	0.003	0.002	0.001	0.000
20	0.820	0.673	0.456	0.312	0.215	0.149	0.124	0.104	0.087	0.073	0.061	0.051	0.043	0.037	0.026	0.019	0.014	0.012	0.005	0.002	0.001	0.001	0.000
21	0.811	0.660	0.439	0.294	0.199	0.135	0.112	0.093	0.077	0.064	0.053	0.044	0.037	0.031	0.022	0.015	0.011	0.009	0.004	0.002	0.001	0.000	0.000
22	0.803	0.647	0.422	0.278	0.184	0.123	0.101	0.083	0.068	0.056	0.046	0.038	0.032	0.026	0.018	0.013	0.009	0.007	0.003	0.001	0.001	0.000	0.000
23	0.795	0.634	0.406	0.262	0.170	0.112	0.091	0.074	0.060	0.049	0.040	0.033	0.027	0.022	0.015	0.010	0.007	0.006	0.002	0.001	0.000	0.000	0.000
24	0.788	0.622	0.390	0.247	0.158	0.102	0.082	0.066	0.053	0.043	0.035	0.028	0.023	0.019	0.013	0.008	0.006	0.005	0.002	0.001	0.000	0.000	0.000
25	0.780	0.610	0.375	0.233	0.146	0.092	0.074	0.059	0.047	0.038	0.030	0.024	0.020	0.016	0.010	0.007	0.005	0.004	0.001	0.001	0.000	0.000	0.000
30	0.742	0.552	0.308	0.174	0.099	0.057	0.044	0.033	0.026	0.020	0.015	0.012	0.009	0.007	0.004	0.003	0.002	0.001	0.000	0.000	0.000	0.000	0.000
35	0.706	0.500	0.253	0.130	0.068	0.036	0.026	0.019	0.014	0.010	0.008	0.006	0.004	0.003	0.002	0.001	0.001	0.000	0.000	0.000	0.000	0.000	0.000
40	0.672	0.453	0.208	0.097	0.046	0.022	0.015	0.011	0.008	0.005	0.004	0.003	0.002	0.001	0.001	0.000	0.000	0.000	0.000	0.000	0.000	0.000	0.000
45	0.639	0.410	0.171	0.073	0.031	0.014	0.009	0.006	0.004	0.003	0.002	0.001	0.001	0.001	0.000	0.000	0.000	0.000	0.000	0.000	0.000	0.000	0.000
50	0.608	0.372	0.141	0.054	0.021	0.009	0.005	0.003	0.002	0.001	0.001	0.001	0.000	0.000	0.000	0.000	0.000	0.000	0.000	0.000	0.000	0.000	0.000

Prepared by Henry Hwang, research specialist, Department of Agricultural Economics, University of Minnesota.

present value of $1 discounted at 4 percent at the end of 10 years) and get $164.87.

Now assume that we are interested in knowing the present value of $1,000 received at the end of each year for 5 years. For variety, let's assume that we are using a discount rate of 10 percent. Using table 8, we can construct a small table of our own.

Year	10% discount factor	Present value of $1,000 received for 5 years
1	0.909	$909
2	.826	826
3	.751	751
4	.683	683
5	.621	621
Total		$3,790

Even though we actually receive $1,000 each year for 5 years, the present value of that income flow is only $3,790.

Let's consider some other applications of the "discount" idea. In the first chapter we indicated that the sequence of dollar income flows is an important variable in determining present value. Assume that alternative 3-year projects offer the same total income flow of $6,000, but that the sequence in project A is $3,000, $2,000, and $1,000, while that in project B is exactly the opposite. Again let's assume a 10 percent discount rate. The difference in present values can be illustrated as follows:

Year	10% discount factor	Project A Income flow	Project A Present value	Project B Income flow	Project B Present value
1	0.909	$3,000	$2,727	$1,000	$ 909
2	.826	2,000	1,652	2,000	1,652
3	.751	1,000	751	3,000	2,253
Total		$6,000	$5,130	$6,000	$4,814

The present value of the income flow from project A is $316 higher than that in project B. Why? Clearly, because the "near" dollars have a higher present value — a bigger weight — than the more distant ones, and project A generates more "near" dollars.

One of the convenient aspects of evaluating income flows on the present value basis is that, given the discount rate, it makes little difference whether the year-to-year income is constant, increasing, decreasing, or entirely irregular. We simply apply the discount factor appropriate for the year in question to the income in that year and proceed

Management of Long-Term Funds—Maximizing Returns

as before. This assumes, of course, that we are able to make reasonable estimates of income for each year in the period under consideration. We shall be dealing later with this problem, so we shall not belabor it here.

A second problem in the present-value approach relates to the selection of the "discount rate." We were rather glib in selecting 4 and 10 percent rates for purposes of our illustrations. Since in this section we are concerned with the "mechanics" of time value, no harm is done. But as a practical matter, the selection of the "correct discount rate" by the decision maker is of crucial concern. Under ideal conditions, a correct estimate of the "cost of capital" — variously referred to as the cutoff rate, the target rate, minimum standard, or hurdle rate — would be an appropriate one to use. In the next chapter we will deal with this concept extensively. Suffice it to say here that at best the discount rate chosen is subject to error. If the rate selected is higher than the "true" rate, the present-value estimate will be too low; if the rate selected is lower, the estimate will be too high. In the first instance, this could lead to rejecting profitable projects, and in the second, to undertaking unprofitable ones.

Discounted Rate of Return. An alternative way of looking at investment proposals is on a discounted rate of return basis. In this case, we are looking for a rate which when applied to net cash flows of a project will make their discounted sum exactly equal to the net investment outlays on the project. We will discuss the relative merits of this approach as compared to the present value approach in a later section. Here we are concerned primarily with the mechanics of determining the appropriate rate. As in the case of present value, there is a formula for computing the discounted rate of return.

Taking the simplest of all possible cases, suppose we have a project which will require an initial outlay of $1,000, will last 1 year, after which the original investment will be returned intact, and which will earn $50 in the year. Using the formula:

$$C = \frac{A_1}{(1+r)}$$

where:
- C = net investment outlay
- A_1 = cash flow
- r = rate of return

$$\$1,000 = \frac{\$50 + \$1,000}{(1+r)}$$

(formula continued on page 58)

58   The Financial Management of Agribusiness Firms

Solving for r we get: $1,000r + $1,000 = $1,050

$$r = \frac{\$50}{\$1000}$$
$$= 0.05$$
$$= 5\%$$

Thus, 5 percent is the rate that just discounts the cash flow to the net investment outlay. This process, as was true in the present-value approach, becomes a great deal more time-consuming as we increase the period under consideration.[12] But again, most analysts use tables rather than the formula to arrive at estimates of the discounted rate of return.

In the examples that follow we will assume that the cash flows in each year are positive, for the obvious reason that a negative income flow in 1 or more years would create difficulties in computing the rate of return.[13] If the cash flow is the same from year to year we can arrive at a reasonably precise estimate of the rate of return. On the other hand, if the flows are uneven we will have to settle for an approximation. Let's examine the uneven flow problem first.

Assume that we are considering an investment of $1,000 which will be completely consumed by the end of its expected 4-year economic life. Projected net cash flows at the end of each consecutive year are $400, $300, $300, and $200. What is the discounted rate of return? We may have to make several approximations before we come close to the "correct" rate. Let's assume initially that the correct rate lies somewhere between 6 and 16 percent. For convenience, let's put our data in a table, as below.

Year	Cash flow	Discount factor 6%	P.V.	Discount factor 8%	P.V.	Discount factor 10%	P.V.	Discount factor 16%	P.V.
0	−1,000								
1	+400	0.943	$377.2	0.926	$370.4	0.909	$363.6	0.862	$344.8
2	300	.890	267.0	.857	257.1	.826	247.8	.743	222.9
3	300	.840	252.0	.794	238.2	.751	225.3	.641	192.3
4	200	.792	158.4	.735	147.0	.683	136.6	.552	110.4
			$1,054.6		$1012.7		$973.3		$870.4

[12] The formula for any number of years is as follows:

$$C = \frac{A_1}{(1+r)} + \frac{A_2}{(1+r)^2} + \frac{A_3}{(1+r)^3} + \cdots + \frac{A_n}{(1+r)^n}$$

where:
 r = rate of return which will exactly equate the income stream to the net investment outlay on the project
 n = projected life of the project
 C = net investment outlay
 A_i = cash flows in the respective years

[13] When negative values do occur the present value approach is usually employed.

Management of Long-Term Funds—Maximizing Returns

Returning to the present-value table (table 8), we apply the discount factors found in the 6 and 16 percent columns to the cash flows in each of the appropriate years and total the result. We see that with the 16 percent rate the present value of the cash flow is about $130 less than the $1,000 initial investment. On the other hand, at the 6 percent rate, the present value of the income flow is about $55 higher than the initial investment. The correct value appears nearer 6 than 16 percent. If we use a 10 percent discount rate we move much closer — but still are about $27 too low. Trying the 8 percent discount rate we are closer still but high by about $13. At this point, we can say that the correct discounted rate of return is between 8 and 10 percent, and closer to the former. For some purposes this may be good enough. If we feel the need for more precision we can interpolate.[14] Carrying out this procedure yields an estimate of 8.6 percent. Given the general crudity of the approximation process, estimates in fractions of percent infer greater precision than actually exists. Rounding off, up or down, may be quite in order.

Estimating the rate of return when the income flow for each year is equal is a little less time-consuming. It involves using table 9 (derived from table 8), which shows the present value of $1 received annually at the end of each year for n years. How might table 9 be used? Let's use an example reasonably close to our last one. Assume an initial investment of $1,000 with a 4-year economic life, no salvage value, and $300 per year net cash flow.

Year	Cash flow	P.V. at 6%	P.V. at 8%
0	−$1,000		
1	300		
2	300		
3	300		
4	300		
Total		$1,039.5	$993.6

[14] For those who may be rusty on interpolation, it works as follows:

Difference in rate of return = 10% − 8% = 2%

Present value at 8% = $1,012.7
Present value at 10% =   973.3
Net Difference $ 39.4

Present value at 8% = $1,012.7
Investment   1,000.0
                      $ 12.7

Then: $\frac{12.7}{39.4} \times 2\% = 0.6\%$

and: 8.0% + 0.6 = 8.6%

Technically, since the values across rows do not change in linear fashion, a small bias is introduced by the interpolation.

Table 9. Present value of $1 received annually at the end of each year for N years

Year (N)	1%	2%	4%	6%	8%	10%	11%	12%	13%	14%	15%	16%	17%	18%	20%	22%	24%	25%	30%	35%	40%	45%	50%
1	0.990	0.980	0.962	0.943	0.926	0.909	0.901	0.893	0.885	0.877	0.870	0.862	0.855	0.848	0.833	0.820	0.807	0.800	0.769	0.741	0.714	0.690	0.667
2	1.970	1.942	1.886	1.833	1.783	1.736	1.713	1.690	1.668	1.647	1.626	1.605	1.585	1.566	1.528	1.492	1.457	1.440	1.361	1.289	1.225	1.165	1.111
3	2.941	2.884	2.775	2.673	2.577	2.487	2.444	2.402	2.361	2.322	2.283	2.246	2.210	2.174	2.107	2.042	1.981	1.952	1.816	1.696	1.589	1.493	1.407
4	3.902	3.808	3.630	3.465	3.312	3.170	3.102	3.037	2.975	2.914	2.855	2.798	2.743	2.690	2.589	2.494	2.404	2.362	2.166	1.997	1.849	1.720	1.605
5	4.853	4.714	4.452	4.212	3.993	3.791	3.696	3.605	3.517	3.433	3.352	3.274	3.199	3.127	2.991	2.864	2.745	2.689	2.436	2.220	2.035	1.876	1.737
6	5.796	5.601	5.242	4.917	4.623	4.355	4.231	4.111	3.998	3.889	3.785	3.685	3.589	3.498	3.326	3.167	3.021	2.951	2.643	2.385	2.168	1.983	1.824
7	6.728	6.472	6.002	5.582	5.206	4.868	4.712	4.564	4.423	4.288	4.160	4.039	3.922	3.812	3.605	3.416	3.242	3.161	2.802	2.508	2.263	2.057	1.883
8	7.652	7.326	6.733	6.210	5.747	5.335	5.146	4.968	4.799	4.639	4.487	4.344	4.207	4.078	3.837	3.619	3.421	3.329	2.925	2.598	2.331	2.109	1.922
9	8.566	8.162	7.435	6.802	6.247	5.759	5.537	5.328	5.132	4.946	4.772	4.607	4.451	4.303	4.031	3.786	3.566	3.463	3.019	2.665	2.379	2.144	1.948
10	9.471	8.983	8.111	7.360	6.710	6.145	5.889	5.650	5.426	5.216	5.019	4.833	4.659	4.494	4.193	3.923	3.682	3.571	3.092	2.715	2.414	2.168	1.965
11	10.368	9.787	8.761	7.887	7.139	6.495	6.207	5.938	5.687	5.453	5.234	5.029	4.836	4.656	4.327	4.035	3.776	3.656	3.147	2.752	2.438	2.185	1.977
12	11.255	10.575	9.385	8.384	7.536	6.814	6.492	6.194	5.918	5.660	5.421	5.197	4.988	4.793	4.439	4.127	3.851	3.725	3.190	2.779	2.456	2.197	1.985
13	12.134	11.348	9.986	8.853	7.904	7.103	6.750	6.424	6.122	5.842	5.583	5.342	5.118	4.910	4.533	4.203	3.912	3.780	3.223	2.799	2.469	2.205	1.990
14	13.004	12.106	10.563	9.295	8.244	7.367	6.982	6.628	6.303	6.002	5.725	5.468	5.229	5.008	4.611	4.265	3.962	3.824	3.249	2.814	2.478	2.210	1.993
15	13.865	12.849	11.118	9.712	8.560	7.606	7.191	6.811	6.462	6.142	5.847	5.576	5.324	5.092	4.676	4.315	4.001	3.859	3.268	2.826	2.484	2.214	1.995
16	14.718	13.578	11.652	10.106	8.851	7.824	7.379	6.974	6.604	6.265	5.954	5.669	5.405	5.162	4.730	4.357	4.033	3.887	3.283	2.834	2.489	2.216	1.997
17	15.562	14.292	12.166	10.477	9.122	8.022	7.549	7.120	6.729	6.373	6.047	5.749	5.475	5.222	4.775	4.391	4.059	3.910	3.295	2.840	2.492	2.218	1.998
18	16.399	14.992	12.659	10.828	9.372	8.202	7.702	7.250	6.840	6.468	6.128	5.818	5.534	5.273	4.812	4.419	4.080	3.928	3.304	2.844	2.494	2.219	1.999
19	17.226	15.679	13.134	11.158	9.604	8.365	7.839	7.366	6.938	6.550	6.198	5.878	5.585	5.316	4.844	4.442	4.097	3.942	3.311	2.848	2.496	2.220	1.999
20	18.046	16.352	13.590	11.470	9.818	8.514	7.963	7.470	7.025	6.623	6.259	5.929	5.628	5.353	4.870	4.460	4.110	3.954	3.316	2.850	2.497	2.221	1.999
21	18.857	17.011	14.029	11.764	10.017	8.649	8.075	7.562	7.102	6.687	6.313	5.973	5.665	5.384	4.891	4.476	4.121	3.963	3.320	2.852	2.498	2.221	2.000
22	19.661	17.658	14.451	12.042	10.201	8.772	8.176	7.645	7.170	6.743	6.359	6.011	5.696	5.410	4.909	4.488	4.130	3.971	3.323	2.853	2.499	2.222	2.000
23	20.456	18.292	14.857	12.304	10.371	8.883	8.267	7.718	7.230	6.792	6.399	6.044	5.723	5.432	4.925	4.499	4.137	3.976	3.325	2.854	2.499	2.222	2.000
24	21.244	18.914	15.247	12.551	10.529	8.985	8.348	7.784	7.283	6.835	6.434	6.073	5.747	5.451	4.937	4.507	4.143	3.981	3.327	2.855	2.499	2.222	2.000
25	22.024	19.524	15.622	12.784	10.675	9.077	8.422	7.843	7.330	6.783	6.464	6.097	5.766	5.467	4.948	4.514	4.147	3.985	3.329	2.856	2.499	2.222	2.000
30	25.808	22.397	17.292	13.765	11.258	9.427	8.694	8.055	7.496	7.003	6.566	6.177	5.829	5.517	4.979	4.534	4.160	3.995	3.332	2.857	2.500	2.222	2.000
35	29.409	24.999	18.665	14.498	11.655	9.644	8.855	8.176	7.586	7.070	6.617	6.215	5.858	5.539	4.992	4.541	4.164	3.998	3.333	2.857	2.500	2.222	2.000
40	32.835	27.356	19.793	15.047	11.925	9.779	8.951	8.244	7.634	7.105	6.642	6.234	5.871	5.548	4.997	4.544	4.166	3.999	3.333	2.857	2.500	2.222	2.000
45	36.095	29.490	20.720	15.456	12.109	9.863	9.008	8.283	7.661	7.123	6.654	6.242	5.877	5.552	4.999	4.545	4.166	4.000	3.333	2.857	2.500	2.222	2.000
50	39.197	31.424	21.482	15.762	12.234	9.915	9.042	8.305	7.676	7.133	6.661	6.246	5.880	5.554	4.999	4.545	4.167	4.000	3.333	2.857	2.500	2.222	2.000

Prepared by Henry Hwang, Research Specialist, Department of Agricultural Economics, University of Minnesota.

In this case, because cash flow is the same for each year, we can employ a shortcut method in arriving at our estimates of discounted rate of return as follows: Divide net investment by net annual cash flow = $1,000/$300 = 3.333. Enter table 9 at the 4-year level. Move across the row until the factor closest to 3.333 is reached. This turns out to be 3.312, which falls under the 8 percent column. Multiplying $300 × 3.312, we arrive at a net present value of $993.6 that is very close to the $1,000 investment outlay. Since 3.333 is between 3.465 (which reflects a 6 percent rate) and 3.312, some may wish to interpolate; but as before, an approximation of 8 percent may be good enough.

For the reader who may be vaguely troubled as to why, in the example above, the rate of return appears to be slightly less than 8 percent, while in the immediately preceding example it was above 8 percent even though the total cash flows in each case were the same, we offer a gentle reminder. In the earlier example, the cash flow was highest in the first year and lowest in the last; since the earlier years have heavier weight in the discounting process, a higher rate of return was realized.

Some Applications

With our grounding in the mechanics of evaluating the impact of time on investment proposals, we are now ready to look at some applications. You will recall that we indicated earlier that most capital uses can be sorted into new, replacement or cost-saving, and service projects. In this section we will develop examples of each of these kinds of problems, using the tools that we have just developed for this purpose.

Analyzing New Investment Proposals. Suppose that the Roseville Grain Corporation is debating whether or not to undertake fertilizer distribution which will call for the construction of a $30,000 building. It is estimated that the building will have a 10-year economic life and will be depreciated on a straight-line basis at $3,000 each year. Table 10 summarizes the projected cash flows from the project. To determine net cash flow for any year, the estimated cash inflows (column 1) are reduced by cash expenses (column 2) and taxes (column 4). Cash outflows associated with interest expense and/or dividends are not included. These are costs of obtaining capital and help determine a cutoff point for the minimum acceptable return on any investment. Capital costs are discussed in chapter 5.

As we suggested earlier, cash inflows (column 1) take into account the positive and negative changes of cash inflows over the entire bus-

62 *The Financial Management of Agribusiness Firms*

iness that result from taking on the new project. If the project was expected to be accompanied by increases in the sales of feed or seed or farm supplies, these increases would have to be taken into account in estimating cash inflows. Similarly, if the project was expected to reduce the cash inflows from some other part of the business, these negative impacts would also have to be included in arriving at an estimate of net inflows.

Estimated cash outflows include such items as labor costs, raw material costs, power costs, and supply costs. As in the case of revenues,

Table 10. Discounted cash flow analysis of a fertilizer storage facility proposal for the Roseville Grain Corporation

Year	(1) Estimated cash inflows	(2) Estimated operating cash outflows *	(3) Estimated total expense †	(4) Estimated tax cash outflow ‡ (25% rate)	(5) Net cash flow §	×	(6) Discount factor (10%)	(7) Discounted cash flow ¶
0		− $30,000			− $30,000	×	1.000 =	− $30,000
1	+ $10,000	− 3,000	$6,000	− $1,000	+ 6,000		0.909	+ 5,454
2	+ 10,000	− 3,000	6,000	− 1,000	+ 6,000		.826	+ 4,956
3	+ 10,000	− 3,000	6,000	− 1,000	+ 6,000		.751	+ 4,506
4	+ 10,000	− 3,000	6,000	− 1,000	+ 6,000		.683	+ 4,098
5	+ 10,000	− 3,000	6,000	− 1,000	+ 6,000		.621	+ 3,726
6	+ 10,000	− 3,000	6,000	− 1,000	+ 6,000		.564	+ 3,384
7	+ 10,000	− 3,000	6,000	− 1,000	+ 6,000		.513	+ 3,078
8	+ 10,000	− 3,000	6,000	− 1,000	+ 6,000		.467	+ 2,802
9	+ 10,000	− 3,000	6,000	− 1,000	+ 6,000		.424	+ 2,544
10	+ 10,000	− 3,000	6,000	− 1,000	+ 6,000		.386	+ 2,316

Net present value + $6,864

* Excludes outlays for interest, dividends, and taxes.
† Column 2 plus $3,000 of depreciation expense each year.
‡ Column 1 minus column 3 times 25%.
§ Column 1 plus column 2 plus column 4.
¶ Column 5 times column 6.

these costs are net in the sense that they take into account changes in costs over the entire business resulting from the new project.

Estimated total expenses (column 3) include depreciation. Why? Because even though depreciation expense does not create an operational cash outflow at the time it is incurred, it is deductible from revenues in determining taxable income.[15] Since depreciation reduces taxable income, it reduces taxes and, therefore, net cash outflow. This is demonstrated below:

[15] Proprietary firms and cooperatives that qualify under the requirements of Section 521 of the Internal Revenue Code of 1954 do not pay corporate income taxes. Cooperatives that do not qualify under the code pay taxes at regular corporate tax rates on earnings they retain as corporate profits.

Management of Long-Term Funds—Maximizing Returns 63

	With depreciation expense	Without depreciation expense
Revenue (I)	$10,000	$10,000
Cash expenses (O)	−3,000	−3,000
Depreciation expense	−3,000	0
Taxable income	4,000	7,000
Taxes (25% of taxable income) (O)	1,000	1,750
Summarizing the inflows (I) and outflows (O):		
Revenue (I)	$10,000	$10,000
Cash expenses (O)	3,000	3,000
Taxes (O)	1,000	1,750
Net cash flow	+$6,000	+$5,250

To highlight the impact of depreciation on cash flow we show what the latter would have been if depreciation had not been considered. We see that since depreciation reduces taxable income from $7,000 to $4,000 it reduces the amount of taxes that must be paid and, therefore, increases net cash flow. In the example, inclusion of depreciation expense "saves" the firm $750. This, of course, is why most firms attempt to charge off as much depreciation expense as the tax laws will allow, as rapidly as possible.

Having arrived at our estimate of net cash flow, we are now in a position to estimate either net present value or the discounted rate of return from this investment. Assuming that the Roseville Grain Corporation has a cost of capital of 10 percent, the appropriate discount factors (table 8) are applied to net cash flows each year.[16] The discounted values are summed to arrive at net present value, which in this case amounts to $6,864.

Alternatively, if we wanted to know the discounted rate of return on this investment, how might we go about it? Since cash flows in each year are equal, we can use the shortcut method discussed earlier in connection with table 9. First, the $30,000 net investment is divided by $6,000, giving us a factor of 5. Entering table 9 at the 10-year level, we find a factor of 5.019 under the 15 percent column. When this is applied to the $6,000 per year net cash flow, the result is $30,114, not far from the net investment figure of $30,000. Thus, we could conclude that this investment would yield a little over 15 percent.

Is this investment proposal a good one or not? It has a positive net present value, $6,864, or, looking at it in a somewhat different light,

[16] Actually, since cash flows for each year are equal, we could have used table 9. We chose the longer method to emphasize the decreased present value of the income flow from later years.

its discounted rate of return (15 percent) exceeds the cost of capital (10 percent), so our immediate impression is favorable. However, since we don't know what other investment opportunities are open to the company, or how this project stands in relation to them, we are not in a position to make a final judgment. We will treat the process of arraying project proposals later in the chapter.

Replacement Decisions. A second major use of long-term capital is to replace existing productive facilities. Trucks, elevators, office equipment, grinders, churns, storage facilities, etc. wear out under continued use. One important problem confronting decision makers is identifying the ideal time to replace a particular item. In this problem we have two elements to take into account: (a) the net operating cash flows that the particular asset generates, and (b) the trade-in or salvage value of the item at any particular point in time. With this in mind, let's work through a hypothetical problem in which the optimum replacement period is to be determined.

Assume that a portable mixer can be purchased for $4,000 and that past experience indicates that it can be operated for 7 years.[17] For purposes of our illustration, assume that the net cash flow from operations and the trade-in value of the mixer in each year are as illustrated below.

Year	Net operating cash flows	Trade-in value of mixer
0	−4,000	
1	1,400	$3,200
2	1,200	2,600
3	1,000	2,000
4	900	1,600
5	500	1,200
6	400	800
7	200	600

We will assume that the decrease in net cash flows from operations is due primarily to increased maintenance costs as the mixer gets older. The decrease in the trade-in value reflects the impacts of time and use. Assume that the cost of capital to the firm is 10 percent. Given the operating cash flow and trade-in value data, we can calculate the present value of an income flow under various assumptions with respect to time of replacement. This is illustrated as follows:

[17] This illustration is purely hypothetical, so neither the value nor the use-life reflects actual experience.

If mixer is traded after 1 year

Year	Cash flow from operations	Cash flow from sale of mixer	Total cash flow	10% discount factor	Discounted cash flow
0			−$4,000	1.000	−$4,000.00
1	$1,400	$3,200	4,600	0.909	4,181.40

Net present value $181.40

If mixer is traded after 2 years

Year	Cash flow from operations	Cash flow from sale of mixer	Total cash flow	10% discount factor	Discounted cash flow
0			−$4,000	1.000	−$4,000.00
1	$1,400		1,400	0.909	+1,272.60
2	1,200	$2,600	3,800	0.826	+3,138.80

Net present value $411.40

If mixer is traded after 3 years

Year	Cash flow from operations	Cash flow from sale of mixer	Total cash flow	10% discount factor	Discounted cash flow
0			−$4,000	1.000	−$4,000.00
1	$1,400		1,400	0.909	+1,272.60
2	1,200		1,200	0.826	+991.20
3	1,000	$2,000	3,000	0.751	+2,253.00

Net present value $516.80

There is an initial cash outlay of $4,000. If the mixer is traded after 1 year, the total cash flow is $4,600, i.e., $1,400 from operations and $3,200 from the sale of the mixer. Applying the 10 percent discount factor (0.909) from table 8, the discounted cash flow is $4,181.40. The net present value would be $181.40. If the mixer is traded after 2 years, we must take into account the cash flow from year 1 ($1,400 discounted by the factor appropriate for that year [0.909]) and the cash flow from year 2 ($1,200 from operations plus $2,600 from the sale of the mixer) discounted by the appropriate factor (0.826) to arrive at a net present value at the end of the second year, $411.40. The same operations are performed again for year 3 and we arrive at a net present value of $516.80 if the mixer is traded at the end of 3 years. The above procedure was used to calculate net present value for all 7 years. These values are summarized on page 66. We see that the net present value is greatest if the mixer is traded at the end of the fourth year. Up to that point the present values are increasing and they decrease thereafter. Thus, the end of the fourth year is the optimum replacement time for the mixer.

Net present value of mixer as related to the year traded

Year	Present value	Net present value	Discounted rate of return, %
0	− $4,000.00		
1	+ 4,181.40	$181.40	15.0
2	4,411.40	411.40	16.5
3	4,516.80	516.80	16.3
4	4,722.30	722.30	17.4
5	4,685.20	685.20	16.4
6	4,576.00	616.80	15.6
7	4,361.60	576.00	15.2

While we don't show the calculations here, we did estimate the discounted rate of return on this investment that would have resulted from replacing the mixer at the end of each of the 7 years. As you can see in the table above, the maximum rate of 17.4 percent at the end of year 4 coincides with the maximum indicated by the present-value approach.

We want to emphasize that if the objective of the analysis is to determine the optimum time of replacement, the problem is treated as though we were examining separate investment proposals for each of the years under consideration. In the example above, we in effect analyzed seven different proposals.

Not all replacement problems are as simple as the one just presented. But the process of analysis is similar. The optimum replacement period will vary greatly from investment to investment. In some cases, we may find that the present values may rise continuously, at least within some reasonably defined economic period. On the other hand, the optimum replacement period for some investments may be as short as a year or two, particularly in the case of machines and other equipment that receive intensive use on a continuous basis and for which maintenance costs may be extremely high. In any case, this tool can be useful to the decision maker who is attempting to establish a replacement policy that is consistent with maximizing net present values or discounted rate of return.[18]

Another problem that arises in the replacement area is what to do when a cost-saving innovation makes an appearance. Suppose, for example, that a firm purchased a processing machine for $20,000 with an estimated use-life of 5 years. The labor costs associated with operating the machine are $40,000 per year. Assume that, within a day after the

---

[18] Some additional complications enter the calculation when the maximum replacement life problem also includes improvements. See Harold Bierman, Jr., and Seymour Smidt, *The Capital Budgeting Decision*, second edition, p. 83–90.

firm is irrevocably committed to the purchase of this machine, a new model comes on the market which would reduce labor requirements and thereby increase net cash flows by $8,000 per year. Assume that the new machine would cost $35,000 and would also last for 5 years. The not-so-old machine could be sold for $10,000. Should the new machine be purchased? Where should the analysis begin?

This is really a problem in identifying the appropriate net investment associated with the purchase of the new machine. If the old machine is sold, the firm incurs a book loss of $10,000. Is this loss properly chargeable to the new investment? The answer is no! The old machine must be regarded as a "sunk cost" incurred by an earlier decision. The decision to purchase the new machine must be based entirely on the *differential cash flows* created by it. Should the $10,000 received from the sale of the old machine be deducted from the cost of the new one? The answer is yes — because the sale of the old machine created a cash flow that was a direct result of the decision to buy the new one.

The correct net investment in the new project is $25,000. What is the present value of an income flow of $8,000 per year for 5 years, assuming that the cost of capital to the firm is 10 percent? Since the income received in each year is the same, we can use table 9 to determine the appropriate discount factor. Entering the table at the 5-year row, we move across to the 10 percent column. We apply the discount factor we find there, 3.791, to the $8,000 per year net cash flow and arrive at a present value of $30,328. When this is compared to the $25,000 net investment we can see that there is a positive net present value of $5,328.

Suppose that the book "loss" of $10,000 had been included in net investment.[19] This would have increased net investment to $35,000. Under these circumstances the proposal to replace the old machine would have had a net present value of −$4,672 and would have automatically been rejected. In so doing, the firm would have lost an opportunity to increase its net present value by the $5,328 which would result from the cost savings generated by the new machine.

In the above example we avoided a rather sticky problem. Suppose that, instead of the new machine appearing almost simultaneously with the purchase of the old one, it appeared a year later. If each machine had an expected use life of 5 years, the "savings" attributable to the purchase of the new one would really only extend over the last 4 years

[19] In our example we have ignored the tax benefits from writing off the loss.

of the life of the old one. This is so because the old machine would have been replaced anyway at the end of 5 years.

Clearly, if the potential cost savings are such that they would generate a positive net present value within the 4-year time period, the investment would still be profitable. In our example above, the present value of an $8,000-per-year income stream discounted at 10 percent over a 4-year period is $25,360 — higher than the $25,000 investment outlay. But suppose that the 4-year net present value was lower. Would the investment be rejected? Since the new machine would have 1 more year of economic life, this may not be a sufficient basis for rejection. Perhaps the easiest way to handle the problem would be to plug in the trade-in or liquidation value of the new machine at the end of the 4th year as income. If this results in a positive net present value, once again the investment could be considered profitable. On the other hand, if it is still negative we may have a sufficient basis for rejecting the proposal.

Not all replacement problems involve simple 1-year overlaps. Replacement opportunities can occur at any time during the life of an investment. Suppose that in our example the new machine had appeared after the 4th year instead of after the first. In this case, the "saving" resulting from its purchase would include only 1 year. Plugging in the trade-in value of the new machine after 1 year may not be a good idea in this case because typically the greatest loss in resale value of machinery and equipment items takes place in the first 1 or 2 years. This would tend to build a low bias into our present-value estimate. We would, therefore, want to be careful about rejecting a proposal on such a basis.

Various methods for handling this problem are discussed in other texts.[20] We won't go into them here because of the somewhat limited objectives of this text. But we do want to emphasize once again the importance of identifying the "correct" net investment associated with a proposal as well as the "correct" net cash flows that are expected to result from the decision.

Assuming that we follow "correct" procedures, are replacement investment proposals automatically accepted if they result in positive net present values? The answer is no, except in the unlikely case of the firm that has unlimited access to funds. In the example above, the replace-

---

[20] See, for example, Erich Helfert, *Techniques of Financial Analysis*, Homewood, Ill.: Richard D. Irwin, Inc., 1963, p. 166–170; see particularly George Terborgh, *Business Investment Policy*, Washington D.C.: Machinery and Allied Products Institute, 1958, for a thorough discussion of the MAPI system of evaluating replacement proposals; for a brief discussion of the MAPI system, see Martin B. Solomon, Jr., *Investment Decisions in Small Business*, Lexington: University of Kentucky Press, 1963, p. 26–29.

ment of the machine, even though determined to be profitable, could have been rejected because other projects competing for the same funds would have yielded a higher net present value. Once again, the importance of not looking at a decision in isolation is stressed.

Service Projects. The discounted cash flow approach breaks down in analyzing service uses of funds. These investments are intended to strengthen employee morale, improve firm image, etc. Examples include the plush board room, attractive offices, the paved parking lot, or a pleasant employee cafeteria which may offer meals at prices less than costs.

Suppose that a firm is planning to remodel a dining room for its employees. The total remodeling cost will be $20,000 and it is expected to operate without major repairs for 5 years. An alternative plan suggests that the present dining room can be repainted and worn tables and chairs replaced for $5,000. After this work is done the cafeteria should also operate without major repair for 5 years. Should the firm invest $20,000 in remodeling a dining room when $5,000 would make it just as functional? Can it be determined if remodeling is worth $15,000? What are the returns from this proposal?

We might attempt to measure the relationship between employee morale and increased productivity (lower costs) with the improved facilities, but it is unlikely that even the best personnel researcher could quantify this with precision. Does this mean that remodeling isn't worth $15,000? Not necessarily. We simply don't know.

Even though the effects of some service-type proposals on productivity can be measured with reasonable accuracy, the most important consideration is frequently neglected. For example, the cost of absenteeism because of injury can be compared with the cost of a new safety device. But these costs fail to measure the impacts of such a device on employee morale and the human value of concern for safety. Some values just cannot be measured in terms of dollars.

Other Measures

Studies of how businessmen actually evaluate investment alternatives suggest that, by and large, they use cruder methods than those just discussed.[21] Perhaps the most popular is the "payback" approach, which simply involves dividing the net investment (I) by the after-tax annual average net cash flow (A) to arrive at a measure of the number of years

[21] See, for example, Martin Solomon, op. Cit., p. 49–56.

(Y) that it takes a project to pay for itself. In equation form:

$$Y = \frac{I}{A}$$

Presumably those projects with short payback periods receive priority attention. It is true, of course, that how long a project will take to pay for itself is a factor in the decision process, particularly in risky ventures. But it certainly isn't the only factor, and blind adherence to the payback approach can lead to wrong choices among alternatives.

Suppose, for example, that we had two project proposals, each requiring a net investment of $1,000 but with project 1 averaging a net cash flow of $335 for 3 years, while project 2 promises an average of $250 per 10 years. For project 1, the payback period is 2.9 years, while that of project 2 is 4 years. Is project 1 superior to project 2? Clearly not, since its total yield above investment is $5 as compared to $1,500 for project 2. Thus, because the payback approach ignores the length of project life it could lead to the wrong choice.

Another important shortcoming is the fact that payback ignores the time-value problem. As we saw earlier, dollars received in "near" years have a higher present value than those received later. In the example below, projects A and B require identical investment outlays of $5,000, and each average $2,000 per year in net cash flow. The payback period for both projects is 2.5 years, suggesting that there is little to choose be-

Year	100% discount factor	Project A Income flow	Project A Present value	Project B Income flow	Project B Present value
0	1.000	−$5,000	−$5,000	−$5,000	−$5,000
1	0.909	3,000	2,727	1,000	909
2	.826	2,000	1,652	2,000	1,652
3	.751	1,000	751	3,000	2,253
			Net present value +$130		−$186

tween them. But income flows in project A are high in the first year and low in the last while the reverse is true in project B. Using the present-value approach we would reject project B because it has a negative net present value. This demonstrates that when we take into account the time value of money we are not indifferent to the choice between the two proposals.

A variation of the payback period approach is its reciprocal, the simple rate of return:

$$R = \frac{1}{I/A}$$

Management of Long-Term Funds—Maximizing Returns

$$= \frac{A}{I}$$

Where:

R = simple rate of return
I = net investment
A = average yearly cash flow

This formulation poses all of the pitfalls that its parent does. It can be demonstrated, however, that if yearly cash flows are equal and the time period considered is long enough, this measure does approach the discounted rate of return approach discussed in the previous section.[22] Since both of these conditions are seldom met as a practical matter, the simple rate of return must be regarded for what it is —a crude approximation of the discounted rate. It should be used with extreme care.[23]

Dealing With the Uncertainty Problem

In his decision-making process, the manager is basically concerned with three estimates. First, he must estimate what additional cash outflows or reductions of current cash inflows will be associated with a proposed course of action. Second, he must determine the additional cash inflows, or reduction in outflows, that will result from it. These first two estimates indicate changes in the net cash pattern. Third, the manager must determine the discount rate that should be used to weigh the cash patterns.

This process is complicated by the fact that not all proposals will have the same degree of certainty attached to them. The manager will have more confidence in some projects than he will in others, for reasons ranging from differences in experience and/or knowledge to uncontrollable factors such as possible changes in regulations or competitive patterns. Perhaps a higher rate of return should be demanded on riskier uses, but how can the proper differential be determined?

In what follows, we will examine a way in which estimates of cash flows and discount rates can be made in an environment of uncertainty.

[22] When annual income flows are equal, the discounted rate of return can be computed as follows:

$$R = \frac{A}{I} - \frac{A}{N}\left[\frac{I}{(I+R)}\right]$$

where:

A = annual cash flow
I = net investment
R = discounted rate of return
N = number of years in life of investment

As N becomes larger, the second term in the equation becomes smaller. With a very high N, the effect of the second term becomes negligible.

[23] For discussion of other "approximations," check the references at the end of this chapter.

72   The Financial Management of Agribusiness Firms

For reasons of simplicity, most of our discussion will center on the present-value approach, but the applications to the discounted rate of return approach will be made clear.

Estimating Cash Flows

Up to this point we have used "single"-valued estimates of income flows in our illustrations, as we do in the simple example below. In a world of perfect certainty, year-to-year cash flows and the cost of capi-

Years from today	Cash change	Discount factor (6%)	Discounted cash change
0	−$100	1.000	−$100.00
1	+30	0.943	+28.29
2	+50	0.890	+44.50
3	+70	0.840	+58.80
4	+90	0.792	+71.28
5	+100	0.747	+74.70
		Net present value	+$177.57

tal are predictable without error. Assuming that no other proposals are open to the firm at a higher net present value and that adequate funds are available, the investment proposed above would be undertaken. But managers operating in the real world of uncertainty are more likely to think in terms of ranges of possible outcomes around some central value rather than the single-valued estimate just illustrated. Can this way of looking at things be translated into an operationally useful method of evaluating alternatives? It is to this problem that we now turn.

Consider the two investment proposals offered below:

Years from today	Expected cash change on both proposals	Proposal 1 Estimated range of cash changes Low	High	Proposal 2 Estimated range of cash changes Low	High
0	−$100	−$90	−$110	−$90	−$130
1	+30	+20	+40	−10	+50
2	+50	+30	+60	+0	+80
3	+70	+60	+80	+20	+100
4	+90	+60	+100	+60	+100
5	+100	+60	+100	+60	+120

The expected cash changes are the same for both. Proposal 1 has a smaller range between the low and high estimates. From the preceding example we know that the expected net present value of both proposals is $177.57 when discounted at 6 percent. It would also be interesting

Management of Long-Term Funds—Maximizing Returns 73

to define the maximum range of net present values for each proposal. This is done by subtracting the high-range cash outlay in period 0 from the discounted low-range cash flows in periods 1-5 to establish the low estimate, and by subtracting the low-range cash outlay in period 0 from the discounted high-range cash flows in periods 1-5 to establish the high estimate. These results are summarized for both proposals below.

Net present value *	Proposal 1	Proposal 2
Low estimate	$ 78.30	−$30.29
Expected estimate	177.57	177.57
High estimate	222.22	281.19

*When discounted at 6%.

Proposal 1 would be profitable even under adverse conditions while proposal 2 would not be. On the other hand, if all goes well, proposal 2 could be more profitable than proposal 1. A manager might drop proposal 2 from consideration if the possibility of a loss would jeopardize the survival of the business. The decision would have to be made in the light of factors such as the firm's capacity to assume loss, and the willingness of the suppliers of capital to assume risk.

In connection with the willingness and capacity to assume risks, evaluation of the probability of possible outcomes would be useful. For example, proposal 2 could lead to a loss, but what is the likelihood — probability — of this happening? If it is only one chance in a thousand, a manager might take that gamble. If it is one chance in five, he might not. Not only is the range of possible outcomes important but the probability of occurrence should also be considered.

Estimates of the probability of occurrence of some particular outcome range from careful studies to simple guesses. Whether he formalizes these estimates or not, the manager uses them every time he makes a decision. He has a "feeling" that one outcome is more likely than another. These subjective estimates of probability arise out of his experience and may be just as valid as those derived by more elaborate means. They can be made even more useful when they are put into a formal probability framework.

The sum of probabilities of all possible outcomes is 1.0. For example, if we say there is a .2 probability (20 percent chance) that the cash inflow in 1 year will be −$10, we're also saying that there is an 80 percent chance that some result other than −$10 will occur. This idea can be illustrated by either of the proposals we discussed above, but we shall use proposal 2. Starting in period 0, with a range of −$90 to −$130, and arbitrarily using $10 units, the possible cash flows in the period are:

$$-\$90, -\$100, -\$110, -\$120, -\$130.$$

Suppose the manager believes that there is a .2 probability (2 chances in 10) that −$90 is the correct figure, .65 probability that −$100 is correct, .10 that it is −$110, .04 that it is −$120, and .01 that it is −$130.

Possible outcome of period 0	Probability of outcome
−$90	.20
−100	.65
−110	.10
−120	.04
−130	.01
	1.00

These estimates indicate that 95 chances out of 100 the initial cash outlay will be $110 or less. There is only one chance in 100 of a value of −$130, and four chances in 100 of a value of −$120. Based on these odds, perhaps the manager would feel justified in using the −$110 as the low estimate instead of −$130. If he is willing to face the odds at 85 out of 100 he would use $100 as the outflow change in the low net present-value estimate.

By revising all estimates, both high and low, at the 85 percent level of occurrence as just illustrated, the following limits are derived for proposal 2. Discounting these cash change estimates, the net present

Years from today	Estimate of high return limit*	Estimate of low return limit*
0	−$90	−$100
1	+40	0
2	+70	+30
3	+80	+30
4	+80	+60
5	+80	+60

* 85% chance of occurring.

value for the high limit is +$200.34 and the low estimate is now positive at +$44.24. The high estimate was lowered by $81 and the low one increased by $75. A manager in this example is taking a calculated gamble by assuming that the 15 chances out of 100 of a higher or a lower value will not occur.

Present-Value Discount Factors

Little was said about the selection of the discount factor in our discussion of cash changes. In the above examples it was assumed to be 6 percent in each instance. We indicated earlier that the selection of discount factor is based on an estimate of the cost of capital, which will be discussed at length in the next chapter. Suffice it to say here that a manager could develop a proposed range of possible discount rates and apply them to the various estimates of cash changes. As the riskiness of a firm's projects increases, the cost of capital will increase because the capital suppliers will demand higher rewards for riskier ventures. Referring to the proposal 2 example in the previous section, assume that the cost of capital range for that firm was estimated to be between 5 and 8 percent. If the manager selects earnings estimates that exclude the possible outcomes that have 15 chances out of 100 of occurring, he should be using a higher discount factor. Perhaps 8 percent would have been more appropriate than the 6 percent used throughout the illustration.

The differences in net present value can be illustrated by using the low estimate of proposal 2 and discounting it at 6 and 8 percent for both the 100 and the 85 percent probability occurrences. As can be seen below, the effect of using the higher discount rates is to lower the net present value in each case. Varying the discount factor is a common method of allowing for risk considerations.

Net present value of estimate of low return alternative discounted at 6 and 8 percent (proposal 2)

100% chance of occurrence estimate		85% chance of occurrence estimate	
6%	8%	6%	8%
−$30.29	−$38.24	+$44.24	+$34.49

At a minimum, the discount rate would always be equal to or larger than the cost of capital estimates. As risk increases, percentage points would be added as a risk "penalty" with the number of points assessed dependent on the amount of risk involved.

Application to Discounted Rate of Return

While what we have said to this point has by and large been focused on net present values, the applicability of the foregoing to determining a "discounted rate of return" should be clear. Rates of returns are often thought of in terms of ranges. The techniques for assessing the probabilities of occurrence of cash flow ranges of varying widths are precisely the same as above. Having established a range of high and low cash flows, we can develop approximations of discounted rates of returns which will equate them to the initial investment. This is done in exactly the same way as was demonstrated earlier in the chapter. Except in the case of equal income flows for each year, estimating rate of return is more time-consuming than estimating present value. The process becomes even more complex — and for all practical purposes ruled out — when negative cash flow values occur in 1 or more years.

How Much Risk?

Can we generalize on how much risk a firm can take? The answer, of course, is no. Some managers who possess great talents, intuition, and a willingness to take a chance can thrive in risk situations in which other managers would quickly perish. The attitudes of owners and lenders towards risks, which vary from firm to firm, will also constrain or otherwise shape the firm's risk posture. Finally, there is a matter of how well the financial structure of the firm is able to withstand the shock of loss. For some firms, a small negative variation in income may mean collapse, while for others it may take a series of catastrophic events to bring about failure. In the final analysis, the interaction of managers, owners, and creditors will determine the limits of risk for the firm. Our treatment above suggests one way of approaching the problem.

Ranking Proposals

Up to this point our discussion of the basic methods of evaluating capital usage programs has centered on return on investment and net present value. Theoretically, projects yielding the highest return on investment (or the largest net present value) are accepted first, followed by all other projects having a return on investment greater than the cost of capital (or a positive net present value) ranked in descending order. To be operational, however, some qualifications are needed.

We indicated that capital projects carry with them varying degrees of certainty and we suggested ways of bringing risk considerations into the analysis. If a new project is being considered, the firm might require it to have an anticipated return which is greater than that from an old tried and tested one by some specified percent. There is danger, of course, that new projects will never get started. In a time of rapidly changing technology, it may be a mistake to burden the new opportunities. But the fact of the matter is that all projects do not have the same degree of certainty attached to them and this needs to be considered in some quantitative or qualitative way when projects are ranked.

Another ranking problem concerns conflicts between the return on investment and net present-value approaches. For example, an investment proposal requiring $1,000 for 1 year at 15 percent has a net present value of only $150. On the other hand, a $10,000 1-year project may have a return of only 10 percent, but a net present value of $1,000. Here the evaluation methods are clearly at odds. Several refinements, not to be discussed here, could be applied to the calculations to resolve this apparent conflict.[24] Normally, net present value is adopted when there are problems of large differences in dollar commitments between projects, significant differences in project life, or negative income flows during the period of the project. On the other hand, the discounted rate of return approach has an advantage in that—once the calculations have been made—it is more easily understood by the decision maker.

A third ranking problem arises because decision makers frequently overlook interdependencies which may exist between projects. It is entirely possible that a particular project, if viewed in isolation, would be dropped from consideration because of low returns or low net present values. Other high-return projects may be so related to it, however, that if it were dropped, overall returns to the firm would fall. Such interdependencies must be identified and taken into account.

At some point, however, the various problems associated with the ranking process must be resolved. Estimates of income flows from alternative projects are made. Risk factors and project interdependencies are taken into account. The manager is now ready to rank the alternative proposal. How might he go about this? Assume, for sake of example, that he chooses the return on investment approach. He could proceed as is illustrated in table 11. In the example, 12 projects in all were taken into consideration. Five were new projects and seven were replacement proposals. The rate of return ranges from 25 to 10 percent and the investment required per project ranges from $3,000 to $25,000. The right-hand column accumulates the individual totals. In effect, this is the firm's demand schedule for capital. How much capital the firm will actually use is dependent on its cost—the topic of the next chapter. For now, we can say that if the cost of capital were 10 percent or less the firm would undertake all of its project proposals for a total investment of $112,000. If the cost of capital were 15 percent, it would drop off the last three projects and invest a total of $88,000. Other

---

[24] See the suggested readings at the close of this chapter. Particularly recommended is Harold Bierman, Jr., and Seymour Smidt, *The Capital Budgeting Decision*, second edition.

Table 11. Project proposals ranked by projected returns on investment and investment requirements

Rank	Type of project	Rate of return, %	Investment required	Cumulative investment
1	New	25	$25,000	$25,000
2	Replace	23	10,000	35,000
3	Replace	22	15,000	50,000
4	New	20	5,000	55,000
5	New	20	3,000	58,000
6	New	18	10,000	68,000
7	Replace	17	5,000	73,000
8	Replace	16	5,000	78,000
9	Replace	15	10,000	88,000
10	New	13	5,000	92,000
11	Replace	11	10,000	102,000
12	Replace	10	10,000	112,000

variations in the cost of capital could be illustrated, but the point to remember is that whether or not a project is undertaken depends not only on its own rate of return, but on its rank in relation to other feasible alternatives, and the cost of capital.

Two Other Considerations in Capital Usage

Two other factors deserve consideration under the topic of capital usage. First, firms too often undertake capital expansion projects without recognizing the impact that the decision will have on working capital. The result is that working capital is frequently reduced to dangerously low levels. This happens when the growth rate of capital investments (fixed assets) outpaces the rate of capital accumulation (long-term debt and equity) to finance them. The only alternative is to shift working capital assets into capital projects. If the firm has maintained excessively large working capital balances, shifting the excess into permanent assets may be desirable. At some point, however, differences in the rate of capital accumulation and the rate of investment would have to be adjusted. If not, working capital shortages may force a reduction in sales, nonpayment or delayed payment of obligations, lower profit levels, and, eventually, bankruptcy.

Table 12 illustrates the changes that occur in the balance sheet structure when the rate of capital investment exceeds the rate of capital accumulation. Even though the capital structure started from a larger base of $8,000 in year 1 and increased at the rate of 5 percent per year, it did not provide adequate capital to finance the 10 percent rate of growth (from a base of $6,000) in net fixed assets. The effect was that

Table 12. Changes in balance sheet structure for a hypothetical firm increasing capital spending by 10% per year and increasing capital accumulation by 5%

	Year 1	Year 2	Year 3	Year 4	Year 5
Current assets	$4,000	$3,800	$3,560	$3,275	$2,940
Net fixed assets	6,000	6,600	7,260	7,986	8,784
Total assets	$10,000	$10,400	$10,820	$11,261	$11,724
Current liabilities	$2,000	$2,000	$2,000	$2,000	$2,000
Capital structure *	8,000	8,400	8,820	9,261	9,724
Total liabilities and equity	$10,000	$10,400	$10,820	$11,261	$11,724
Net working capital (Current assets-current liabilities)	$2,000	$1,800	$1,560	$1,270	$940

* Long-term debt plus all equity accounts.

net working capital, current assets minus current liabilities, declined from $2,000 in year 1 to $940 in year 5. Capital investment is clearly being financed out of working capital. Current assets and current liabilities are approaching equality. Unless the trend is reversed, the firm will find it increasingly difficult to meet current obligations. Creditors may think it necessary to undertake drastic action to protect themselves.

The point emphasized here is that, as capital investment expands, the firm's working capital demands will also increase. Assuming an efficient working capital balance to begin with, working capital must expand also.

A second capital usage problem is that investments may be made today only to find that a new proposal offering a greater return appears tomorrow. No matter how much effort or ingenuity is exerted, it is impossible to anticipate all proposals that are on the horizon. From a practical standpoint, since funds available to the firm are rationed in the short run, if it invests up to the limit of its resources it gives up the flexibility needed to undertake a high-return project that may appear later on short notice. How much flexibility should be built in will depend on many factors, such as rate of innovation in the particular industry, expenditures on research and development, the range of returns likely on unknown projects, as well as recent experiences with respect to returns on new projects. As in the case of the liquidity-profitability conflict, the manager must seek to strike a happy balance between flexibility and profitability. If he is in a position to take on any or all new projects as they come along, he is no doubt foregoing some profits. On the other hand, if his funds are so committed that he must reject any and all windfall proposals, he may also be denying the firm the opportunity for additional profits.

Suggested Readings

Archer, Stephen H., and Charles A. D'Ambrosio. *Business Finance: Theory and Management.* New York: Macmillan Company, 1966, p. 227–240.

Bierman, Harold, Jr., and Seymour Smidt. *The Capital Budgeting Decision,* second edition. New York: Macmillan Company, 1966.

Dean, Joel. *Managerial Economics.* Englewood Cliffs, N.J.: Prentice-Hall, Inc., 1951, 621 pages.

Helfert, Erich. *Techniques of Financial Analysis,* revised edition. Homewood, Ill.: Richard D. Irwin, Inc., 1967, p. 139–170.

Horngren, Charles T. *Cost Accounting, a Managerial Emphasis.* Englewood Cliffs, N.J.; Prentice-Hall, Inc., 1962, p. 735–741.

Johnson, Robert W. *Financial Management,* third edition. Boston: Allyn and Bacon, Inc., 1966, p. 161–195.

Levin, Richard I., and C. A. Kirkpatrick. *Quantitative Approaches to Management.* New York: McGraw-Hill Book Company, 1965, p. 79–111.

Quirin, G. David. *The Capital Expenditure Decision.* Homewood, Ill.: Richard D. Irwin, Inc., 1967.

Weston, J. Fred, and Eugene Brigham. *Managerial Finance,* second edition. New York: Holt, Rinehart, and Winston, Inc., 1966, p. 138–182.

PROBLEM SET
I. Mechanics of Discounting
For the four investment proposals listed below, determine:
   (a) Net present value using a "cost of capital" of 10 percent.
   (b) Rate of return.
   (c) Payback.

	Investment proposals			
	A	B	C	D
Initial cash outlay	$1,000	$1,000	$1,000	$1,000
Net cash inflows in year				
1	300	400	250	(1,000)*
2	300	300	250	400
3	300	200	250	400
4	300	200	250	600
5	300	100	250	600
6	0	0	250	600
7	0	0	250	0
8	0	0	250	0

* Denotes outflow.

II. Replacing a Useful Asset
One year ago the Waldo Farm Equipment Company bought an automatic lathe for $12,000. The lathe was believed to have a 6-year life and create a $4,000-a-year profit before taxes. A year later the company calculates that by scrapping the original and buying a new model, it could increase the profit before taxes to $5,600. The new lathe would cost $14,000 and would have a 5-year life. Currently, the firm
   (a) is in a 25 percent marginal income tax bracket,
   (b) uses straight line depreciation,
   (c) could sell the original lathe (now 1 year old) for $9,000,
   (d) believes that both assets would have a salvage of $0,
   (e) uses a 10 percent discount factor in evaluating capital proposals.

Determine whether the new lathe should be purchased to replace the existing one.

III. Cash Flows and Discounting Tools
The Egertson Livestock Marketing Company is considering the purchase of a new asset with a total cost of $20,000. It has an anticipated 10-year life with no salvage value. It is to be depreciated on a straight-line basis amounting to $2,000 per year. The project's earnings before depreciation and taxes are expected to average $4,500 per year for the first 7 years and $3,000 per year for the last 3 years. The firm is in the 30 percent marginal tax bracket and believes that it must receive a return of 10 percent to justify the undertaking.

Determine:
   (a) Net cash flow for each year.
   (b) Discounted rate of return.
   (c) Net present value.
   (d) Payback period.
   (e) If the project should be adopted.

CHAPTER 5
Managing Long-Term Funds—Minimizing the Cost of Capital

In the last chapter we focused our attention on the process of analyzing returns from alternative investment opportunities. We made frequent reference to the "cost of capital" as being the final determinant of how much investment could be undertaken profitably by a firm. It is to the problem of measuring the cost of capital that we now turn.

We must acknowledge at the outset that there are some conceptual as well as measurement problems associated with the quantification of the cost of capital. Thus, what is presented in this chapter cannot be regarded as the final word on the matter. On the other hand, it is our intention to present a way of looking at the cost of capital which, in spite of any shortcomings it may have, is far better than ignoring the problem altogether or relying on uneducated guesses in arriving at estimates.

The cost of capital is usually thought of in a percentage or rate sense. It is commonly referred to as the cutoff, hurdle, target, or minimum rate of return which must be achieved if an investment proposal is to be minimally acceptable. If, for example, the cost of capital is estimated to be 10 percent, only projects yielding 10 percent or more would be considered as feasible alternatives. If the present-value approach is used in analyzing investment proposals, the cost of capital is the rate at which future income flows are discounted. Thus, its role in the investment decision process is crucial.

Two major factors affect the cost of capital—quality considerations and the composition of capital used. By quality we mean the end results of the bargaining between the owners of capital and the firm seeking it in reference to such matters as risk, claims on assets, earnings, voting rights, tax considerations, control, and income.

The composition of the capital used—the capital structure—also affects the cost of capital. Different proportions of equity and debt can be used to satisfy long-term capital needs. Within limits, as we shall see later, the total cost of capital can be varied by varying these proportions.

Let us now turn to a more detailed consideration of these two factors. We will deal first with the quality aspects of various types of securities. Then we shall consider the problems associated with measuring the costs of individual components as well as the "mix" of the capital structure of the firm.

Quality Aspects

Suppliers of capital seek to maximize the returns from the funds they allow others to use while at the same time attempting to minimize the probabilities of incurring losses. On the other hand, the users of capital — business firms — seek to obtain capital at minimum costs and with a minimum of restrictive agreements or covenants imposed by suppliers. These two points of view create a gap which is bridged either by direct negotiation or through the workings of impersonal market transactions. If suppliers of capital negotiate for certain features to enhance their safety, they may be forced to settle for a lower yield; or they may simply restrict the amount they are willing to offer at a given yield; or they may impose other conditions relating to such things as the repayment period or the security required. On the other hand, if a firm demands a flexibility feature that reduces the supplier's safety, it may have to pay a higher yield, or accept a smaller amount than it initially sought, or agree to specific restrictive covenants.

Security Features

While there are no real limitations on the final form a contract may take, there has been some standardization of provisions included in them. Table 13 summarizes the major features with respect to risk and other factors affecting quality which are typically found in debt, preferred, and common security issues. A review of the table indicates that from a "safety" point of view the suppliers of debt capital typically receive maximum protection from loss while at the other end of the spectrum the holders of common stock — the residual equity claimants — assume maximum risk. The owners of preferred stock have an intermediate position. But lenders pay a "price" for safety in the form of lower, although fixed, returns on their funds as compared to providers of equity capital.

Let's look at the major features of the basic security types to see how each modifies risk or potential economic gain. We will take them in turn.

Due Date. Debt capital typically must be repaid at face value within some specified period of time. Long-term debt maturities range from 1 to 15 years, but the greatest number, at least as far as agriculturally

Managing Long-Term Funds—Minimizing the Cost of Capital 85

Table 13. Major features of basic securities with respect to risk and other factors affecting quality *

Features	Term loans, bonds, and other debt instruments	Preferred stock	Common or residual equity
Due date	Yes	No	No
Claims on earnings	First	Second	Third
Claims on assets	First	Second	Third
Tax-deductible claim on earnings	Yes	No	No
Voting status	None	Limited	Yes
Returns variability	Fixed	Relatively fixed	Variable
Risk level:			
Supplier	Low	Intermediate	High
Firm	High	Intermediate	Low
Risk modifications:			
Favoring supplier	Pledge of assets; agreed on debt limits; amortization or sinking fund plans; dividend restrictions	Sinking funds; voting rights under specified conditions	Preemptive rights which protect against possible dilution of existing stock by new issue
Favoring firm	Repayment linked to earnings; accelerated maturity	Voluntary retirement	Residual claim on income and assets
Cost to firm	Low	Medium	High

*Adapted from Arnold Haseley and Leon Garoian, "Financing Long Term Capital Needs," *Management News for Agricultural Business*, Oregon State University, Corvallis, Ore., March 1962.

related firms are concerned, are in the 5- to 10-year range."[25] It is not uncommon for a loan agreement to call for its amortization through specified installments during its term. Similarly, bonds, although not commonly used by agricultural marketing and supply firms, may call for the establishment of "sinking funds," into which the firm must periodically pay in specified amounts to insure retirement of the obligation. Such features, of course, are designed to maximize the safety of the "lenders."

Normally, residual equity issues do not carry a due date. Preferred stock could have such a feature and may even call for the establishment of a sinking fund. By and large, however, if the equity holder wishes to liquidate his share of the business, he must find his own "market." This may be particularly difficult in the case of stocks that are not

---

[25] Writers often refer to short-, intermediate-, and long-term debt. Short-term includes loans maturing in 1 year or less; intermediate, 1-10 years; and long-term, over 10 years. As was pointed out in chapter 3, short-term debt is retired by working capital shifts. Intermediate- and long-term debt are both retired over a longer period of time out of earnings generated by the firm. For this reason, a distinction has been made between short- and long-term debt on the basis of period to retirement. In this text, instruments maturing 1 or more years in the future will be considered long-term.

widely traded, or where evidence of equity is simply reflected as "book credits" for which no organized market exists.

Maturity dates on debt instruments are subject to negotiation. A firm may wish a prepayment privilege, i.e., the option to repay the loan before the maturity date. This is generally referred to as a "call" feature. It puts the lender at a disadvantage because he is not assured of an income flow from interest for a specified period as is typically the case. He will, therefore, usually demand a premium for providing this kind of repayment flexibility. Preferred stocks frequently include the call feature.

Claims on Earnings. Interest on debt instruments takes priority over dividends to preferred stock or residual equity, in that order. The amount of interest due at any point in time is fixed and must be paid regardless of how good or poor business conditions are. If the firm is not able to meet its interest obligations, it either must restructure its debt if this is possible, or liquidate the assets of the business to satisfy the security claims of its creditors.

While preferred issues usually carry a "fixed" dividend provision, nonpayment cannot result in the dissolution of the firm. Preferred holders may demand "cumulative rights," in which case dividends passed over in any prior period must be paid out before residual equity holders may receive a dividend. Residual equity holders, as the name implies, get what is left. If nothing is left, they get nothing. On the other hand, should the firm strike a bonanza, all of the rewards above the fixed commitments are theirs.

Prior Claims on Assets. Most claims on assets are secured by the general credit of the firm. A debenture bond is an example of such a claim. In the case of default, holders of these securities have a general claim on assets that are not mortgaged or otherwise specifically pledged. Some firms may find it necessary to offer potential lenders claims on specific assets — a mortgage on land and buildings or liens on particular items of equipment or inventory — particularly if their financial condition is questionable. The lender can liquidate the pledged assets to satisfy his claim in the event of default. The protection thereby offered the lender may allow the firm to obtain the funds at a lower rate of interest than would otherwise be possible. A mortgage bond is an example of such a claim.

Some lenders are willing to "subordinate" their claims on assets to other debt holders. In the event of default, they receive payment only after those with specific and general claims have been taken care of. A subordinated claim typically carries with it a relatively high interest yield.

Equity holder claims are satisfied only after those of debt holders have been covered. Preferred holders take precedence over residual holders.

Voting Status. Lenders are not given voting privileges. The right to elect the board of directors or to vote on major company issues is reserved to the owners of equity capital. Even preferred shareholders usually have limited voting rights. We emphasize that the "right to vote" does not give the individual a voice in operating decisions. This is reserved to management. But it does give the shareholder a voice in the development of the firm's general policies and the control of its affairs through the board of directors.

This lack of a voice in policy and control is a risk element for which the lender expects compensation. In view of the general protection he receives in the form of priorities of claims on income and assets, his risks are typically not great. But if he feels they are, the lender can exercise some control through restrictive covenants. For example, he may impose as a condition of his loan a limit on the additional debt that the firm can take on; or he could reserve the right to demand the return of his capital unless certain conditions with respect to methods of operations or return are met. These, or other conditions, may be the only ones under which he would be willing to supply the funds. However, the more protection the lender demands, the lower is the interest yield he can expect.

Tax-Deductible Yield Payments. Interest payments are deductible from net operating income. This is not true in the case of dividends paid on equity issues and this increases the attractiveness of borrowing to corporations that pay corporate income taxes. The net impact of deductible interest payments is to reduce the cost of debt capital. We will be coming back to this interest deductibility advantage of debt capital later in the chapter.

Other Features. To make them more attractive to lenders, loan agreements can offer options such as the right to convert debt claims into equity at some later date. This provides the lender with the safety of debt ownership but also opens up the possibility of sharing in profits, should they develop, by shifting to an equity position.

A feature frequently provided to common stockholders is a preemptive right to purchase a prorata share of any new issue. When new stocks are issued there is frequently a "dilution" (a reduction) in the market value of the old stock. Under a preemptive right one can obtain shares of the new issue at a price designed, in theory, to offset the decrease in the value of the old holding. The dilution problem can be largely avoided by the judicious use of debt, which is another compelling factor for utilizing it.

Summary and Appraisal of Quality Factors

The choice between risk and reward underlies the bargaining between suppliers and users of capital. Each party seeks in his own way to maximize the possibility of his own (or his firm's) gain while minimizing the probability of loss. But these objectives are essentially in conflict. Low-risk opportunities usually promise low returns while high-risk opportunities must promise higher returns. Between these two ends of the spectrum there is a continuum which is bridged by negotiation.

From the point of view of the firm, and this is the point of view emphasized in this book, debt capital costs the least; but it also carries the greatest risk, since the survival of the organization is dependent on its ability to meet fixed obligations on time. As the firm seeks to achieve greater flexibility and, thereby, to modify its risk position through the bargaining process, it moves across the qualitative spectrum in the direction of equity. In so doing, its cost of capital rises commensurate with the increased risk the suppliers are asked to take.

It must be emphasized that for a given level of risk the cost of capital is reflected not just in the rate paid but on the conditions imposed by the agreement as well. The firm must weigh both conditions and rate in evaluating costs.

What prevents the entrepreneur with a high-risk preference from operating in large part or entirely with borrowed capital? Simply because as lenders supply larger and larger portions of total capital they would be assuming greater risks and would, therefore, demand greater rewards. The cost of debt capital to the firm would approach and eventually equal that of equity capital. Further, lenders would demand greater management control and at some point demand all of it. Typically, therefore, some combination of debt and equity is used. Assuming that proper attention has been paid to the qualitative aspects, the determination of the combination which minimizes the cost of capital is dependent on the ability of the firm to identify and meas-

Managing Long-Term Funds — Minimizing the Cost of Capital

ure the costs associated with each source. It is to this problem that we now turn.

Measuring the Cost of Capital

In this section we will focus on methods of estimating the cost of capital quantitatively. First, we shall consider the evaluation of costs of fixed payment obligations — which include such securities as notes, preferred stock, and bonds; then we shall examine methods for determining the cost of residual equity capital; finally, we will discuss the overall cost of capital and financial leverage.

Fixed-Payment Obligations

Perhaps the easiest of all costs of capital to estimate are those related to fixed-payment obligations — debt instruments such as notes or bonds, and preferred stock. Such obligations normally specify in precise terms the total amount involved and the associated interest (or dividend). In the case of a debt obligation, the repayment plan and the due date are also specified.

Term Loans. Let's begin our discussion by identifying the relevant considerations in estimating the cost of a term loan. The problem really centers around identifying the "effective rate" — what is actually being paid — of interest as opposed to the quoted or published rate. For example, if we borrow $5,000 from a bank for a year at 5 percent interest, it is common practice for the lender to deduct the interest charge at the outset. This would mean that we would receive a net of $4,750. Since the interest payment is $250, the effective rate of interest would be $250 ÷ $4,750 = 5.3 percent. Thus, the "effective rate" is 0.3 percentage points higher than the published rate.[26]

For firms subject to corporate income taxes, a second consideration enters. Interest expense is tax deductible. The cost of debt capital is reduced by the amount of "tax saving" involved. If the firm in the above example paid out 40 percent of its income in federal taxes, its net interest cost would be as follows:

$$\text{Interest cost} = \text{effective rate} \times (1 - \text{tax rate})$$
$$= 5.3\% \times (.6)$$
$$= 3.18\%$$

Consider now a somewhat more complicated problem. Assume that a firm borrows $200,000 for 4 years at 5 percent interest as earned.

[26] Some banks require that a compensating balance — a minimum deposit balance in relation to the loan outstanding — be maintained. Under these conditions the effective rate is also higher than the published rate.

Assume that the loan is amortized at the rate of $50,000 per year paid at the end of each year. Table 14 summarizes the total transaction.

Table 14. Summary of transactions in a hypothetical amortized loan

Date	Principal outstanding	Due date	Principal payment	Interest payment*
Jan. 1, 1974	$200,000	Dec. 31, 1974	$50,000	$10,000
Jan. 1, 1975	150,000	Dec. 31, 1975	50,000	7,500
Jan. 1, 1976	100,000	Dec. 31, 1976	50,000	5,000
Jan. 1, 1977	50,000	Dec. 31, 1977	50,000	2,500
				$25,000

* 5% of beginning year outstanding principal.

Closing costs and other fees associated with negotiating the loan were $2,000. We could set up the problem on a basis quite similar to the one we used to estimate the discounted rate of return in the previous chapter. But since we already know the quoted rate and are simply interested in making an adjustment to determine the effective rate, the following formula may be used to provide a reasonable estimate of it.[27]

$$\text{Effective rate} = \frac{\text{Total finance charges}}{1/2 \text{ of original loan}} \times \frac{\text{no. of payments}}{\text{no. of years}} \times \frac{1}{(\text{no. of payments} + 1)}$$

Using data from the problem above, we have:

$$\text{Effective rate} = \frac{\$25,000 + \$2,000}{\$100,000} \times \frac{4}{4} \times \frac{1}{(4+1)} = 5.4\%$$

Once again, if the firm pays corporate income tax at the 40 percent rate, the after-tax cost to the firm would be 5.4 percent $(1-.4) = 3.24$ percent. We will come back to the importance of the income tax-deductibility aspect of borrowed capital later in the chapter.

Preferred Stock. The computation of the cost of preferred stock is relatively simple, assuming that no sinking fund is involved. (If a sinking fund is involved, one could follow the same procedure we outlined for our amortized debt example.) Here, as in the case of borrowed capital, the payment—now a dividend—is usually specified. If the net amount (after flotation costs) of an issue of 6 percent $25 par value preferred stock received by the company is $23 per share and the dividend payment is $1.50 per year, then the effective rate is $1.50 \div \$23 = 6.5$ percent. Since dividends are not a tax-deductible

[27] The formula is applicable to loans requiring monthly, quarterly, or other installment repayment schedules.

expense, this 6.5 percent net cost to the company is in sharp contrast to the tax benefits associated with debt capital.

Residual Equity

Residual equity capital is generated either by retaining part or all of a firm's earnings or by selling common stock. Retained earnings constitute a large part of the residual equity used in agricultural marketing and supply firms but from time to time these firms also find it useful or necessary to sell common stock.

Before we get into our discussion of residual equity capital, however, it will be helpful to remind the reader of some of the distinctions between proprietary corporations, cooperatives, and proprietorships and partnerships in regard to firm objectives, methods of distributing net proceeds, and taxation. This is necessary because these factors have a bearing on what must be taken into account when estimates of the costs of residual equity capital are being made for each of these types of organizations.

Proprietary corporations are profit-making organizations whose business activities are designed to benefit their owner-stockholders on the basis of their ownership. The residual equity supplier (common stockholder) receives what is left of income after debt and preferred stock obligations are taken care of. These net earnings can be paid out to him in the form of dividends or they can be retained in part or wholly by the corporation, in which case they add to the book value of his shares.

The proprietary corporation must pay federal corporate income tax on profits. If profits are retained, the stockholder pays no personal income tax on his share, but he does pay taxes on any dividend that he receives.[28] Insofar as retained earnings increase the value of his holdings, should he sell them he would be liable for a capital gains tax, which is assessed at a lower rate than personal income tax.

Cooperatives, on the other hand, are organized to benefit their member-patrons on the basis of their patronage. In part, these benefits are reflected in the "net margins" (profits) from the enterprise in which the cooperative is engaged, and in part by insuring the farmer-member competitive prices in the sale of his products or on his purchases of services and supplies. Placing a value on the latter benefits is difficult at best and we make no effort to do so here. But it is a factor that must be taken into account by those who are evaluating the profitability of a specific cooperative.

[28] Under the federal personal income tax laws, the first $100 received in dividends by an individual is tax-free. With minor adjustments, all other dividends are taxed at the personal income tax rate.

As in the case of proprietary corporations, what is left of net margins after the debt and preferred obligations are covered is paid out to the patron-owner in the form of cash patronage refunds (dividends) for which he is given a pro rata credit, or retained in part or wholly by the cooperative. Unlike the proprietary corporations, the "payout" to the patron-owner is made on the basis of his share of *total patronage* rather than the *amount of stock* he holds.

Under Section 521 of the Internal Revenue Code of 1954 and subsequent amendments, a cooperative is permitted to use a patronage refund to reduce its gross income in computing its federal income tax liability. To "qualify," the cooperative must pay out in cash, property, or qualified written notices of allocation those patronage refunds meeting statutory definition within 8½ months following the close of the fiscal year. The cash portion of a qualified allocation must be at least 20 percent of the total patronage refund. The patron treats the receipt of "qualified" refunds — cash and noncash — as current ordinary income and pays personal income taxes on them accordingly. Cooperatives pay taxes at regular corporate rates on earnings they retain as corporate profits.[29]

Not all agricultural marketing and supply firms are cooperatives or proprietary corporations. Proprietorships and partnerships are organized to benefit their owner(s). They pay no Federal corporate income tax, but the residual owner(s) must include earnings as personal income for tax purposes. In what follows we will not give separate attention to proprietorships and partnerships because in large part what we will say about the cost of "retained earnings" can be applied in estimating residual equity capital costs for such organizations.

With this general background, we are now ready to look at the cost of residual equity capital. We will begin our discussion by focusing on proprietary corporations and then suggest such modifications as may be necessary for cooperatives.

Proprietary Corporations

Much of the literature relating to evaluating the cost of residual equity capital focuses on firms which have ready access to security markets. And, of course, many corporations — particularly the larger ones — do have common stocks that are continuously and publicly traded. For such securities, arriving at some estimate of market value is not difficult. On the other hand, many or most firms serving agriculture

---
[29] For details on tax laws affecting cooperatives see David Volkin and D. Morrison Neely, *The Amended Laws Affecting Cooperatives and Their Patrons*, U.S. Department of Agriculture Report 87, February 1967.

Managing Long-Term Funds — Minimizing the Cost of Capital

have securities that are either closely held or otherwise not commonly traded. It is difficult to establish meaningful market values in this situation. These differences in the marketability of securities have considerable impact on how one goes about analyzing their costs. In what follows we will first discuss the cost of capital in the case of readily marketable securities and then suggest modifications necessary in valuation procedures when they are not.

New Common Stock. Sale of new common stock, although not a major source of equity funds in agriculturally related firms at present, could play a more important role in financing in the future. It is important, therefore, to include a discussion of new common stock in our considerations of the cost of capital.

How does one go about this analysis of the cost of an equity issue? Actually, the same fundamental procedures we discussed in connection with determining the rate of return on investment (chapter 4) are applicable here. The stockholder is in a sense "buying revenue" when he purchases a share of stock. The cost of capital to the firm is the amount it must pay the stockholder to induce him to part with his money. Unlike fixed return securities, however, we are not dealing with some firmly stipulated amount but rather with what the firm and the stockholder "expect" to realize if all goes well in the enterprise.

It is conventional to think of the cost of "old common" as that discount rate (k_0) which will equate the expected flow of earnings per share to the market price per share. If earnings are assumed to be constant from year to year, this rate is given by the following formula.[30]

$$k_0 = \frac{EPS}{MP}$$

where:
EPS — expected earning per share
MP = market price

If the expected earnings per share, for example, are $8 per year and the market value of the stock is $80, then the cost of old capital is $8/$80 or 10 percent.

When we are trying to estimate the cost of new capital, however, we need a somewhat different formulation than the one above. Since the issuance of new stock can dilute the net worth of present stockholders through its impacts on earnings per share of existing shares, we need a formulation that will identify and, if management chooses, "screen

---
[30] Because common stock does not carry a due date (is assumed to exist perpetually), various time factor adjustments drop out of the formula, as we suggested in our discussion of the simple rate of return in chapter 4.

out" proposals that would cause such dilution. Ezra Solomon has described such a measure.[31] In this case, the cost of common equity is a rate that will discount expected future earnings from the enterprise which would have resulted *if the investment proposal was not undertaken* to the net price per share of the new issue. By net price we mean market price less any flotation cost.

When we are dealing with the case of constant expected future earnings, the cost of new equity capital is given by the following formula: [32]

$$k_n = \frac{E_n}{P_n}$$

where:

E_n = expected earnings if the investment is not undertaken
P_n = net proceeds per share from the sale of stock

If, for example, expected earnings per share without the proposed investment were $3, and the net proceeds per share (market price less flotation costs) were $27 for the new issue, the cost of the new issue would be $3/$27 = 11.1 percent. Suppose that the stockbuyers' attitudes toward the new issue were such that the net proceeds per share which could be realized from its sale were only $20. The cost would then be $3/$20 = 15 percent. This higher cost of capital would "cut off" investment proposals which fail to yield at least 15 percent.[33] Conversely, if the market valued the issue so that net proceeds were $30 per share, cost of capital would be reduced to 10 percent and the "cutoff" point on investment proposals would be similarly reduced. Because earnings on shares are not tax deductible, the costs so calculated are automatically "after tax."

We hasten to point out that real-world estimates may be more complicated than the simple formulation above suggests, but hardly any more so than the estimation of rate of return or net present value, which we discussed in chapter 4. In short, we may have to be satisfied with estimates that are a great deal less than perfect; but the procedures that are suggested are structurally sound and can, therefore, steer us away from major errors on this ground alone.

---

[31] For a thorough development and defense of this formulation, see Ezra Solomon, *The Theory of Financial Management*, New York and London: Columbia University Press, 1963, p. 38–46.

[32] Where earnings are expected to increase over time at a constant annual rate, the formula becomes:

$$k_n = \frac{E_n}{P_n} + G$$

where G represents the annual increase in the value of earnings as a percent. For formulations relating to more complicated growth patterns, see J. Fred Weston and Eugene F. Brigham, *Managerial Finance*, second edition, New York: Holt, Rinehart and Winston, 1966, p. 300–304.

[33] We are assuming here that the investment is to be financed entirely with common stock. As we shall see later, a "mix" of debt and equity might reduce the overall cost of capital so that lower return proposals would be acceptable.

Retained Earnings. The largest single source of equity capital for agricultural marketing and supply firms is derived from retained earnings. Do retained earnings have a cost in the same sense that equity issues that are sold do? In spite of a widely held belief to the contrary —even among some sophisticated managers who should know better —the answer is yes. When a firm retains earnings for its own purposes, it automatically denies these funds to its stockholders for their personal use. In short, there is an opportunity cost to them. This is the "real cost" of retained earnings. But can it be measured?

If we abstract, for the moment, from problems relating to personal income tax, and assume that we are dealing with stockholders who are alike with respect to risk preferences and to alternative investment opportunities, estimation of the opportunity costs of retained earnings would be no problem. If the best rate of return our homogeneous group of investors could hope to obtain from alternative opportunities is 7 percent, then the firm would have to earn at least this much by reinvesting earnings to be justified in not returning them to the stockholders. But again the "real world" is more complicated than this. Investors do have different attitudes toward risk, so they are not alike with respect to their preferences between alternative investment opportunities. Furthermore, once we introduce the income tax factor, we greatly multiply the complications of arriving at an opportunity cost that is applicable to the group. Recall that in a proprietary corporation stockholders pay no income tax on retained earnings but do so on any dividend that they receive. Insofar as retained earnings are reinvested profitably by the firm, the stockholder will enjoy a capital gain—but the tax rate on such gains is at least 50 percent less than on dividends, and the tax payment is deferred until the stock is sold. Thus, for example, if the rate of earnings on a particular stock, i.e., EPS/MP, is 7 percent and an individual stockholder is in the 50 percent personal income tax bracket, a payout of the entire earnings would net him only a 3.5 percent return. Thus, the "opportunity cost" to him of retained earnings is lower than it would be if there were no tax.

One formulation which "builds in" the income tax factor in the estimation of the cost of retained earnings as as follows:

$$k_r = \frac{E_n(1-t)}{MP}$$

where:

k_r = cost of retained earnings
E_n = expected earnings per share
t = marginal personal tax rate
MP = market price per share

In this case, since there are no flotation costs associated with retained earnings, the market price per share is net. The apparent simplicity of this formulation breaks down, however, when we attempt to measure the marginal tax rate. The relevant rate is one that applies to capital gains which, as we indicated before, is about half the personal income tax rate. But as we know, there can be a great variation in the rates at which individual stockholders pay income tax. Arriving at an "average" marginal rate which is reasonable for all stockholders is impossible simply because some would be below and some above the average and their individual opportunity costs would vary accordingly. Unsatisfactory as this measure may be, however, it is by far and away better than assuming that retained earnings are costless to the firm.

An alternative formulation for arriving at the cost of retained earnings is offered by Solomon.[84] It suggests that the appropriate "opportunity cost" that the firm must take into account in judging internal investment proposals is the rate of return possible from the best alternative investment opportunities "outside" the firm.[85] The major advantage of this formulation is that it makes it unnecessary to estimate the marginal personal tax rate. The cost of capital under this approach would be as follows:

$$k_o = \frac{E_o}{MP_o}$$

where:

k_o = rate of return on best outside alternative
E_o = expected earnings per share from outside investments
MP_o = market price for outside investment share

If the rate of return from an internal proposal exceeds k_o — the opportunity cost of internal investment — it would be considered acceptable.

It would be incorrect, of course, to assume that every time an internal investment proposal exceeded the screening rate it would be accepted. Stockholders are not uniformly interested in capital gains. Most, in fact, demand some level of dividends. If they become dissatisfied with a firm's dividend policy, they can liquidate their holdings. If enough do so, the market price per share will decrease and thus raise the firm's equity capital costs. Management is, or should be, aware of this view and must take it into account when it weighs internal investment decisions.

Some Modifications. Up to this point, we have assumed that common

---
[84] Ezra Solomon, op. cit., p. 51–55.
[85] The firm's investments in an outside opportunity would have to be large enough to give it majority control for income tax reasons. See Ezra Solomon, op. cit., p. 67.

stocks were actively traded and that values were determined in a free and open market system. The fact is that most corporations serving agriculture do not have stocks which are actively traded. Since market value is an integral part of the cost of residual equity, evaluation becomes a problem. One alternative way of meeting this problem is to employ an appraised value of whatever securities we are dealing with. An appraised value does not mean that stock can be sold for the appraised price, but rather that it is worth that price if a buyer can be found. The appraised value can and should be modified by what is known — if anything — of market conditions.

Generally speaking, as the marketability of a stock declines, the flexibility of the stockholder declines also. The risk he assumes, therefore, is greater. Other things being equal, then, the cost of residual equity capital (new common or retained earnings) under these conditions would be greater than if it were freely marketable. In any case, once a value has been placed on the securities, the same fundamental logic used in determining the cost of freely marketable equity capital applies here as well.

Cooperative Corporations

As we suggested earlier, a cooperative exists to serve its member-patrons. The member-patron is rewarded not on the stock he holds but rather on the basis of his patronage. These rewards can come to him in the form of earnings generated by the organization and/or by insuring him a "competitive market" for products and supplies. We will not attempt to place a dollar value on the latter here. In what follows, we will assume that cooperatives price at competitive levels and we will concentrate on the distribution of earnings.

One problem in evaluating residual equity in cooperatives is the lack of standardization in equity accounts. We suggest that equity securities, whether they be stocks, book credits, or other forms of equity certification, which are residual in their claim on assets or income be classified residual equity, irrespective of name.

Since the sale of new common stock which is truly residual is a rarity among cooperatives, we can, for all practical purposes, rule it out of consideration here. Cooperatives rely very heavily on retained earnings for residual equity. There is a clear advantage from the firm's point of view in doing so because of income tax considerations discussed earlier in this chapter. Furthermore, as is true of financing out of retained earnings for any corporation, there are no flotation costs.

What are the costs of retained earnings for cooperatives? As in the case of proprietary managers, many cooperative managers view them as "costless" and, of course, they are just as wrong. Again, some opportunity cost concept is relevant, but which one?

Since, at least under present conditions, "outside" investment opportunities for cooperatives are somewhat limited, some measure of patron opportunity cost is probably most appropriate. While farmers are by no means alike with respect to incomes, alternative opportunities, or tax brackets, they are a great deal more so than the conglomeration of stockholders in a proprietary firm. Most of their investments are on the farm or in related activities. They use roughly the same credit facilities and while their personal money costs may vary, they would probably cluster in a reasonably narrow range. While no measure of personal opportunity cost will fit the entire group, the dispersion around some chosen rate would not be as great as would be the case of a proprietary firm's stockholders.

A cooperative could, for example, estimate the rate of return to the farmer on an additional $100 investment in a farm which is more or less typical of those in the area it serves. Or, it might examine the cost of various types of credit to its farmer patrons. These are, after all, reflections of the opportunity cost to the farmer of having earnings retained. Out of the feasible opportunities examined, a cooperative could choose the one carrying the highest rate as the cost of retained earnings. If the expected rate of return exceeded the "screening rate," the new proposal would be acceptable.

Several other factors must be taken into account in evaluating the opportunity costs of retained earnings as far as the member-patron is concerned. One is that, unlike the proprietary stockholder, he pays taxes on retains when they are allocated as though they were cash. Thus, there is no personal income tax advantage to him by having earnings retained. A second factor relates to the revolving fund method of financing, which is commonly used by cooperatives, and its impact on present value of earnings. For example, the present value of $1,000 earned this year and not received for 10 years is not $1,000. Using a 6 percent discount rate, it would be $558. If we take into account the income tax — paid in the year earned — it is even less. Further, there is no opportunity for offsetting capital gains on retained earnings. Since there is little or no trading in cooperative equity issues, they are paid off at face value.

On the above grounds, if one looks at a member-patron and the organization as completely separate entities, it is easy to see potential conflicts of interest when it comes to choosing between returning net proceeds as cash patronage dividends or reinvesting them in the organization. The preference of the patron for a bird in the hand instead of two-thirds or one-half of a bird 10 years from now is quite understandable. Indeed, if the revolving period is long enough, the present value of his share in the revolving fund, appropriately discounted, may be negligible. Looked at in purely financial terms, under such conditions he might have reasonable grounds to question whether or not there are any net benefits deriving from the organization's existence. This assumes, of course, that in the cooperative's absence he could obtain marketing services and supplies at prices comparable to those existing when it was in business. This is a good question. Many argue that it is in this difficult-to-document "police role" that the cooperative may make its greatest contribution to its members, and that this role carries a "price tag" which the principal beneficiaries should be willing to — indeed must — support. Since how well an individual cooperative performs its "police role" can be objectively tested only in its absence, the member may be, in some cases, hard put to place a value on it. This is less of a problem in "well-run" cooperatives that price competitively and produce adequate margins which are revolved in reasonably short periods of time. But there are some well-run and effective organizations which, by virtue of their peculiar competitive environment, are unable to produce significant margins; and there are others who use the "police role" as a coverup for poor performance. It is distinguishing between the latter two that may present the greatest difficulty in evaluation.

Some Alternatives. There is growing evidence that some cooperatives are beginning to experiment with modifications of revolving fund plans, for example, paying interest on balances in the funds, while others have turned to different methods entirely. Some are employing "per unit capital retain financing" whereby a specified amount of each unit sold is held by the organization, under specific agreement with the member-patron, to support its capital structure.[36] Still others — particularly those that have been notably effective — have had little difficulty in selling securities to their members. These carry a fixed-return provision and are, therefore, not residual equity. Such instruments represent only part of the total capital structure and we mention them here only because they represent at least a partial alternative to the traditional revolving fund method.

[36] In this case, the member is furnishing the cooperative capital on the basis of the dollar value or physical volume of products he markets through it. This compares with the alternative of investing a portion of his patronage refund arising from operations to support the structure, or making an out-of-pocket investment in, for example, additional shares of stock.

Overall Cost of Capital

Up to this point we have discussed ways in which the cost of various securities (debt, preferred and residual equity) can be calculated under various forms of business organization. As we suggested at the outset of this chapter, the process at best is difficult and, to be sure, far from precise. Whatever the means he employs, however imperfect, a manager can and should arrive at some estimate of the costs of various types of capital as far as his firm is concerned. When he has done this, the calculation of the overall cost of capital — the cutoff rate used in the investment decision process — becomes a matter of arithmetic. It is simply the weighted average of the cost of the several sources employed. The process is illustrated in the table below:

	Amount used	Proportion, %	After-tax cost, %	Weighted cost, %
Long-term debt	$300,000	30	3	0.9
Preferred stock	100,000	10	8	0.8
Common stock	100,000	10	14	1.4
Retained earnings	500,000	50	7	3.5
	$1,000,000			6.6

The weighted average overall cost of capital in the example is 6.6 percent. It reflects the proportion and cost of each type of capital used. Projects promising a return of less than 6.6 percent would be rejected. A question that immediately arises is whether or not this is the "least cost" combination of debt, preferred and residual equity.

Since long-term debt is clearly "lowest cost" to the firm, why not use more of it and less of, say, retained earnings? It would appear that for each $100,000 of debt the firm took on, its cost of capital would increase by 0.3 percent ($100,000 × 3 percent ÷ $1,000,000), while for each $100,000 of retained earnings released, cost of capital is reduced by 0.7 percent ($100,000 × 7 percent ÷ $1,000,000), for a net reduction in the cost of capital of 0.4 percent. If the firm could acquire the additional debt at no, or even a small, increase in the rate of interest, it would clearly pay to do so. The reasons firms don't move entirely to debt financing is the fact that, as we suggested earlier in the chapter, lenders would be incurring greater risks and would, therefore, demand greater rewards in the form of higher interest. Recall also that as the proportion of debt goes up risks to the residual equity holders also increase because of their last-place claims on income and assets should things not go well for the firm. Thus, they would also tend to demand greater rewards for their risks and the cost of equity capital could also rise. While still a matter of controversy, there is substantial evidence that through certain ranges the addition of fixed-return capital to the overall capital structure will decrease costs but that at some point these benefits are offset by the increasing risk to the lender as well as to the residual equity holder. Identifying that point, or probably more correctly, that area, should be a major preoccupation of the financial manager.

The concept of substituting long-term debt or preferred equity for residual equity capital is referred to as leverage. We turn now to a more complete development of that concept.

The Concept of Financial Leverage

The key element in the concept of financial leverage is the impact of the use of fixed-return securities — various forms of debt and preferred stock — on the returns to residual equity capital. Table 15 helps to illustrate this point. It shows how, with a total capitalization of $1 million, various mixes of debt and equity influence residual equity returns. These comparisons are made under the assumption that net operating income is the same for each mix. So that we can work with round numbers, we assume that the firm is in the 50 percent corporate income tax bracket.

Table 15. Illustration of the effects of financial leverage on returns to equity capital

Financial statement items	100	70/30	60/40	60/30/10
Sales	3,000,000	3,000,000	3,000,000	3,000,000
Cost of goods sold	2,400,000	2,400000	2,400,000	2,400,000
Gross margin	600,000	600,000	600,000	600,000
Operating expense	400,000	400,000	400,000	400,000
Net operating income	200,000	200,000	200,000	200,000
Interest expense @ 6%	0	18,000	24,000	18,000
Net income	200,000	182,000	176,000	182,000
Taxes (50% rate)	100,000	91,000	88,000	91,000
Preferred dividends	0	0	0	6,000
Net residual income "A"	100,000	91,000	88,000	85,000
Capital structure				
Debt	0	300,000	400,000	300,000
Preferred	0	0	0	100,000
Residual equity "B"	1,000,000	700,000	600,000	600,000
Return on residual equity "A"/"B"	10.0%	13.0%	14.7%	14.2%

With 100 percent residual equity financing (column 1), net residual income is $100,000 and the rate of return on residual equity capital is 10 percent. If instead of an all-equity capital structure the firm introduced 30 percent debt (column 2) with an interest rate of 6 percent, residual equity income decreases to $91,000 — but residual equity capital is now only $700,000, and the rate of return on it is therefore 13 percent. If the lending public's faith in our hypothetical firm is strong it might be willing to support 40 percent of the capital structure (column 3) at 6 percent interest. A 14.7 percent return on equity capital would result. Suppose, on the other hand, the lending public had reached its limit when it supplied 30 percent of total capital. The firm might then decide to issue preferred stock — and again to keep things in round numbers let's assume it continues to use 30 percent debt but now issues preferred stock equivalent to 10 percent of the total capital structure on which it promises to pay dividends of $6,000. A return of 14.2 percent on residual equity results — not as good as with 40 percent debt, but certainly better than the 13 percent possible with the 70/30 mix.

The somewhat lower rate of return when preferred is introduced (column 4), as compared with the 40 percent debt structure (column 3), is a reflection of the tax deductibility advantage of interest payments as opposed to dividends. With the 60/40 mix, the $24,000 paid in interest was wholly tax deductible. But in the 60/30/10 mix, even though a total of $24,000 was paid out in interest and dividends also, only the $18,000 interest part of the total was tax deductible. The $6,000 of dividends came out of after-tax income. The lack of tax deductibility of dividends in a sense "costs" the firm $3,000 ($88,000 v. $85,000) in net residual income.

Since the return on residual equity increased as debt and preferred stock were added to the financial structure, leverage in the above example would be termed favorable. But why did this increase in residual equity return take place? Quite simply, because the firm was "paying" less for debt and preferred stock than either one of them was earning. The rate of return on the total capitalization of $1 million in the all-equity case was 10 percent. But the after-tax cost of debt was only 3 percent — 6 percent × (1–tax rate) — and the after-tax cost of preferred stock was 6 percent. In effect, for every dollar of debt the firm employed it was making 7¢ (10¢ – 3¢) and for every dollar of preferred stock, 4¢ (10¢ – 6¢). For example, in the 60/30/10 mix, residual equity income is equal to:

$600,000 \times 10¢ = \$60,000$
$300,000 \times 7¢ = \$21,000$
$100,000 \times 4¢ = \underline{\$\ 4,000}$
$\$85,000$

This is precisely the value that was arrived at in table 15.

But leverage need not always be favorable. Let's develop another example using the same firm with the same alternative capital structures, but in this case with net operating income at $50,000 instead of $200,000. The situation is illustrated in table 16.

Table 16. Illustration of the effects of unfavorable financial leverage

Financial statement items	Capital mix			
	100	70/30	60/40	60/30/10
Net operating income	50,000	50,000	50,000	50,000
Interest expense	0	18,000	24,000	18,000
Net income before taxes	50,000	32,000	26,000	32,000
Net income after 50% tax	25,000	16,000	13,000	16,000
Preferred dividend @ 6%	0	0	0	6,000
Net residual income	25,000	16,000	13,000	10,000
Capital structure				
Debt	0	300,000	400,000	300,000
Preferred stock	0	0	0	100,000
Residual equity	1,000,000	700,000	600,000	600,000
Return on residual equity	2.5%	2.3%	2.2%	1.7%

In the all-equity case (column 1), net residual income is $25,000 and the rate of return on residual equity is a low 2.5 percent. But matters get worse as we move across the table. With the 70/30 mix, rate of return falls to 2.3 percent; with a 60/40 mix, it is down to 2.2 percent; and finally, with the 60/30/10 mix, it is down to 1.7 percent. Why? Because in this case the firm was "paying" more for debt and preferred stock than either was earning. The residual rate of return in the all-equity case was 2.5 percent but the net after-tax costs of debt capital and preferred stock were still 3 and 6 percent, respectively. In this case, for every dollar of debt the firm employed it was losing 0.5¢ and for every dollar of preferred stock, 3.5¢. Using the 60/30/10 mix as before, residual equity income under unfavorable leverage conditions is equal to:

$600,000 \times (2.5¢) = \$15,000$
$300,000 \times (-0.5¢) = -1,500$
$100,000 \times (-3.5¢) = \underline{-3,500}$
$\$10,000$

This value also coincides with the one arrived at in table 16 (column 4).

We have now seen both sides of the financial leverage coin. On one side it tends to magnify returns to residual equity; on the other it can accelerate reductions in returns. What factors, therefore, must be taken into account when the use of "fixed-charge" capital is being contemplated? First, of course, as has been suggested in our previous discussion, the ratio of after-tax net operating income (as in an all-equity situation) to total capitalization must be greater than the ratio of after-tax dollar cost of debt or preferred stock to the dollar amount of each employed.

A second important factor that must be considered is the level and variability of operating income. If the level of operating income in relation to total capitalization is such that the rate of return on residual equity is only slightly higher than the cost of fixed-payment securities, only minor negative variations in income can accelerate the reduction in profitability to residual equity. Even when the expected level of operating income is high in relation to capitalization, but varies widely, use of a high proportion of fixed-return capital can be equally disastrous. If operating income drops far enough, required interest and dividend payments can quickly absorb whatever earnings there are. At the limit, if these claims exceed the earnings available to pay for them, the firm may face bankruptcy.

A third factor is the matter of flexibility — a firm's capacity to take advantage of an unexpected opportunity. Even though a firm might be well below its "debt limit," it may choose not to take on added fixed payment commitments so that if the unexpected possibility of a windfall did occur it would be in a position to take advantage of it. The "loaned-up" firm has no place to go in such a case. As in other decisions, the "returns" from flexibility must be considered in relation to costs. One element of the cost of flexibility is the difference in the cost of capital between the structure the firm actually operates under and the one it could operate under were it to be fully "levered." The other element of the cost of flexibility, of course, is the returns foregone.

In summary, the financial leverage concept has important implications for those who are striving to minimize the overall cost of capital. It is the financial manager's function to identify which among alternative mixes of residual equity and fixed-return securities is truly "least cost." In performing this function, he must take into account the qualitative as well as quantitative aspects of capital costs. The tools outlined in this chapter would be useful to him as he performs this task.

Other Sources of Long-Term Funds

Noncash Expenses

Another major source of investible capital is the revenue available after deducting earnings and cash expenditures from total revenue. This difference represents noncash expenses, of which the prime example is depreciation expense. Capital from noncash expenses usually represents substantial sums. In theory, at least, the same kind of criterion used for other internally generated funds is applicable here. As a practical matter, the firm normally finds a use for these funds. They are usually reinvested before other internally generated earnings and always before new debt or external equity sources are sought.

Leasing

Leasing is a source of capital to many firms. A company may choose to lease an asset and thus acquire the right of use for a designated time period without taking ownership. The ultimate question is whether it is more or less costly to purchase or lease.

The lease or purchase question only comes up after it has been determined that (a) the option to lease or buy an asset exists and (b), regardless of how acquired, the asset can be justified as a bona fide use of the firm's capital.

Leasing is often considered the equivalent of debt financing. There are some similarities since both leasing and debt obligations call for a contractual commitment for future payments. In the case of debt, the borrower must pay back the principal and interest charges. In the case of leasing, the payment schedule is considered a charge for the use of equipment. The charges are tax deductible in both instances. Since the risk factor for debt and lease financing is quite similar, a purchase or lease decision boils down to determining whether it is cheaper to lease the asset or borrow to finance its purchase.[37]

Suppose a company has the choice of leasing an asset for $10,000 a year for the next 5 years or borrowing $40,000 at 6 percent interest and buying the asset. Assume that the interest is payable at the end of each year and the principal is to be repaid at the end of the 5th year. If the firm does not pay income taxes, the alternative cash flows would be as shown at the top of page 106.

If it is also assumed that the equipment will be scrapped after 5 years with no salvage value, the costs of financing identify all the cash flows

---

[37] It should be emphasized that this only holds true if it is known that the use of the asset will generate a positive net present value to the firm.

106 The Financial Management of Agribusiness Firms

Year	Lease	Borrow and buy
0	0	+$40,000 and −$40,000 = 0
1	−$10,000	−$ 2,400
2	−$10,000	−$ 2,400
3	−$10,000	−$ 2,400
4	−$10,000	−$ 2,400
5	−$10,000	−$ 2,400 + (−$40,000) = $42,400

involved.[38] Using the 6 percent interest cost as a cutoff rate, we see in the table below that the net present value of the borrow-and-buy approach is lower by about $2,000, and that purchase of the equipment rather than leasing it would be most economical.

Comparison of cash changes and present value for a hypothetical lease-buy problem (no taxes)

Year	Cash changes	×	6% Discount factor	=	present value
			Lease costs		
1	−$10,000		.943		−$9,430
2	−10,000		.890		−8,900
3	−10,000		.840		−8,400
4	−10,000		.792		−7,920
5	−10,000		.747		−7,470
				Net present value	−$42,120
			Borrowing costs		
1	−$2,400		.943		−$2,263.20
2	−2,400		.890		−2,136.00
3	−2,400		.840		−2,016.00
4	−2,400		.792		−1,900.80
5	−42,400		.747		−31,672.80
				Net present value	−$39,988.80

When income taxes are a consideration, the problem becomes more complicated. In the first place, both interest and lease costs are tax deductible. Assuming a 50 percent tax rate, the effective after-tax charge is halved in both instances. Also, when borrowing and buying, the firm would be allowed to depreciate the equipment. Since this is a noncash expense, its impact on cash would be due to tax saving. For example, if the firm used straight-line depreciation methods, annual depreciation expense would be $40,000 divided by 5, or $8,000. An

[38] If there was a salvage value or the asset had a productive life of more than 5 years, this would have to be accounted for in the calculations. Since the lease approach does not give the firm ownership rights, only the purchase alternative would show benefits from value beyond the fifth year. In the case where the useful life extends beyond 5 years, the lease charge would still be considered debt financing, but since the loan in the borrow-and-buy approach would be paid off, the alternatives would not be equivalent from a risk standpoint. Except for extremely large projects, this may not have major impact anyway.

increase in expenses of $8,000 leads to a decline in taxes of 50 percent of that amount, or $4,000. Therefore, if we again use the 6 percent discount factor, the annual cash flow after taxes on the two approaches would be as follows:

Comparison of cash changes and present values for a hypothetical lease-buy problem (50 percent tax rate)

Year	Cash changes	×	6% discount factor	=	Present value
			Lease costs		
1	−$5,000		0.943		−$4,715
2	−5,000		.890		−4,450
3	−5,000		.840		−4,200
4	−5,000		.792		−3,960
5	−5,000		.747		−3,735
			Net present values		−$21,060
			Borrowing costs		
1	+$2,800		0.943		+$2,640
2	+2,800		.890		+2,492
3	+2,800		.840		+2,352
4	+2,800		.792		+2,218
5	−37,200		.747		−27,788
			Net present value		−$18,086

It is clear that borrowing and buying is still better, now by close to $3,000.

A firm does not always have a lease or buy choice. Some items are only available through leasing while others can only be purchased. When the alternative does exist, there are often other complications. The example used above considered a straight financial lease, that is, the firm was acquiring only the use of the asset. Often, leasing companies will provide other services such as maintenance and repairs and technical assistance. When this is the case the value of these services must either be deducted from the lease figures or added to the borrow-and-buy figures to make them comparable.

Suggested Readings

Bierman, Harold, Jr., and Seymour Smidt. *The Capital Budgeting Decision*, second edition. New York: Macmillan Company, 1966, p. 143–180, 218–235, 283–358.

Childs, John F. *Long-Term Financing*. Englewood Cliffs, N.J.: Prentice-Hall, Inc., 1961.

Engberg, Russell C. *Financing Farmer Cooperatives*. Bank for Cooperatives, 1965.

Griffin, Nelda. *Financial Structure of Regional Farm Supply Cooperatives.* U.S. Department of Agriculture, Farmer Cooperative Service General Report 124, 1965.

———. *How Adjustable Revolving Fund Capital Works.* U.S. Department of Agriculture, Farmer Cooperative Service General Report 111, 1963.

Helfert, Erich. *Techniques of Financial Analysis,* revised edition. Homewood, Ill.: Richard D. Irwin, Inc., 1967, p. 105–135.

Henning, G. F., and Marshall Burkes. *Changes in the Financial Structure of Agricultural Business Organization.* Wooster, Ohio: Ohio Agricultural Experiment Station, Research Bulletin 952, 1963.

Henning, G. F., and R. E. Laubis. *Financial Structure of Agricultural Business Organizations.* Wooster, Ohio: Ohio Agricultural Experiment Station, Research Bulletin 880, 1961.

Johnson, Robert W. *Financial Management,* third edition. Boston: Allyn and Bacon, Inc., 1966, p. 233–291.

Neely, D. Morrison, and David Volkin. *Per Unit Capital Retains: Tax Treatment by Cooperative Patrons.* U.S. Department of Agriculture, Farmer Cooperative Service Information Bulletin 51, 1966.

Quirin, G. David. *The Capital Expenditure Decision.* Homewood, Ill.: Richard D. Irwin, Inc., 1967, p. 95–146.

Solomon, Ezra. *The Theory of Financial Management.* New York and London: Columbia University Press, 1963, p. 38–46.

Volkin, David, and D. Morrison Neely. *The Amended Tax Laws Affecting Cooperatives and Their Patrons.* U.S. Department of Agriculture Service Report 87, February 1967.

Weston, J. Fred, and Eugene F. Brigham. *Managerial Finance,* second edition. New York: Holt, Rinehart, and Winston, 1966, p. 253–306.

PROBLEM SET

I. Lease or Buy

A firm has already determined that it needs a new semi-tractor trailer unit. The manager has the option of borrowing $16,000 and buying the unit or leasing it at a cost of $3,000 per year. The asset is expected to have a 5-year life.
Other details are:
   (a) The lease is for 5 years.
   (b) If purchased, the asset will be depreciated on a straight-line basis over a 5-year period. No salvage value is anticipated.
   (c) Interest charges will be 6 percent on the unpaid balance. One-fifth of the loan is to be repaid each year.
   (d) The firm has a 10 percent cost of capital.
   (e) The firm is in the 25 percent marginal tax bracket.

Which alternative would you choose?

II. Cost of Capital

The Clark County Farm Supply Corporation wishes to determine its overall weighted average cost of capital. In preparation, the staff has gathered the following information:
   (a) The current capital structure is made up of:
      1. A $20,000 10-year term loan which will mature in 5 years at an effective cost of 4 percent.
      2. $10,000 of 6 percent preferred stock.
      3. $70,000 of residual equity, almost all of which is retained earnings.
   (b) To obtain a loan today, a 5 percent interest charge would have to be paid. This is not a reflection on the firm's risk position, but is due to a change in debt charges for all firms.
   (c) If additional preferred stock was desired it could still be sold for a 6 percent yield.
   (d) The residual equity is not marketable, but the value of the total residual equity position has been appraised at $100,000. The annual earnings available to the residual owners have averaged around $10,000 per year. While earnings are expected to increase in the future, this growth will be gradual.
   (e) The firm is in the 22 percent corporate tax bracket.
   (f) After a careful study of the firm's 100 residual equity owners, it was estitimated that with few exceptions the individuals were in the 20-30 percent personal income tax brackets. It is suggested that a 25 percent rate be applied.

Problems:
   1. Estimate the overall weighted average cost of capital.
   2. It has been suggested that the cost of capital could be lowered if more debt were used. What factors and what additional information would be necessary to properly answer the question?

CHAPTER 6
Profit Planning

The kinds of analysis implied by the preceding chapters make profit planning a requirement for any and all business organizations. In its most uncomplicated form, profit planning begins with a search for proposals compatible with the firm's objectives. It calls for an appraisal of what the company is and what its owners want it to be. Management must clearly understand its firm's capacity for survival and growth. It needs answers to questions such as the following: Does the firm have any real competitive advantages in relation to products, services, or the location of its major markets? Have customer-patrons been clearly identified? Has management identified those factors which influence customer-patron willingness to deal with or through the organization? Has it realistically appraised the firm's public image?

On the other side of the coin, has a clear appraisal of its competition been made? Is the competition gaining or losing in respect to its relative market shares? What devices are competitors utilizing to attract customers? Do their pricing and credit policies depart substantially from the firm's own policies in these areas?

Finally, of course, the firm must take into account the general economic environment in which it is operating. It should know about such things as changes in land use patterns, community growth or decline, income changes in its market and/or supply area, as well as changes in technology which have a direct bearing on the business. Most of these factors are well outside the control of the firm but they all have relevance, in varying degrees, to its success or failure.

When the above analysis has been completed the firm is in a position to develop its profit plan. In this chapter, we will present tools that are useful in the profit planning process.

Profit planning can encompass a month, a year, or much longer periods of time. As we suggested in earlier chapters, long-term investments imply the need for long-term profit planning because it is really on the basis of some estimate of future profits that the investment is made. For convenience of presentation, most of the discussion in this chapter will focus on profits generated by a business in a year. But the same techniques could be employed to examine a profit stream for a series of years. To be sure, the degree of uncertainty increases as the time period considered is lengthened. We suggested in chapter 4 how the uncertainty problem could be dealt with.

Benefits from Planning

Before we turn to our discussion of profit planning tools, we would like to outline what we consider to be the major advantages of the planning process. As we suggested at the outset of this chapter, the initial phase of planning involves a "paper" dissection of the business. This dissection process is one of the prime benefits of planning. It makes management ask, for example, why labor costs are as high as they are and what can be done about them. It makes it ask why the firm is losing business in some parts of its trade territory or why the sale of a particular item is falling off, and what can be done about it. A plan forces a manager not only to ask what can be achieved, but also what must be done if certain target levels of sales and costs are to be realized. Larger sales or lower costs cannot be achieved simply by wishing for them; management must cause these things to happen through the execution of a plan.

In addition to helping management understand its own business, the plan offers other benefits. It provides a yardstick by which business performance can be measured. The only meaningful measure of success or failure is the achievement — or nonachievement — of some previously established objective. Managers often point with pride to the growth in the volume of sales of their organization, but if asked why the volume is growing at that rate, or whether or not it is the maximum rate of increase consistent with good business practice, they are often hard put to answer. It is entirely possible that a firm would be better off with a different rate of increase — higher or lower — than the one it is currently experiencing. There are many examples of companies that have experienced sales increases but declining profits because increased costs have exceeded the increases in revenues.

Another advantage of a plan is that if business takes an unfavorable turn, such a deviation from planned results can be quickly detected and corrective measures taken. Furthermore, since an effective plan must be in writing, it is easily promulgated among the members of the organization and provides them with a clear concept of what the firm's overall profit objectives are. This is unquestionably superior to the situation where objectives are tightly locked in the minds of management.

Profit Planning 113

Finally, and most importantly, a firm's survival might hinge on the development and execution of a plan. Greatly increased investment requirements, rapid technological change and accelerated obsolescence, greater customer-patron sophistication, changing marketing methods and channels, and the demands by lenders and other suppliers of capital have made formalized profit planning a "must" rather than an option for business organizations.

In the remainder of this chapter we will discuss the tools relevant for profit analysis, cash budgeting, and the development of pro forma balance sheets.

Profit Analysis

In forecasting profits for a firm, estimates of future revenues and costs are required. Revenues are affected by the total volume of sales, prices, product mix, and channels of distribution. Costs are affected by processing and handling techniques, prices paid for materials and services utilized, and rate of output. In this section, we will deal with sales forecasting, elements of cost analysis, product mix considerations, profit forecasting, and break-even analysis.

Sales Volume Forecasting

An important part of the total profit planning process is forecasting the probable attainable alternative sales volumes and choosing from among these the one that will most likely achieve the income objectives of the organization. The process is not a simple one. First of all, there are the obvious difficulties of forecasting probable attainable volumes. Second, even though the forecasts are extremely accurate, other economic, technical, or operating factors can enter which can cause realized sales to depart from planned sales. Thus, it becomes important for the sales forecaster to think in terms of ranges of possible outcomes. This does not mean that the forecaster cannot specify some single target level of volume, but it means that in so doing he simply expects realized volume to fall within some range of it.

Where does one begin to predict future sales for a particular firm? One logical place would be to look at past sales trends. This may give us a first approximation of what is likely to happen in the future. Sales for a hypothetical firm for the last 10 years are shown below.

1966	$800,000	1971	$930,000
1967	840,000	1972	900,000
1968	820,000	1973	940,000
1969	880,000	1974	970,000
1970	910,000	1975	1,000,000

This firm had a 25 percent growth in sales for the period, from $800,000 in 1966 to $1 million in 1975. In 8 of the 10 years, sales increased over the previous year, the largest gain being $60,000 in 1969. In 1968 and 1972, revenues declined by $20,000 and $30,000, respectively. In the absence of additional information, one might conclude that in the years ahead there is an 80 percent chance that sales will increase from $20,000 to $60,000 per year with an expected increase of about $30,000 per year. In 20 percent of the years, sales will decline $20,000-$30,000. Based solely on these figures, the 10-year period from 1976 to 1985 might appear as follows.[39]

1976	$1,030,000	1981	$1,180,000
1977	1,060,000	1982	1,210,000
1978	1,090,000	1983	1,240,000
1979	1,120,000	1984	1,270,000
1980	1,150,000	1985	1,300,000

Past experience suggests that the range of outcomes would run from $30,000 greater to $60,000 less than the expected values.

But using past operating experiences as the sole basis for estimating future sales can be hazardous because factors which affected previous outcomes may have changed. Furthermore, trends really don't tell the firm whether it is exploiting as much sales volume as is available. To answer this question calls for additional information.

The first thing that must be known, of course, is the geographic extent of the market and/or supply area being served. For most agricultural marketing firms, the supply area — the geographic area from which it draws its raw materials for processing and marketing — is an important factor in determining its sales volume. For farm supply firms, on the other hand, the geographic area in which it "sells" is the relevant one. These boundaries should not be considered static and they should be examined each year, as competitive factors and other forces that influence them change.

Once the geographic boundaries are identified, the next step is to determine the potential volume in the area. This means identifying all potential customers and/or suppliers. It also means estimating the average use of a particular item per customer, in the case of supply firms, or the average production per supplier, in the case of marketing firms. Such information can be derived from the firm's own experiences; and

---

[39] The estimates anticipate a $30,000 annual increase. The maximum gain in the preceding 10 years was $60,000, or $30,000 greater than the average annual expected gain. The largest decrease from a previous year was $30,000, which, in turn, is $30,000 less than the expected value for the following year, or a total of $60,000 less than expected.

Profit Planning 115

this can be supplemented from outside sources. For example, county agents may have estimates of the average utilization of fertilizer per farm or per acre in the area; trade associations frequently have this kind of information also. The Crop and Livestock Reporting Service develops estimates of acreages planted in various crops, production of milk, poultry, etc., and these data may be helpful.

Given the number of potential customers or suppliers and the average purchases or production of each, an estimate of the total volume potential in the area is easily made. This potential can be shrinking or growing for a number of reasons. It may be expanding, for example, because the number of potential buyers is expanding. Or it may be expanding because average consumption of the item in question is expanding. Or the reverse might be true. Whoever makes the volume estimates must constantly remind himself that this is not a once-in-a-lifetime activity.

Given the total volume potential of an area, a firm's share of the market can be estimated simply by dividing its own volume by the total potential volume. The trend in a firm's share should be watched continuously. It is an effective gauge of how well it is doing relative to its competitors as well as a useful device in making the sales forecast. Many firms find it easier to forecast volume for their entire market or supply area rather than for just themselves. Then they apply their estimated share to arrive at a forecast for the firm itself. For example, if the forecast of sales volume for a particular analysis fertilizer in the market area is 100,000 tons and the firm's estimated market share is 20 percent, it would expect to be able to sell 20,000 tons.

A number of economic factors must be taken into account in the forecasting process. How well the economy as a whole is doing must be considered. For agricultural marketing and supply firms, how well agriculture is doing in relation to the rest of the economy is important. Many of the commonly published indicators of national or agricultural economic health (such as national income estimates, farm income estimates, employment, etc.) are of little value when the market or supply area under consideration is small relative to the nation as a whole. Even though nationally the economic picture may be favorable, certain areas may be lagging far behind. Other areas, on the other hand, may be doing much better than average. Even periods of national economic decline have different impacts on different geographic areas. Thus, the generally available indicators must be modified to take local conditions into account. Consultation with the local banker, credit bureaus, agricultural extension agents, and other representatives of the state university who may have a direct interest in the economic progress of an area may provide the firm with useful economic information.

Beyond this general picture, the firm must be concerned with some rather specific factors that may influence the demand for its products and/or the supplies available for processing and marketing. Shifts in the type of farming can have direct influence on the kinds of farm inputs demanded as well as products produced. Improved technologies may render certain inputs obsolete while creating a demand for a whole new set of inputs. The price level of the goods or service in question will have a direct influence on the quantity demanded or supplied. Prices of substitute commodities must also be considered. The competitive environment must be scrutinized for changes or expected changes in competitive strategy. The firm's own plans for advertising and promotion or other activity designed to influence sales must also be considered.

All of these factors will have an influence on the sales forecast. Some firms have employees who are competent to conduct statistical analyses of economic data which may show how changes in the magnitudes of one or more of these variables will affect sales or supplies available. Other firms base estimates of expected sales volume on surveys of what customers say they will buy or on estimates by salesmen or others who are in close contact with the customers.

As the last step in the process, the person responsible for the forecast mentally sorts these factors, combines them with his own experience of past performance as well as his considered judgment of probable future events, and makes the projection. Such forecasts are typically made for only a year or two ahead, but increasingly, as firms begin to realize the advantages of longer range planning, they are being made for longer periods.

Returning to our hypothetical firm, assume that it took into account the factors that we discussed above and came up with revised estimates of sales for the years 1976-1985, as below.

Year	Expected	High	Low
1976	$1,020,000	$1,050,000	$1,000,000
1977	1,040,000	1,060,000	1,020,000
1978	1,070,000	1,080,000	1,030,000
1979	1,090,000	1,110,000	1,040,000
1980	1,100,000	1,130,000	1,040,000
1981	1,100,000	1,140,000	1,040,000

Year	Expected	High	Low
1982	1,120,000	1,170,000	1,050,000
1983	1,140,000	1,200,000	1,060,000
1984	1,170,000	1,230,000	1,080,000
1985	1,200,000	1,270,000	1,100,000

Acknowledging its inability to predict the future with exactness, it developed high, low, and expected sales estimates. Notice that the range between the high and low estimates becomes larger in later years because the ability to predict future events declines as the time horizon is extended. Each year these projections would be revised in the light of experience and new data. If events in the interim are such as to suggest that a revision is called for, it should be made. No projection, however carefully made, must be considered sacrosanct.

With this background on sales forecasting let us now turn to consideration of the cost analysis side of profit forecasting.

Cost Analysis

Many firms are "output conscious." Some believe, wrongly, that any increase in output is desirable. In large part this attitude arises from the increasing pressure for firms to get larger. While there are some clear benefits to be derived from carefully planned expansion, not all volume increases are necessarily profitable. Any planned expansion or contraction must be examined in relation to its impacts on costs. In the discussion that follows, we will attempt to identify those costs that are relevant to the decision process.

Cost Concepts. *Accounting Costs*—Many decision makers equate accounting costs with those appropriate for use in the decision-making process. Since accounting costs are routinely recorded on the books of the firm, they take on an aura of concreteness and precision that has great appeal to the harried manager. But the fact of the matter is that accounting costs, useful as they are in describing the overall asset status of the firm as well as the sources and uses of funds for some past time period, have distinct limitations as far as the decision-making process is concerned.

The first limitation is that accounting costs are historical. Profit projections require forecasts of future costs which may be quite different than those experienced in the past. For example, technology may change so that output of product or service per unit of input is greater than before. Or the prices paid for materials, labor, equipment, or other items used in the process may change. Similarly, over time the combination of products handled could be altered and this also has impacts on the cost structure.

Additional limitations on the usefulness of accounting data are the standard, and arbitrary, conventions used in deriving these costs. Particularly damaging is the arbitrary allocation of joint or overhead costs among various product lines. There is no really scientific basis for making such allocations other than conventional techniques that have been adopted for reasons of expediency. Some commonly used bases are the portion of total sales volume represented by a given product, warehouse or shelf space occupied by a product, actual direct labor cost, actual direct labor hours, standard direct labor hours, standard direct labor cost, and standard machine hours.[40] All have distinct limitations which could lead to serious errors if such costs are utilized in the decision-making process.

If indeed accounting costs are not the appropriate ones for use in making cost forecasts, which costs are? As a starting place, it is clear that anticipated or future costs are the relevant ones for this purpose. Such costs would take into account expected changes in wage rates, material costs, or changes in methods of operation. Beyond this, several other cost concepts have relevance.

Opportunity Costs — At this stage in this text, the concept of opportunity costs is no longer foreign to us. We have used it earlier in our discussion of maximizing returns on investments and minimizing capital costs. In the context in which we use it here the opportunity cost of any product or service is the profit which would have accrued from feasible alternatives had the resources of the business been directed to their production. According to Dean, the opportunity cost concept is most relevant when the supply of input factors is limited.[41] This is particularly true when we are considering a short time period such as an operating year when a number of factors in a business may be fixed. For example, at any given time the capacity of a feed company for mixing feed is limited. The opportunity cost of producing pig starter in this case is the value of dairy cattle feed which could be produced alternatively by using the same "scarce" mixing capacity. On the other hand, the opportunity costs of factors or products readily available in the market and, therefore, not "scarce" in the above sense, are explicitly contained in their prices.

Opportunity cost data never appear in accounting records but are

---

[40] Joel Dean, *Managerial Economics*. New York; Prentice-Hall, Inc., 1951, p. 317. Chapter 5, p. 247–348 presents an excellent discussion of costs.
[41] Ibid., p. 260.

Profit Planning 119

perfectly relevant for the manager who is evaluating profit prospects. Additionally, the opportunity cost concept serves as a constant reminder that alternatives should be explored. Too often the decision maker is boxed in by some narrowly defined concept of what the business is rather than what it might be.

Fixed and Variable Costs — In considering alternative levels of output for the firm, it is useful to distinguish between fixed and variable costs. This distinction is particularly relevant where the opportunities for adjusting the size of plant or the amount of machinery or some other factor used in producing marketing or farm supply services are limited.

Total variable costs are those that change with changes in volume. They may include such things as the cost of labor, fuel and power, repairs associated with day-to-day operations, packaging materials, and other supplies. Total fixed costs, on the other hand, do not vary with output. They typically include such items as depreciation on buildings, machinery and equipment, interest, insurance, property taxes, and salaries.

The distinction between fixed and variable costs is not hard and fast. Given enough time, almost any fixed cost can be varied. For example, the size of the building or the amount of machinery and equipment can be increased or decreased if enough time is allowed. On the other hand, if the time period considered is short enough, even those costs typically considered variable may, for all practical purposes, be fixed. For example, certain conventions which have grown up through custom or union negotiation have tended to fix the amount of labor required in very short-run situations such as a day or a week or, in some cases, even a month. It is the decision maker, of course, who must finally determine which of the costs are to be classified as variable and which fixed for the time period he has under consideration. In any case, why should he go to the trouble of making this distinction?

Perhaps an example will serve to illustrate its importance. Assume that the total output capacity of a fertilizer blending plant for some time period, say a month, is 1,000 tons. At that level of output, total costs are $60,000, of which $40,000 are variable and $20,000 are fixed. Since fixed costs are in no way related to output, in this particular situation even though the plant produces nothing in the period, $20,000 (fixed costs) would, therefore, be sustained.

Next assume that the price per ton of fertilizer is $55 and that the expected total revenue for the period from the sale of 1,000 tons is

$55,000. If the firm insists on recovering its total costs of $60,000, it would not produce fertilizer at all in this time period. Losses of $20,000 (fixed costs) would therefore be sustained.

If instead of considering total costs the decision maker focused his attention on variable costs, he may have arrived at a different decision. If variable costs of $40,000 at capacity are subtracted from revenue, a balance of $15,000 is left. This balance is conventionally called the "contribution margin." In this case the contribution margin is large enough to cover all but $5,000 of fixed costs. By not producing at all, the firm would have lost $20,000 (fixed cost). By producing the 1,000 tons of fertilizer, losses could be held to $5,000.

Out of this illustration comes a simple principle. So long as the expected increase in revenue from the sale of a particular commodity exceeds the expected increase in costs, under short-run conditions it may pay the firm to produce. If, on the other hand, expected increases in revenue are less than expected increases in costs, i.e., the expected contribution margin is negative, production should clearly be halted. If, in the example, expected total revenue had been $39,000, to have produced the 1,000 tons would have resulted in losses of $21,000 — $20,000 in fixed costs and $1,000 in variable costs.

Decisions to produce at less than full cost must be tempered by consideration of the possible impacts on future customer attitudes toward the price of the product. If, in the previous example, customers would expect fertilizer prices never to exceed $55 per ton—which would cover variable costs of $40 but not full costs of $60—and on this basis would refuse to pay more than that in the future, the manager might be well advised not to produce at that price.

Product Mix Considerations

As we suggested earlier in this section, the arbitrary allocation of overhead costs can lead to "bad" decisions. This is particularly true in the case where the firm is attempting to select its product or enterprise mix. By using the contribution margin concept we can avoid this problem. Table 17 shows how. Let's first assume that the firm illustrated produces and/or sells five products (items A, B, C, E, and F) and one service (item D). Assume for simplicity that the six items represent all of the feasible alternatives open to the firm and that each item is essentially independent of any other item in respect to demand. Assume also that the costs of handling one item are not appreciably affected by the other items handled. Gross profit is arrived at by subtracting cost of goods sold from total sales. The contribution margin represents the difference between gross profit and direct variable costs. Adjusted gross profit is derived by subtracting direct fixed costs from the contribution margin. By *direct* variable and fixed costs we mean those costs that can be assigned to a given item. Note that no direct fixed costs are assigned to item C. Let it represent a short-run opportunity product that requires no additional investment and whose costs are entirely variable. Nonassignable costs, both direct and fixed, are included in overhead. No effort is made to allocate overhead costs among the several items nor should there be in this decision-making exercise. Such an allocation would simply clutter up the process. These overhead costs may be assigned later for the benefit of department heads who may wish to know what kind of overhead burden they are expected to carry. But they are not relevant here.

The items are arranged in descending order according to expected adjusted gross profit. Visual inspection immediately highlights items E and F, since they both show negative adjusted gross profits. The case for dropping item F is clear. As can be seen, it has a negative contribution margin of –$50. Item F also has a direct fixed cost of $50, so that whether the firm produces it or not it will incur costs of $50. But by not producing it in this case, the firm "saves" the $50 by which direct variable costs exceed gross profits. Thus, adjusted gross profit would increase from $5 to $55 if item F were dropped.

What is true of item F is not true of item E. Item E has a positive contribution margin of $20 which offsets one-half of the $40 of direct fixed costs associated with that item. If item E is dropped, the full $40 of direct fixed costs must be borne by the business. Adjusted gross profit

Table 17. Hypothetical array of products on the basis of profitability

Sales	Total	Item A	Item B	Item C	Item D	Item E	Item F	Overhead
Sales	$5,400	1,000	1,100	700	800	600	1,200	
Cost of goods sold	3,400	600	800	500		500	1,000	
Gross profit	2,000	400	300	200	800	100	200	
Direct variable cost	1,680	200	150	100	700	80	250	200
Contribution margin	320	200	150	100	100	20	(50)	(200)
Direct fixed cost	315	50	25		50	40	50	100
Adjusted gross profit.	5*	150	125	100	50	(20)	(100)	(300)

Adjusted gross profit
Without item F = 5 + 50 = 55
Without item E = 5 + 50 − 20 = 35

* Total adjusted gross profit is equal to net profit for the firm as a whole.

would decline by the amount of the contribution margin, or by $20. Thus, if both E and F were dropped, gross profits would be $35 as opposed to $55 if only item F were dropped.

If, rather than assuming that the firm is choosing among products it is already producing, it is assumed that the firm is producing only item A, and items B, C, D, E, and F are the only feasible alternative products open to it, a somewhat different decision would be rendered. Clearly E and F would be ruled out of consideration immediately, since in this case the firm has no fixed commitments in them. Thus, the combination of products and services A, B, C, and D would yield an adjusted gross profit of $125 ($150 + $125 + $100 + $50 − $300).

If this firm could handle only one opportunity item, item C would be carried as long as it generated a positive contribution margin or until a feasible substitute generating a higher contribution came along. For example, if a new item G appeared on the scene and if it would generate a contribution margin of $125, C would be dropped and G would be added if a choice had to be made.

The above illustration was based on a number of simplifying assumptions. One was that there were no demand interrelations between the several items. Demand interrelationships frequently do exist among products and these must be accounted for. For example, the sale of item A might be positively related to the sale of item E. To realize a profit in A, it may be necessary to absorb a loss from E even though the latter, by itself, appears to be unprofitable. Similarly, certain production or cost interrelationships may make it feasible or even necessary to continue an item that would normally be dropped if it were technically independent of all other products in the mix.

Profit Forecast

After due consideration of the sales forecasts for various products handled by the firm, associated costs, and product mix, we are now in a position to formalize our estimates of these factors. For purposes of illustration let's assume that we are asked to prepare profit estimates for The Lauderdale Farm Marketing Company, which handles grain and a number of farm supplies.

A sales budget for Lauderdale could be prepared as in table 18. Expected total sales would be derived from a previously developed sales forecast. Of the several levels of volume and associated prices projected, that one which fits the total profit plan of the firm is selected. Thus, column R in table 18 is derived simply by multiplying expected price per unit for the particular item in question times the expected sales volume. To arrive at an estimate of gross profit for the particular item it is necessary to estimate the total cost of goods sold. This is directly tied to the volume estimate. Cost of goods sold is derived by adding purchases to the beginning inventory for the period under consideration and subtracting estimated ending inventory.

Table 19 represents the hypothetical cost budget associated with the above sales budget. The figures presented must not be regarded as standards for any of the items included. Direct costs and overhead costs are handled separately. For each of these categories, costs are identified

Table 18. Hypothetical sales budget for Lauderdale Farm Marketing Company

Product	(R) Expected total sales (selling price × quantity)	(U) Cost of goods sold	Gross profit (R)-(U)
Feed and seed			
Dairy	$90,000	$76,500	$13,500
Hog	50,000	42,500	7,500
Beef	95,000	80,750	14,250
Poultry	...	...	...
Total	405,000	340,000	65,000
Fertilizer			
Analysis A	40,000	32,000	8,000
Analysis B	25,500	18,000	7,500
Analysis C	...	...	...
Analysis D	...	...	...
Total	80,000	64,000	16,000
Petroleum products			
Gas, station	58,000	43,000	15,000
Gas, bulk	...	...	...
L.P.	...	...	...
Oil	...	...	...
Total	97,000	69,000	28,000
Service and merchandise			
...	...	...	...
...	...	...	...
...	...	...	...
Total	33,000	11,000	22,000
Grain			
...	...	...	...
...	...	...	...
Total	810,000	770,000	40,000
Total	1,425,000	1,254,000	171,000

124   The Financial Management of Agribusiness Firms

as being variable or fixed. As we suggested earlier, variable costs are those that change with changes in output. The job of classifying a cost as variable or fixed is not an easy one. Given enough time, almost any cost can be made to vary. Contrariwise, if the time period is short enough even costs that are commonly classified as variable may be for all practical purposes fixed. The breakdown in table 19 is more or less typical for time periods of a year or less.

Selling costs are included in the variable costs category in the illustration as a matter of convenience. The advertising and promotion elements of this item present some problems of classification. For example, if a particular product is not to be sold, it is not advertised. On the other hand, if it is to be sold and the decision to advertise is made, there is usually some fixed amount budgeted which usually does not vary with changes in output. In this sense, it is not a true variable cost, and some budgeters prefer to handle it as a separate item.

Table 20 brings the sales budget and the cost budget together into a profit budget. This is frequently called a pro forma income statement. For those who may be concerned that the format used departs somewhat from income statements typically presented, we wish to point out that our interest here is focused on a planning-decision-making tool for use inside the firm. The manager can adopt conventional methods of presentation, if he wishes, for purposes of reporting to the stockholders.

As in our earlier illustration, the contribution margin of each product line is derived by subtracting the total variable costs from gross profit. In this illustration the contribution margin of each of the products is positive. Note that the adjusted gross profit from the several individual products does not include any overhead allocations, since this would simply confuse the decision-making process. Department heads, of course, would wish to know the overhead burden assigned to them and management would typically make an allocation for this purpose. Insofar as such an allocation does not influence the decision process, no harm is done.

Under ideal circumstances an annual budget is broken down into monthly or quarterly statements that take into account seasonal variations with respect to sales and costs. It is imperative that intermediate goals be established to check on the progress toward achieving the annual budgetary objectives. Only by frequent readings on progress throughout the year is the firm able to ascertain whether or not it will achieve its targets. As suggested earlier, since budgets are developed on

Table 19. Cost budget for Lauderdale Farm Marketing Company

	Feed and seed	Fertilizer	Direct costs Petroleum products	Service and merchandise	Grain	Overhead	Total
Variable							
Wages	$32,100	$4,071	$12,299	$4,575	$4,071	$3,650	$60,766
Fuel, heat, light	2,100	223	675	252	223	100	3,573
Repairs	600	112	337	125	111	150	1,435
Supplies	700	91	270	100	90	200	1,451
Telephone	400	147	446	166	148	200	1,507
Selling costs	1,100	123	373	139	124	200	2,059
Miscellaneous	300	33	100	37	33	200	703
Subtotal	$37,300	$4,800	$14,500	$5,394	$4,800	$4,700	$71,494
Fixed							
Building depreciation	900	300	964	1,338	2,042	1,000	6,544
Equipment depreciation	1,600	300	2,532	3,513	5,361	500	13,806
Salaries	4,000	4,000	0	0	0	18,750	26,750
Interest	600	0	821	1,140	1,739	700	5,000
Insurance	500	200	599	832	1,269	600	4,000
Property taxes	700	0	1,052	1,458	2,226	600	6,036
Miscellaneous	200	0	0	0	0	3,100	3,300
Subtotal	$8,500	$4,800	$5,968	$8,281	$12,637	$25,250	$65,436
Total	$45,800	$9,600	$20,468	$13,675	$17,437	$29,950	$136,930

Table 20. Profit budget for Lauderdale Farm Marketing Company

		Direct costs					
	Total	Feed and seed	Fertilizer	Petroleum products	Service and merchandise	Grain	Overhead costs
Total sales	$1,425,000	$405,000	$80,000	$97,000	$33,000	$810,000	
Cost of goods sold	1,254,000	340,000	64,000	69,000	11,000	770,000	
Gross profit	171,000	65,000	16,000	28,000	22,000	40,000	
Total variable cost	71,494	37,300	4,800	14,500	5,394	4,800	4,700
Contribution margin	99,506	27,700	11,200	13,500	16,606	35,200	(4,700)
Total fixed cost	65,436	8,500	4,800	5,968	8,281	12,637	25,250
Adjusted gross profit	34,070	19,200	6,400	7,532	8,325	22,563	(29,950)
Overhead allocation		0	0	0	0	0	
Net operating profit	34,070						

the basis of estimates of future events, variations from target levels can be expected. It is essential that management establish acceptable ranges for this variation. If, for example, sales of a particular item during the year should fall outside the acceptable range, action would immediately be undertaken to discover the underlying reasons. It is entirely possible that some unanticipated element is at work that will make the achievement of the target outcome impossible. In such a case, an adjustment in the plan is called for. On the other hand, it is possible that the target is being missed because some factor internal to the firm, and therefore under its control, is acting up. In such a case, immediate corrective action can be taken. If the particular item stays within acceptable range of variation over the year, the manager need not worry about it.

The manager who has carefully studied his cost and revenue picture is in good position to analyze the impact of variations of sales on profits. If, for example, it becomes necessary to reduce the planned sales of a particular item, he is in a position to allocate the released resources to other feasible alternatives in such a way as to minimize the impact of the reduction on the firm's profitability. This can only be done if cost and revenue behavior from the alternatives are known.

Break-Even Analysis

Another widely used tool in profit forecasting is "break-even analysis." Its primary contribution to the process is that it explicitly takes into account the impacts of variations in volume on profitability. It builds on the concepts of fixed and variable costs that we discussed in the previous section. Recall that variable costs are those that change directly with changes in the volume of output, while fixed costs remain unchanged regardless of the number of units produced. Drawing from our example in the previous section, let's apply break-even analysis to the fertilizer department of the Lauderdale Company. From table 19 we see that fixed costs in the fertilizer department are $4,800. This can be graphed as shown in figure 2. Note that as volume increases (measured along the horizontal axis), fixed costs (measured along the vertical axis) are unchanged. Next, assume that variable costs — in this case the price per unit we pay for raw product plus variable operating costs — are $68.80 per ton. Graphically, variable costs would appear as shown in figure 3.

This graph implies that at zero output, variable costs are zero and at an output of 1,000 tons, variable costs are $68,800.

Figure 2. Fixed cost illustration.

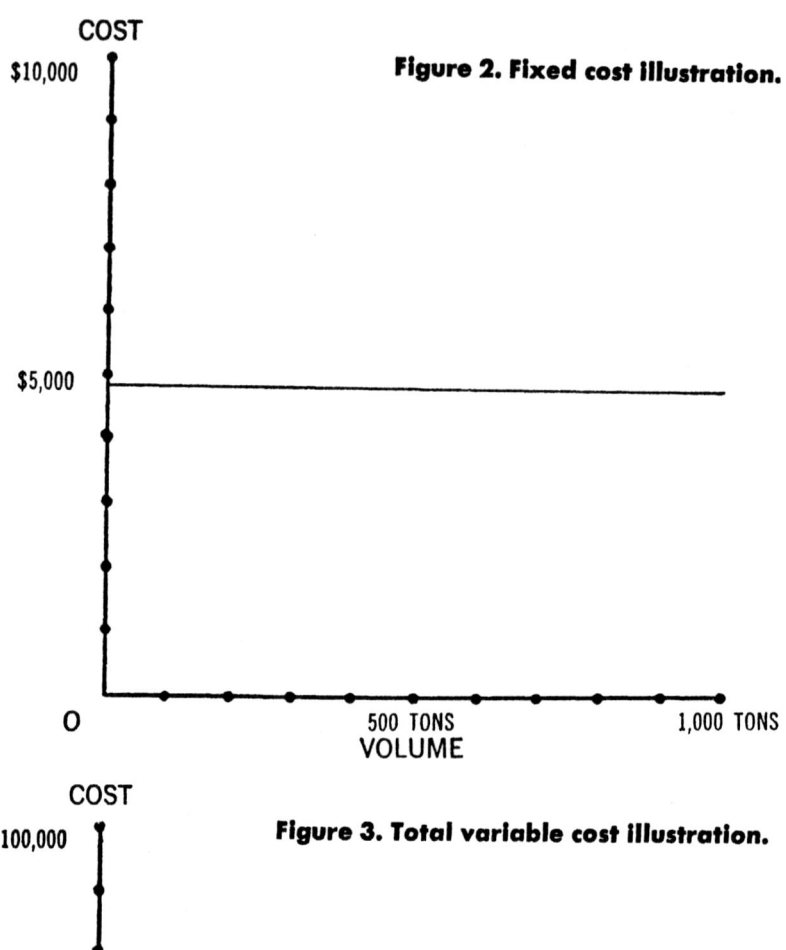

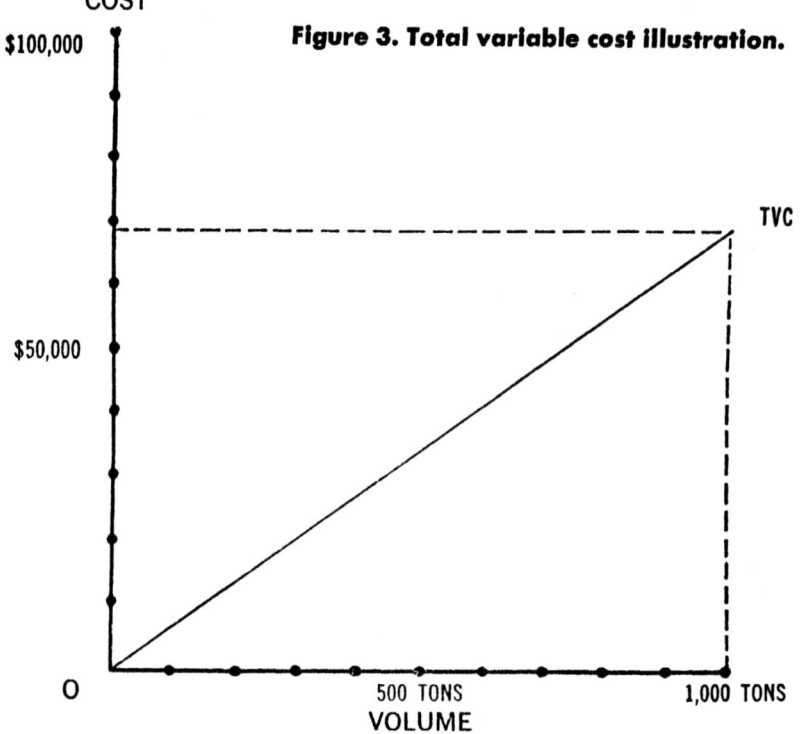

Figure 3. Total variable cost illustration.

Now let's put fixed and variable costs on the same graph, as shown in figure 4.

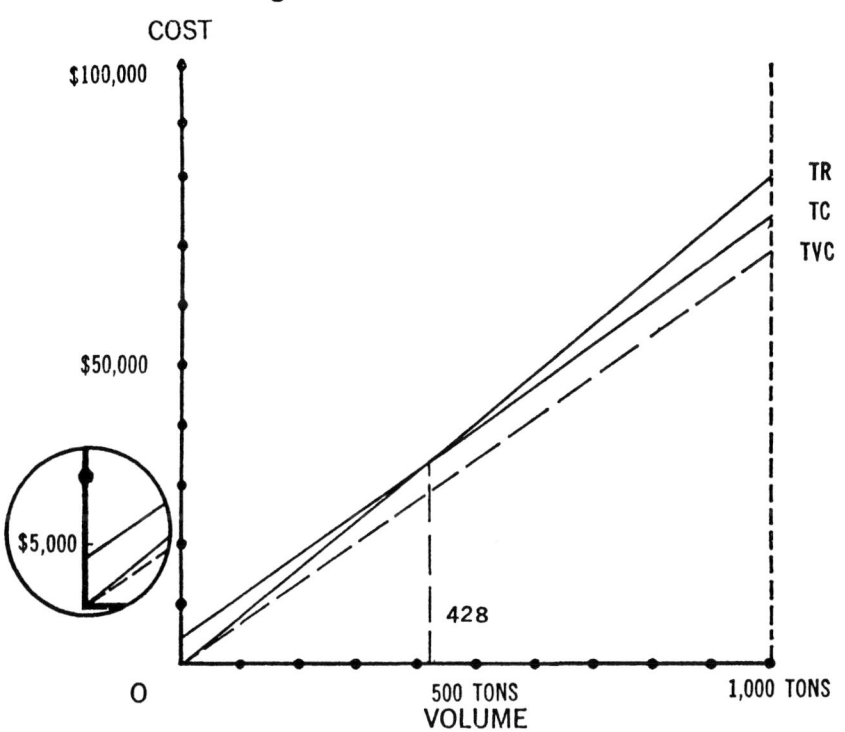

Figure 4. Break-even chart.

Variable costs are represented by the dotted line. The vertical difference between total variable costs and total costs represents fixed costs. The graph of total cost tells us that at zero output, total costs are $4,800, and at an output of 1,000 tons, $73,600. Now let's assume that the firm can sell fertilizer at $80 per ton. Multiplying this price times the number of units sold gives us estimated total revenue for each planned volume of sales. Total revenue appears on our graph as the line identified by TR. We can see (if we have sharp eyes) that break-even volume occurs at an output of around 428 tons.[42] Below that volume the firm in-

---

[42] The break-even point can be calculated algebraically as follows: Let

$$\text{Profit} = PQ - VQ - F$$

where:
P = sales price per unit
Q = number of units sold
V = variable cost per unit
F = total fixed costs

Therefore, if profit = O, then
$O = 80\,Q - 68.80\,Q - 4,800$
$11.20\,Q = 4,800$
$Q = 428$ tons

130   *The Financial Management of Agribusiness Firms*

curs losses on the sale of fertilizer. Any volume increase above it results in an increase in profits. If we assume that the firm operates at an output of 1,000 tons, then total profits are $6,400.

Suppose that total costs remain as before, but that selling price increases to $85 per ton, as illustrated in figure 5. Now the total revenue

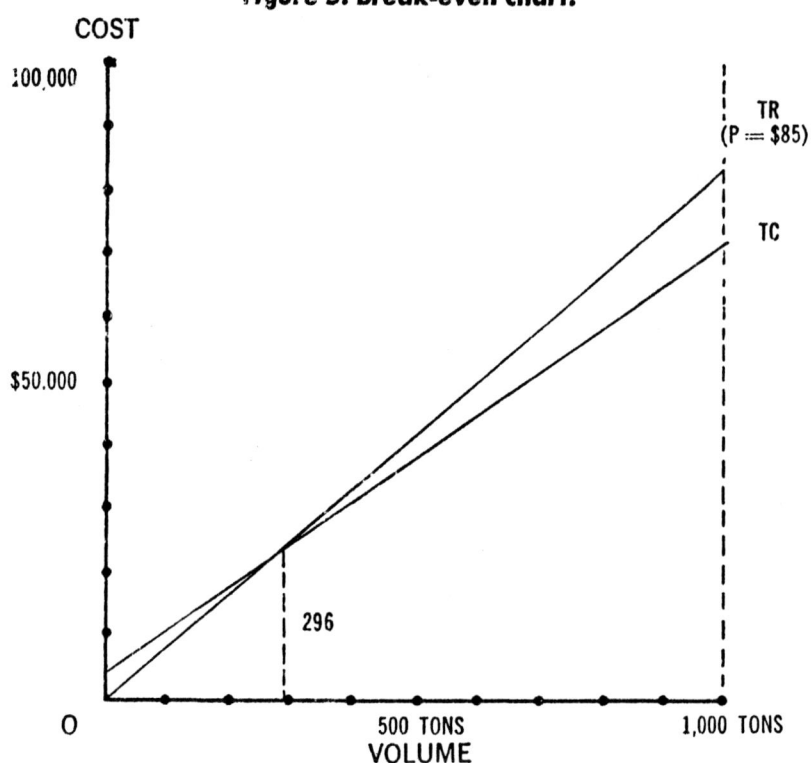

Figure 5. Break-even chart.

line is steeper than previously and the break-even point is lower than before — 296 tons.[48] The opposite would be true, of course, if price per ton had fallen. The break-even point would have been to the right, at higher volume, in this case. Similarly, higher variable and/or fixed costs would tend to move the break-even point to the right, and vice versa.

Profit-Volume Analysis and Price Policy. The tendency for the break-even point to shift with changes in prices has important applications in the development of price policy by a firm. Suppose, for example, that a firm was charging $85 per ton (as reflected by TR_1 in figure 6)

[48] Using the profit equation at break-even:
$$0 = 85Q - 68.80Q - 4,800$$
$$16.20\ Q = 4,800$$
$$Q = 296 \text{ tons}$$

Figure 6. Break-even chart.

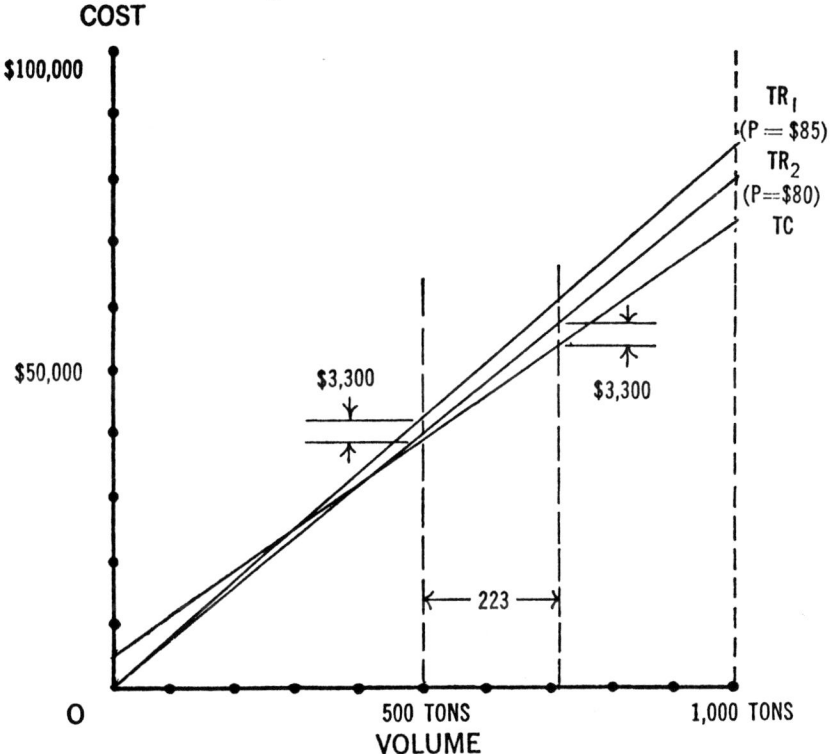

for fertilizer and was selling 500 tons. Let's assume, as before, that variable costs per ton are $68.80 and fixed costs $4,800. Under these conditions, profits are $3,300.[44] Now suppose that the firm is considering a price reduction to $80 per ton (as reflected by TR_2 in figure 6). Assume that no changes in cost rates are anticipated and that the firm wishes to maintain the same level of profits — $3,300 — as before. To accomplish this it would have to sell 723 tons — 223 more than before.[45] In effect, a 6 percent reduction in price would require nearly a 44 percent in-

[44] Using the profit equation, we have,

$$\begin{aligned}\text{Profit} &= \$85(500) - \$68.80(500) - \$4,800 \\ &= \$42,500 - \$34,400 - \$4,800 \\ &= \$42,500 - \$39,200 \\ &= \$3,300\end{aligned}$$

[45] Given a specific profit target, a formula for determining the volume required is as follows:

$$Q = \frac{\text{profit target} + \text{fixed cost}}{\text{selling price} - \text{unit variable cost}} = \frac{T + FC}{(P - V)^*}$$

In the example above:

$$Q = \frac{\$3,300 + \$4,800}{\$80 - \$68.80} = \frac{\$11.20}{\$8,100} = 723 \text{ tons}$$

* Price per unit of product less variable cost per unit is defined as the contribution margin in break-even analysis.

crease in volume to maintain profits at their previous level.[46] Under the best of circumstances, such an increase might be difficult to achieve. While in our particular example (figure 6) it appears possible, in many cases capacity limitations would "cut off" such an expansion.

The above formulation is particularly useful when management has some discretion as far as selling prices are concerned. Unless it is willing to accept "surprise" profit results, the firm must develop price policy in light of cost—volume relationships, profit targets, and its physical capacity. Frequently, of course, price adjustments are forced on the firm. In this case, the above framework is useful in analyzing the adjustments that must be made in volume to dampen the impacts of a price decrease on profitability.

What we have been saying about the impacts of varying prices on profitability could also be said about variations in cost. An increase in variable costs would make the total costs curve (figure 6) steeper. With a given total revenue curve, the break-even volume would, as in the case of lower prices, move to the right. An increase in fixed costs would have a similar impact. This emphasizes the need for careful cost control in profit planning.

Operating Leverage Considerations. In chapter 5 we discussed financial leverage. The key element in that concept was the proportion of fixed return capital in the overall capital structure. We saw that when firms employed a high proportion of fixed return capital (were highly levered), rates of return on residual equity were magnified if all went well, on the one hand, but that declines in returns were exaggerated in the event that realized revenues fell short of those planned, on the other hand. Financial leverage has a direct parallel in the concept of operating leverage. In the latter case, the fixed element is fixed costs. If the proportion of fixed cost to total cost is high, the firm has a high degree of operating leverage. Variations in volume in this case exaggerate net operating profit positively or negatively, depending on the direction of the change.

In our examination of operating leverage, we will first consider profit behavior around the break-even point as volume varies and then take a closer look at just how fixed costs affect that behavior. Let's again consider an example using the fertilizer department of Lauderdale. Assume that the price per ton for fertilizer is $80, that variable costs per

[46] Percentage change in price $= \dfrac{\$85 - \$80}{\$85} = 0.06 = 6\%$.

Percentage change in quantity $= \dfrac{500 - 723}{500} = 0.44 = 44\%$.

Figure 7. Illustration of operating leverage.

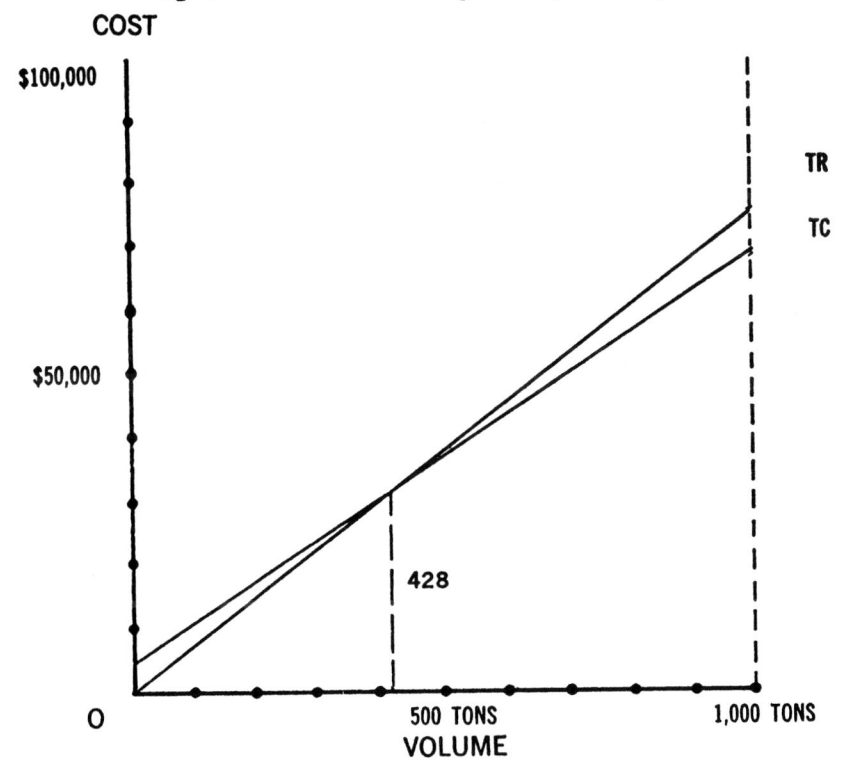

ton are $68.80, and that total fixed costs are $4,800. The revenue and cost picture appears as in figure 7.

The break-even level of output occurs at 428 tons. Now, observe profit behavior as we increase output by increments of 10 percent from the break-even point. This is done in the table below.[47] Since at the

Volume	% change in volume	Profit	% change in profit
428	0	0	0
471	10	475	infinite
518	10	1,002	108
569	10	1,584	58
700	—	3,040	—
770	10	3,824	26
847	10	4,682	23

[47] Because visual interpretation of the break-even point with small net increments is difficult, we used the profit equation to estimate alternative profit points.

$P = \$80(471) - \$68.80(471) - \$4,800 = \$\ 475$
$P = \$80(518) - \$68.80(518) - \$4,800 = \$1,002$
$P = \$80(570) - \$68.80(570) - \$4,800 = \$1,584$
$P = \$80(700) - \$68.80(700) - \$4,800 = \$3,040$
$P = \$80(770) - \$68.80(770) - \$4,800 = \$3,824$
$P = \$80(847) - \$68.80(847) - \$4,000 = \$4,686$

break-even point profits are zero, as we increase output from 428 to 471 tons (10 percent) profits increase by infinity. A practical interpretation of this is that around the break-even point, any small percentage increase in output will result in quite a large percentage increase in profits. Increasing volume another 10 percent, from 471 to 518 tons, results in a profit increase of 108 percent. As we move further away from the break-even point, profits continue to increase, but do so at a decreasing percentage rate. In short, the further to the right of break even that a firm can operate, the smaller are the impacts of volume changes on relative profitability. But what can go up can also come down, and here is where the operating leverage concept has its major impact. As volume sold moves back toward break even, profit declines at an increasing percentage rate. If a firm's volume is varying around the break-even point, the percentage variation in operating profits will be extremely high.

While we asserted earlier that the relative proportion of fixed costs is key to the concept of operating leverage, just how these costs affect it may not be clear. Let's probe a little deeper. Suppose that we have two firms selling an identical product for $100 per ton. Assume further that variable operating costs are also identical at $60 per ton. But now assume that firm A has fixed costs of $20,000 while firm B has fixed costs of $10,000. This situation might appear as in figure 8.

Assume that both firms are operating at an output of 750 units. In this case A's profit is $10,000 and B's is $20,000.[48] Now let us vary output by 10 percent on either side of 750 units and observe the impact on profitability. This is done in the table below.

Volume	% change from 750 tons	Firm A Profits	% change	Firm B Profits	% change
675	−10	$ 7,000	−30	$17,000	−15
750	↕	10,000	↕	20,000	↕
825	+10	13,000	+30	23,000	+15

In firm A—the one with the highest proportion of fixed costs and, therefore, the one with the greatest operating leverage—a 10 percent upward or downward change in volume results in a 30 percent change in profit; this compares to a variation of only 15 percent in profits for firm B with exactly the same volume changes.[49]

[48] Using the profit equation for A, $P = \$100 (750) - \$60 (750) - \$20,000 = \$10,000$
for B, $P = \$100 (750) - \$60 (750) - \$10,000 = \$20,000$

[49] The degree of operating leverage at any level of output can be measured as follows:
$$Q = \frac{Q(P-V)}{Q(P-V)-F}$$
(Formula continued on page 135)

Profit Planning 135

This difference is due entirely to differences in fixed costs. The illustration emphasizes the profit vulnerability of firms which are carrying a high degree of operating leverage. This vulnerability is particularly acute at or near the break-even point. If one were to couple high operating leverage with high financial leverage the risk impacts would be extreme. Only the foolhardy or adventuresome would put them together in the same firm.

Appraisal of Break-Even Analysis. Break-even analysis has a role in overall profit planning. It calls to management's attention the impor-

Figure 8. Illustration of operating leverage.

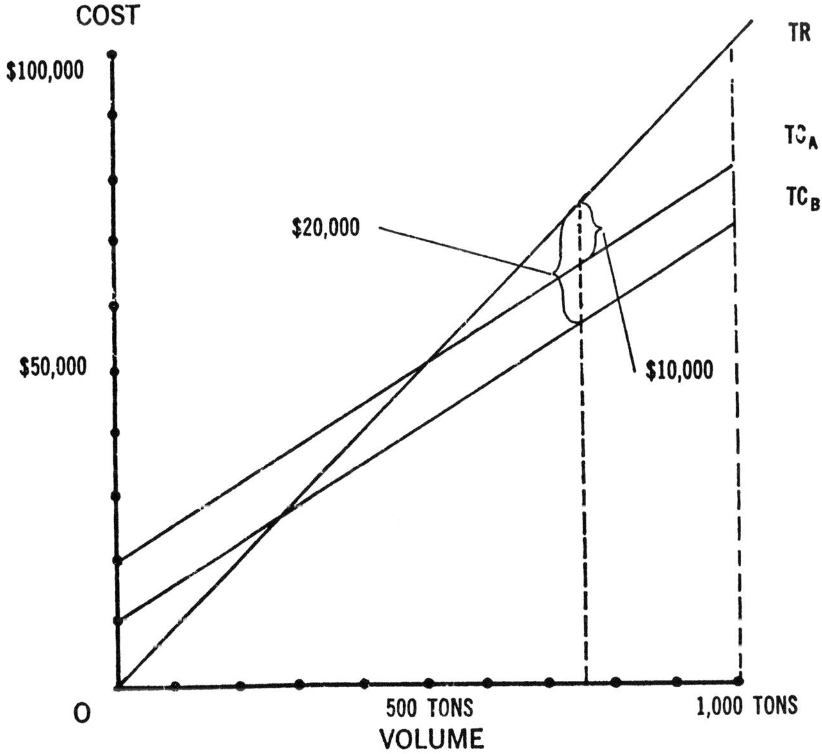

where:
Q = specific level of output
P = price per unit
V = variable costs per unit
F = total fixed costs

Notice that with high fixed costs, the denominator would tend to be small relative to the numerator. In this case the degree of operating leverage would be high. In the example in the text, the degree of operating leverage at an output of 750 units would be as follows:

For firm A $\quad \dfrac{750(100-60)}{750(100-60)-20,000} = \dfrac{30,000}{10,000} = 3.0$

For firm B $\quad \dfrac{750(100-60)}{750(100-60)-10,000} = \dfrac{30,000}{20,000} = 1.5$

which are equivalent to the 30 and 15 percent changes in profits in the example above.

tance of taking into account cost-volume relationships as it attempts to develop the firm's price-profit policy. In this connection it serves to demonstrate how variations in fixed and/or variable costs as well as variations in product prices can affect profitability. It is also useful in the assessment of risks, as reflected in measures of operating leverage.

On the other hand, it does have some limitations. First of all, it assumes that both revenue and cost functions are linear. Within fairly narrowly defined volume limits, such an assumption may not unduly violate the actual relationships. But at extremely low or high output levels, actual values may depart considerably from those implied by the assumption of unvarying costs and prices — and, therefore, must be used with extreme caution.

Secondly, the break-even approach is best suited to the analysis of one product line at a time. The unsophisticated user could do his firm great harm, therefore, if he overlooked potential product and/or cost interrelationships — either one or both of which could have significant impacts on overall firm profitability.

A third problem relates to sorting variable and fixed costs. As we suggested earlier, there is nothing magic about the process. But how we make the split is important to break-even analysis, as our just completed discussion clearly implies. Over- or underestimating one or both of these cost categories can have severe implications for the break-even point.

Finally, of course, there may be a dangerous tendency to stick with break-even charts long after the underlying data have changed. New production techniques, new factor costs, and different combinations of factors employed all have impacts on the level and slope of the cost curves. Further, while we would normally expect a firm to be extremely sensitive to price changes, if it fails to take them into account when it considers revenues in relation to costs — as in a break-even chart — wrong decisions can result. Break-even charts must be regarded as being as variable as the environment in which they are used, and must be changed accordingly if they are to be a positive assistance to the decision process.

In the final analysis, how useful this tool is will depend in large part on the capacity and understanding of the person using it. It is not a substitute for intelligence or correct data; the results will only be as good as the data used in the analysis as well as the quality of the interpretation of the outcome. In general, this tool is best used in conjunction with an operating budget such as we suggested in the previous section.

Cash Budget

Another important projection in overall profit planning is the cash budget. It lists cash inflows and outflows over some future time period — usually a year, broken down into months or quarters. Such a budget is illustrated in table 21, which shows an annual cash budget as well as sample monthly budgets for the hypothetical Lauderdale Farm Marketing Company.

Some but not all of the information used in preparing the income statement is included in the annual cash budget. Depreciation, which is a noncash expense, would be excluded. Because of the accrual method of accounting, some cash expenses recorded in the income statement may not be paid until the following year; likewise, some of the payments made in the period under consideration may reflect purchases made in a previous period. The same is true of sales when credit is granted. For example, merchandise sold in December on 60-day terms will not be paid for until February of the following year.

When preparing a cash projection for a period as long as a year, the problems created by accruals usually are not too significant because there is a tendency for the collection or payment of prior-period revenue or expense to be balanced off by the period-ending accruals. Under these circumstances a firm might well be justified in using items from the projected income statement as a basis for the projected cash budget, with additions or subtractions of cash flow items not related to the income statement. This is what we did in our example of Lauderdale's cash budget.

Cash increases from operations for the year were projected at $59,420. This value less income tax payments of $3,000 ($56,420) would be the cash flow generated by the business (discussed in chapter 4). The annual cash budget also tells us that Lauderdale is planning to purchase $30,000 of new assets, plans to borrow an additional $20,000, and pay out $5,000 in interest and $5,000 in dividends. The net change in cash balance for the year is planned to be $36,420 and this, coupled with a $12,000 beginning cash balance, will yield a planned ending cash balance of $48,420.

So much for the annual cash budget. Let us now turn our attention to shorter-term cash budgeting problems. Shorter-term cash budgets are extremely useful in planning for seasonal cash needs. It is not uncommon in highly seasonal businesses for monthly cash outflows to exceed monthly inflows, with the result that the firm may have to borrow addi-

Table 21. 1976 cash budget for Lauderdale Farm Marketing Company

Cash changes	Annual	September	October	November
From operations:				
Cash receipts				
Cash sales	$415,000	$40,000	$65,000	$60,000
Accounts receivable	1,010,000	200,000	185,000	175,000
Total	1,425,000	240,000	250,000	235,000
Disbursements				
Accounts payable	1,254,000	225,000	230,000	175,000
Labor	60,766	7,000	6,500	5,000
Fuel, heat, light	3,573	500	500	500
Repairs	1,435	200	200	200
Selling expenses	2,059	300	300	300
Telephone	1,507	200	200	200
Supplies	1,451	250	250	250
Salaries	26,750	2,315	2,315	2,315
Insurance	4,000	350	350	350
Property taxes	6,036	0	0	3,018
Miscellaneous	4,003	265	265	265
Total	1,365,580	236,380	240,880	187,398
Cash increase from operations	59,420	3,620	9,120	47,602
From sale or purchase of fixed assets	−30,000	−30,000	0	0
From income tax payments	−3,000	0	0	0
From financing changes and dividends				
Interest payments	−5,000	0	0	−5,000
Dividend payments	−5,000	0	0	−5,000
From increase or decrease in long-term debt or equity	+20,000	+15,000	−5,000	+5,000
Net change in cash balance	36,420	−11,380	4,120	42,602
Beginning cash balance	12,000	2,000	−9,380	−5,260
Ending cash balance	48,420	−9,380	−5,260	37,342
Minimum desired cash balance		6,000	6,000	6,000
Cash overage or shortage		−15,380	−11,260	31,342

138

tional funds or liquidate certain of its securities for the purpose of tiding it over that period. If such seasonal drains on cash are anticipated, adequate funds, from whatever the source, can be provided. The firm can thereby, at a minimum, avoid losing discounts on the goods it purchases (see our discussion in chapter 3), or, more seriously, damage its credit rating, or, at the extreme, run the risk of bankruptcy. On the other side of the coin, it may discover that during certain periods of the year its cash balances are somewhat higher than they need be and such cash can be put to more productive use in the form of short-term securities and/or other investments in the firm.

Let's assume that Lauderdale is a highly seasonal business and that its interests would be best served by a monthly cash budget. Where does the process of developing a monthly cash budget start? Clearly, we need some estimate of monthly sales and monthly disbursements. We know from our annual budget that cash receipts of the year are expected to be $1,425,000. The historical seasonal distributions of sales by month can be helpful to us as a first approximation of what month-to-month sales are likely to be. If, for example, 10 percent of the year's sales are in January, estimated sales for that month would be $142,500. A second factor affecting cash receipts is the credit policy of the firm. Lauderdale might extend credit on a net 30-day basis. If everybody paid up on time but not before (as we suggested was good practice), then sales made in one month would be converted to cash in the next period. As a practical matter, not everyone pays his bills on time and firms can pretty well estimate what kind of lag they can expect on the basis of their previous experience. For example, Lauderdale may find that about 20 percent of its customers pay their bills in the same month that they are incurred, 65 percent in the following month, 10 percent in the third month, 1 percent in the fourth month, and 4 percent take longer than 4 months. Thus, for every $1,000 of sales anticipated in January, for example, it would expect to receive $200 in cash in January, $650 in February, $100 in March, and $10 in April. It may be hard put to tell when it will receive the other $40. But in any case it can account for the bulk of sales being transformed into cash in the month indicated and the expected collection date of accounts receivable would be assigned accordingly.

Cash disbursements are handled in a similar fashion. Again, the problem is to identify when actual cash flows out of the firm. Certain kinds of raw material are paid for almost immediately. The firm should always plan its payment schedule to take advantage of any discounts offered. For some merchandise, however, no discount is offered and the firm is well advised not to pay until the last day that it is required to do so. This means that in some cases items purchased in January may not be paid for until February or March. Similarly, various accrual items are not recorded until actual cash outlays are made.

With these factors in mind, we developed cash budgets for a sample of months, September, October, and November, for Lauderdale. Similar budgets could have been prepared for other months in the year. In any case, it is clear that Lauderdale is indeed in a highly seasonal business. We see in September, for example, that the net change in cash balance for the month was a negative $11,380. Since the beginning cash balance for the month of September was $2,000, there would be a negative ending cash balance of $9,380. Let's further assume that Lauderdale wishes always to have a minimum cash balance of $6,000 in any month. It would, therefore, need to obtain $15,380 of additional cash. For this purpose it may have to rely on its established credit sources or liquidate certain securities which it may have set up just for this purpose, or for that matter liquidate any other asset. In October, it is once again in a deficit cash position (negative $5,260 ending cash balance plus $6,000 minimum) but by November receipts begin to lead disbursments by a considerable margin. In that month, it produced a surplus over minimum cash needs of $31,342. Presumably, Lauderdale's cash position would improve in the month of December to a point where its ending cash balance would be $48,420, as indicated by the annual cash budget.

For firms in which receipts and disbursements are uniform from month to month, quarterly or even semiannual cash budgets may be adequate. Whatever the time period chosen, the short-term (e.g., monthly or quarterly) cash budget is designed primarily to protect the liquidity position of the firm as well as to insure that surplus cash balances are identified so that they can be siphoned off into other more productive uses.

Pro Forma Balance Sheet

A third very useful statement in the overall planning process is a projected balance sheet. In preparing a cash budget and a projected income statement, we have accumulated much of the information needed. Let's return to our illustration of the Lauderdale Farm Marketing Company. Its balance sheet as of December 31, 1975, is shown in table 22.

Table 22. Lauderdale Farm Marketing Company balance sheet

Balance Sheet
December 31, 1975

Current Assets		Current Liabilities	
Cash	$ 40,000	Accounts payable	$420,000
Accounts receivable	130,500	Notes payable	5,000
Inventory	463,000	Accruals	25,900
	$633,500		$450,900
		Long-Term Debt	41,000
Fixed Assets		Equity	100,000
Net	93,365	Retained Earnings	134,965
Total Assets	$726,865	Total	$726,865

By combining data from the projected income statement (table 20) and the cash budget (table 21) with the 1975 balance sheet above, a projected balance sheet for 1976 (table 23) was developed. For simplicity of illustration, certain accounts were assumed to remain unchanged. The adjustments in cash, the debit entry for net assets, long-term debt, and the debit entry for retained earnings all derive from the cash budget (table 21). The credit entry for asset adjustments came from our cost budget (table 19) and the credit entry adjustment for retained earnings came from the income statement ($34,070 minus $3,000 in income tax).

The illustration in table 23 is carried a step farther to show changes in the sources and uses of funds (last two columns). The increases in cash and net asset accounts (uses) are offset by changes in long-term debt and retained earnings accounts (sources).

Other accounts could have been treated similarly. Typically, inventory requirements and accounts and notes payable do change, particularly when the period considered is as long as a year. Estimates of these changes can simply be plugged in as were those illustrated above.

While our primary focus in the Lauderdale Company illustration was on yearly statements, the same procedures that we followed in developing them could be used for shorter or longer periods. Further, estimates are frequently made for a range of possible outcomes rather than for just a single expected one. Variations of the basic projections can also be explored. For instance, a firm might prepare a set of projections assuming a particular investment program is undertaken and another set assuming that it is not. By examining the differences, additional insights as to the acceptability of a proposal can be gained.

Table 23. Lauderdale Farm Marketing Company, worksheet for projected balance sheet, December 31, 1976

	Balance sheet December 31, 1975		Adjustments		Projected balance sheet December 31, 1976		Projected sources and uses of funds statement	
	Debit	Credit	Debit	Credit	Debit	Credit	Use	Source
Cash............	$40,000		$36,420		$76,420		$36,420	
Inventory........	463,000				463,000			
Accounts receivable.	130,500				130,500			
Net assets.......	93,365		30,000*	$20,350†	103,015		9,650	
Accruals payable...		$420,000				$420,000		
Notes payable....		5,000				5,000		
Accounts payable..		25,900				25,900		
Long-term debt....		41,000		20,000*		61,000		
Equity...........		100,000				100,000		$20,000
Retained earnings..		134,965	5,000*	31,070‡		161,035		26,070
	$726,865	$726,865	$71,420	$71,420	$772,935	$772,935	$46,070	$46,070

* From annual cash budget (table 21).
† From cost budget (table 19). Depreciation expense was $6,544 for buildings and $13,806 for equipment for a total of $20,350.
‡ Net operating income before income taxes was $34,070 and the firm paid out $3,000 in income tax for a net of $31,070.

It must be emphasized that sound estimates are dependent on more than internally derived data. Studies undertaken by other organizations, such as the U.S. Department of Agriculture, universities, banks, and research institutes, can add valuable insights. Some firms also find it useful to employ private consulting firms to delve into particular problems.

Questions are often asked by managers concerning the length and frequency of the planning period. Should estimates be prepared monthly, quarterly, or annually? How many years in the future should we attempt to project? How often should estimates be revised? There is no single answer to these questions that is applicable to all firms. The frequency of the planning period depends in large part on the environment in which the firm is operating as well as on its own financial strength. A strong firm operating in a relatively stable industry might get by on quarterly or semiannual estimates. Where the firm is weak and/or the industry is volatile, a closer watch must be maintained. The question of how far into the future it should project the cash flow from certain projects is, of course, dependent on its projected economic life.

Suggested Readings

Boch, R. H., W. S. Farris, C. B. Cox, and J. S. Day. *Long Range Planning for Agricultural Marketing Firms*, revised edition. Layfayette, Ind.: Purdue University, Agricultural Economics Department, 1960.

Committee on Management Services. *Budgeting for Profit in Small Business.* New York: American Institute of Certified Public Accountants Bulletin No. 2, 1959.

Gavett, J. William, and John M. Allderidge. *Operational Analysis is Small Manufacturing Companies.* Small Business Administration Research Report, 1962, section I.

Helfert, Erich. *Techniques of Financial Analysis.* Homewood, Ill.: Richard D. Irwin, Inc., 1963, p. 37–53, 83–97.

Johnson, Robert W. *Financial Management*, third edition. Boston: Allyn and Bacon, Inc., 1966, p. 200–224.

Knight, W. D., and E. H. Weinwurm. *Managerial Budgeting.* New York: Macmillan Company, 1964.

Lindsay, Robert, and Arnold W. Sametz. *Financial Management.* Homewood, Ill.: Richard D. Irwin, Inc., 1963, p. 79–91.

Levin, Richard I., and C. A. Kirkpatrick. *Quantitative Approaches to Management.* New York: McGraw-Hill Book Company, 1965, p. 17–43.

Mattessich, Richard. "Budgeting Models and System Simulation," *Accounting Review.* Vol. 36, No. 3, July 1961, p. 384–398.

Phillips, Richard. *Managing for Greater Returns.* Des Moines, Iowa: Farmers' and Grain Dealers' Association of Iowa, 1957.

Scott, Burnham H. "Budgets Can Generate Profits," *Budgeting.* Vol. 14, No. 2, September 1965, p. 22–29.

Smith, Frank J., Jr., and James Gresham. *Budgeting for the Farm Supply Business*. University of Minnesota Special Report 18, 1965.

Weiner, Julius. "Separation of Fixed and Variable Costs," *Accounting Review*. Vol. 35, No. 4, October 1960, p. 686–691.

Welsch, Glenn A. "Budgeting for Management Planning and Control," *The Journal of Accountancy*. October 1961, p. 38.

Weston, J. Fred, and Eugene F. Brigham. *Managerial Finance*, second edition. New York: Holt, Rinehart, and Winston, Inc., 1966, p. 185–219, 229–236.

Wright, Roland M. "Crossroads: The Crucial State in Introducing Budgeting," *Budgeting*. May 1965, p. 7–11.

———. "The Effect of Business Size on the Organization Structure and Budgetary Practices," *Budgeting*. January 1964, p. 15.

———. "Management Advisory Services and Budgeting: The Views of Some Consultants," *Budgeting*. November 1964, p. 23.

PROBLEM SET

Budgets and Pro Forma Statements.

From the following information prepare:
- (a) a projected income statement for the 3-month period ending May 31,
- (b) a projected balance sheet as of May 31,
- (c) a cash budget for each of the months of March, April, and May.

Factors:
1. Sales are projected as follows:

    March $36,000   May   24,000
    April   42,000   June   24,000

   Of total sales, 70 percent are cash and the remaining 30 percent are collected in 30 days.
2. The firm attempts to maintain an inventory of merchandise equal to 120 percent of the following month's projected sales needs. Cost of goods averages around 70 percent of sales and goods are paid for 30 days after purchase.
3. Labor costs and general administrative expenses (excluding depreciation) vary little from month to month. They average $5,000 and $2,000 per month, respectively, and are paid in the month incurred.
4. In late May, the firm expects to purchase a new storage shed for $10,000 by borrowing this amount from the bank to be repaid over a 5-year period.
5. In late May, taxes totaling $4,500 for the period from July to December of the preceding year are due. Tax estimates for the 3-month period under consideration are to be recorded as liabilities for future payment. The firm's tax rate is 30 percent.
6. The cash account is always kept somewhere between $3,000 and $5,000. If it should drop below $3,000, the firm borrows in $1,000 units (notes payable, short-term) until the minimum level is reached. If the balance exceeds $5,000, short-term notes payable are retired in $1,000 units until it is below the maximum. Monthly interest charge on short-term debt is .5 percent. It is paid on the last day of each quarter (May 31).
7. Depreciation expense is estimated at $5,000 per quarter and is recorded on the last day of the quarter.
8. The balance sheet as of February 28 is as follows:

    Current assets
      Cash $4,000
      Accounts receivable 8,400
      Inventory 30,240
        Total current assets $42,640
    Fixed assets
      Land, plant and equipment
        Gross 200,000
        Accumulated depreciation on
          plant and equipment 70,000
        Net   130,000
    Total assets $172,640

Current liabilities
    Accounts payable $23,520
    Notes payable, short-term   10,000
    Taxes payable   6,000
                                       ──────
        Total current liabilities $39,520
Owner's equity   133,120
                                                  ───────
Total liabilities and equity $172,640

CHAPTER 7
Financial Analysis and Control

Achievement of profit objectives is not an automatic process. Strategies employed by management to move the firm toward its objectives are seldom without flaw. Since the planning process of necessity deals with the uncertain future, even the best-laid plans can go awry in spite of near-perfect strategies. Thus, management needs continuous readings of the firm's progress, or lack of it, toward previously established goals. For this purpose the firm needs an adequate set of records which will generate the right kinds of information about important aspects of the business at the right time. Many a business has failed simply because management discovered too late that something had gone wrong. Earlier recognition of the problem through frequent checking of performance, which can be measured by an adequate system of records, may have, in many cases, allowed time for corrective action.

An essential element of an effective control system is the predetermination, by management, of desired results. Goals with respect to profit, growth, market share, etc., and supporting performance standards relating to such matters as sales and operating efficiency provide benchmarks by which realized results can be measured. These benchmarks highlight key decision areas and dictate the kind of information that is needed. Only those data relevant to the decision process, or required by law, should be collected. Data on which no decision is to be based are redundant as far as management is concerned. At a minimum, management will need regular information on the following.[50]

1. The firm's cash position, so that at any point in time cash balances on hand and inflows offset outflows. This insures the firm's ability to meet payrolls on time, take advantage of trade discounts, purchase raw materials in economic quantities, and handle minor contingencies.

2. Trends in sales revenues; selling expenses; production costs, including raw materials costs, wage and salary expenses; and overhead costs — with particular reference to administrative salaries and general office expenses.

3. Trends in production and/or service performance measured in terms of previously defined quality standards and customer satisfaction.

[50] See R. A. Willson and F. J. Smith, Jr., *Managing the Farm Supply Business — 10 areas*, Agricultural Extension Special Report 16, University of Minnesota, September 1965, p. 9–99.

148   *The Financial Management of Agribusiness Firms*

4. Trends in the firm's capital structure, a timetable for new capital expenditures, and the sources of funds available to the firm.

In addition to the above, the firm should have regular readings on its market share, its prices in relation to those of the competition, customer acceptability of products as reflected in new orders or reorders, and sales backlogs. Astute management will develop other measurements that suit its firm's peculiar situation. With these general requirements in mind let us now turn to a consideration of ratio analysis as one method of arriving at readings of the general economic health of the business.

Ratio Analysis

Ratio analysis is frequently employed in measuring the performance of various aspects of a business. If properly used and its limitations understood, it can be a very useful management tool. A number of reasons account for the wide use of ratio analysis. First of all, ratios are relatively easy to calculate. Most ratios compare two figures readily available from the income statement and/or the balance sheet. Because the data are readily available, not much time or expense is required to develop it. Ratios allow easy comparison of the firm's past with its present performance, as well as comparisons between like firms in an industry. They are also readily understood by various interested parties within a firm. Not all members of the management team are financially oriented and ratios can provide basic overview information to the heads of such departments as production, marketing, personnel, as well as to the general manager and the board of directors. Finally, ratios are helpful in communicating the firm's financial position to interested parties outside of management. This would include the stockholders, cooperative patrons, and suppliers. The financial community may also use ratios as part of an analysis to determine the credit worthiness of a firm.

In spite of these advantages, it must be emphasized that ratios are merely indicators. If a particular facet of the business is headed for trouble, a change in a ratio can sound a warning. But the ratio change does not isolate the underlying cause of the problem. Additional analysis is usually required before appropriate corrective action can be taken. Furthermore, interfirm comparisons are sometimes misleading because financial ratios vary with the accounting practices that underlie them. Methods employed in asset and inventory evaluation, overhead cost allocation, as well as rates of depreciation chosen, differ from firm to firm. Thus, casual comparisons of ratios between firms can lead to mistaken judgments of performance.

It must be remembered also that balance sheet ratios are products of information recorded at one point in time. In many cases, these data are prepared just once annually. Comparing a firm's asset picture on one day this year with one day last year may provide a very distorted picture, if we allow it to, of what has happened in the interim. The fact of the matter is that two such readings may be virtually meaningless unless buttressed by monthly and/or quarterly readings.

With this general background on the advantages and disadvantages of ratios in mind, we can now move on to a discussion of some widely used financial ratios.

It would be difficult in this general text for us to prescribe which ratios would be particularly significant for any specific agricultural marketing or farm supply firm. Each firm must carefully evaluate its peculiar operations and develop a set of ratios that best suits its own needs. Over the years, however, a group of ratios designed to measure performance in certain areas of a business has been developed. These ratios are usually presented under the headings profitability, liquidity, solvency, and operating efficiency. In what follows we will discuss the development of several ratios in each of these categories from which a firm could choose one or more which best suits its needs.

To assist us in illustrating the development of ratios, we present condensed versions of an income statement and a balance sheet for the Lauderdale Farm Marketing Company in table 24. The income statement simply reflects a rearrangement of items in the expense budget (table 19) and the profit budget (table 20) that we presented in the previous chapter. Dollar values of certain accounts will be drawn from these statements to illustrate various ratios.

Profitability

A fundamental measure of how efficiently a firm is being managed is its profitability in terms of return on investment as well as profits on sales. A particularly useful way of looking at factors affecting profitability and how they are related is shown in figure 9. It indicates that return on investment is directly affected by (a) the intensity with which the assets of the firm are used, as measured by the number of times assets turn over in a period (total sales ÷ total assets), and (b) the kinds of earnings a firm is able to generate on sales (earnings ÷ sales).

Table 24. Condensed income statement and balance sheet of Lauderdale Farm Marketing Company, December 31, 1976

Income statement		Balance sheet	
Sales	$1,425,000	Current assets	
Cost of goods sold	1,254,000	Cash	$76,420
Gross margin	$171,000	Accounts receivable	130,500
Plant expense		Inventory	463,000
Labor	60,766		$669,920
Other	42,355	Net fixed assets	103,015
Selling expense	2,059	Total assets	$772,935
Administrative expense	26,750	Current liabilities	
Operating income	$39,070	Accounts payable	$420,000
Interest expense	5,000	Notes payable	5,000
Income before tax	$34,070	Accruals	25,900
Income tax	3,000		$450,900
Income after tax	$31,070	Long-term debt	61,000
Dividend paid	5,000	Equity	100,000
Retained earnings	$26,070	Retained earnings	161,035
			$772,935

Let's look at these in turn. The asset turnover concept suggests that the higher the sales volume produced with a given set of assets, the higher the return on investment. For example, as more milk is processed through a given-sized dairy plant, or more grain is moved through an elevator, the more effectively are the associated assets being utilized— up to a point! A firm could, of course, push volume to a level where physical processing or handling capacity is reached. Squeezing out additional volume in such a case may be so costly as to be prohibitive. But as a practical matter, most agricultural marketing and supply firms have some "slack" in this regard, and are typically struggling to maintain or increase volume through their facilities. Figure 9 indicates that turnover can be increased by increasing sales relative to total investment; or, if this is impossible, management might devise ways of cutting back on total investment, perhaps by selling off redundant fixed assets, reducing inventories, investing cash outside of the firm, or reducing accounts receivable after the impacts of such a move on sales had been considered.

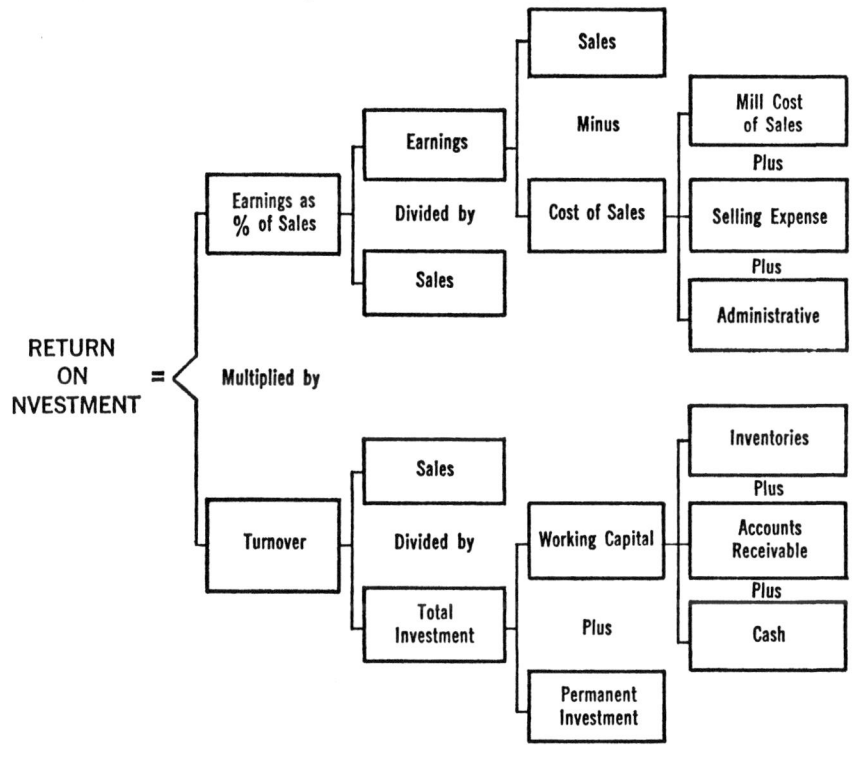

Figure 9. Relationship of factors affecting return on investment.

```
                          ┌─ Sales
                  ┌─ Earnings ─┤ Minus            ┌─ Mill Cost of Sales
                  │            │                  │ Plus
         ┌ Earnings as  Divided by─ Cost of Sales─┤ Selling Expense
         │   % of Sales │                         │ Plus
         │            └─ Sales                    └─ Administrative
RETURN ON│
INVESTMENT = Multiplied by
         │                                        ┌─ Inventories
         │            ┌─ Sales                    │ Plus
         └ Turnover ──┤ Divided by─ Working Capital┤ Accounts Receivable
                      │                           │ Plus
                      └─ Total Investment         └─ Cash
                                      Plus
                                Permanent Investment
```

Reproduced by permission of E. I. DuPont de Nemours and Company
from Executive Committee Control Charts, p. 6.

* Other versions of this scheme substitute "cost of goods sold" for "mill cost of sales."

Looking at the earnings side of figure 9 brings us face to face with questions of operating efficiency and price policy. On the cost side, careful control of such factors as labor expense, administrative expense, and selling costs is called for. But even the most efficiently operated business can be unprofitable unless careful attention is paid to price policy. Management discretion in this regard may be limited, depending on the competitive environment in which the firm is operating. But such limits should be clearly identified and pricing policy developed accordingly. At the extremes, low prices may generate zero profits on the one hand while high prices may result in zero sales on the other. No firm can exist for long at either end of this spectrum. We suggested ways in which profit-price-volume problems could be analyzed in chapter 6.

Let us now take a look at how return on investment for the Lauderdale Company could be measured by the above formulation.

$$\text{Return on investment} = \frac{\text{earnings before interest and taxes}}{\text{sales}} \times \frac{\text{sales}}{\text{total assets}}$$

$$= \frac{\$39,070}{\$1,425,000} \times \frac{\$1,425,000}{\$772,935}$$

$$= \frac{\$39,070}{\$772,935} = 5.1\%$$

The return on overall assets is 5.1 percent. We remind the reader that the $39,070 of operating income is net after depreciation has been charged and before taxes and is not the same as the cash flow we considered in our discussion of returns on investment in chapter 4. This measure, therefore, is not the equivalent of the internal rate of return that was discussed earlier, although it is commonly used by firms and financial institutions in evaluating investments. Note also that this formulation does not explicitly deal with the time value of money. This measure should be used simply as an *indicator* to provide insights as to the direction of a firm's profitability.

Managers often find it useful to look at income after interest and taxes as a percentage of sales as a measure of profitability. This ratio is presented below for Lauderdale:

$$\text{Profit on sales} = \frac{\text{income after interest and income taxes}}{\text{sales}}$$

$$= \frac{\$31,070}{\$1,425,000}$$

$$= 2.18\%$$

Since equity holders usually do not own all of the assets of a firm, their interest naturally focuses on the return on *their* net investment. A ratio commonly used for this purpose is as follows:

$$\text{Profit on equity capital} = \frac{\text{income after interest and income taxes}}{\text{net worth}}$$

$$= \frac{\$31,070}{\$100,000 + \$146,035}$$

$$= \frac{\$31,070}{\$261,035}$$

$$= 11.9\%$$

Another frequently used profit ratio is gross margin — total sales less cost of goods sold (including losses from shrinkage, theft, or obsolescence) ÷ total sales. Gross margins are affected by prices received for merchandise sold, the particular combination of products handled, the net prices paid for goods purchased for processing and/or handling, and "leakage." This ratio is an indicator of how well these aspects of the business are being managed. For Lauderdale, gross margin was measured as follows:

$$\text{Gross margin} = \frac{\text{sales} - \text{cost of goods sold}}{\text{sales}}$$

$$= \frac{\$1,425,000 - \$1,254,000}{\$1,425,000}$$

$$= 12\%$$

There are themes and variations on the above ratios relating to profitability.[51] Management, of course, can and should "tailor make" ratios to fit its peculiar needs.

So far, we have consciously avoided saying whether the profit performance of Lauderdale, as measured by our sample of indicators, was good or not. The fact of the matter is that, given what we know about this hypothetical company, we are not in a position to say much. On a superficial basis, Lauderdale's profit performance, as indicated by the several measures, appears adequate as compared to the *general* experience in the grain and farm supply business. But, because this is just an illustration, we don't have trend data on these indicators so we can't say whether Lauderdale is doing better or worse than it had done previously. And while the return levels appear adequate, we don't know how they stack up with those of like firms in its own *particular* market. We typically measure performance in relation to something—firm goals, past trends, or performance by similar organizations. It is up to the firm's management to develop this type of information. Trade associations, commercial auditing firms, credit bureaus, banks, universities, and extension services can provide helpful assistance along these lines.

In table 25 we present a sample of profitability ratios for a variety of agriculturally related firms. For convenience of presentation we have included other ratios to be discussed in following sections on liquidity, solvency, and efficiency. We do so simply to outline the "ball park" in which such ratios might typically fall. There is nothing sacro-

---

[51]For example, since dairy marketing cooperatives can pass savings along to member-patrons in the form of higher pay prices as well as net margins, focusing entirely on the latter may give a distorted profitability picture. Such cooperatives, therefore, frequently find it useful to develop a "return to producers" ratio. This ratio compares the advance payments made to producers for products they sell through the organization, plus the net margin, with the total dollar sales volume as follows:

$$\text{Return to producers} = \frac{\text{advance payments} + \text{net margins}}{\text{total dollar sales volume}}$$

The Financial Management of Agribusiness Firms

Table 25. A sampling of financial ratios for firms serving agriculture (1)

Line of business (and number of concerns reporting)	(2) Current assets to current debts, times	(3) Net profits on net sales, %	(4) net profits on tangible Net worth, %	(5) Net sales to tangible net worth, times	(6) Collection period, days	(7) Net sales to inventory, times	(8) Current debt to tangible net worth, %	(9) Total debt to tangible net worth, %
Retailing								
5252 Farm equipment (95)	2.48 / 1.89 / 1.52	3.87 / 2.12 / 0.92	17.14 / 10.44 / 3.99	7.03 / 4.87 / 3.03	15 / 26 / 45	5.7 / 4.1 / 2.8	52.5 / 91.5 / 149.4	90.6 / 147.6 / 199.7
5969 (68) Farm & garden supplies	6.77 / 3.17 / 1.56	4.67 / 3.16 / 0.86	12.43 / 7.93 / 3.64	3.95 / 2.79 / 2.00	* / * / *	14.8 / 7.7 / 4.4	12.8 / 24.9 / 63.8	33.2 / 52.9 / 113.2
5541 (82) Gasoline service stations	3.77 / 2.37 / 1.66	6.10 / 2.78 / 1.37	16.19 / 9.60 / 4.40	4.69 / 3.01 / 1.94	* / * / *	26.7 / 9.5 / 6.7	14.8 / 30.8 / 65.7	41.6 / 65.8 / 112.4
5411 Groceries & meats (164)	2.56 / 1.91 / 1.31	1.78 / 1.10 / 0.56	16.21 / 10.56 / 4.49	12.52 / 8.83 / 6.28	* / * / *	25.4 / 16.6 / 12.6	30.9 / 48.9 / 76.6	49.5 / 83.6 / 131.8
5211 Lumber yards (142)	7.80 / 3.65 / 2.26	3.27 / 1.70 / 0.48	8.82 / 4.66 / 1.18	3.56 / 2.36 / 1.70	41 / 59 / 86	6.5 / 4.9 / 3.7	11.0 / 29.1 / 61.7	32.0 / 66.2 / 114.2
5531 Tires, batteries & accessories (65)	3.79 / 2.45 / 1.66	4.22 / 2.08 / 1.04	15.25 / 7.61 / 4.23	4.97 / 3.59 / 2.57	* / * / *	10.6 / 6.1 / 4.4	31.2 / 49.8 / 103.8	68.0 / 103.7 / 179.3
Wholesaling								
5029 Chemicals Allied products (56)	4.23 / 2.29 / 1.83	2.96 / 1.70 / 0.99	14.88 / 7.69 / 4.88	5.59 / 4.22 / 2.61	31 / 37 / 61	15.7 / 11.8 / 6.8	23.9 / 50.1 / 81.4	58.9 / 107.1 / 137.6
5043 Dairy products (57)	2.12 / 1.60 / 1.17	1.64 / 1.34 / 0.45	12.56 / 7.70 / 3.66	10.54 / 6.47 / 4.30	19 / 27 / 32	67.1 / 37.2 / 22.7	34.0 / 63.4 / 88.7	60.7 / 84.5 / 252.2
5083 Farm machinery & equipment (52)	4.12 / 2.79 / 1.91	4.59 / 1.93 / 0.95	18.51 / 9.45 / 4.48	6.43 / 3.78 / 2.41	24 / 47 / 63	9.7 / 6.0 / 5.0	18.5 / 42.7 / 84.1	64.9 / 104.7 / 122.4
5048 Fruits & produce, fresh (60)	3.80 / 2.42 / 1.57	1.79 / 0.83 / 0.33	17.98 / 11.50 / 4.45	14.54 / 11.07 / 7.19	11 / 16 / 27	91.5 / 40.7 / 15.2	23.3 / 47.3 / 77.5	68.2 / 93.7 / 114.9
5042 Groceries (206)	3.63 / 2.18 / 1.58	1.12 / 0.64 / 0.31	12.69 / 6.42 / 3.27	19.30 / 10.76 / 7.02	9 / 14 / 21	16.5 / 11.3 / 8.4	34.4 / 67.6 / 133.6	74.9 / 134.5 / 206.7
5098 Lumber & building materials (164)	4.00 / 2.48 / 1.63	3.27 / 1.69 / 0.63	11.55 / 7.26 / 3.00	6.71 / 4.09 / 2.89	34 / 47 / 64	9.8 / 6.9 / 4.8	22.6 / 50.2 / 110.5	48.7 / 108.1 / 147.7
5047 Meats & meat products (61)	3.74 / 2.39 / 1.57	1.73 / 1.18 / 0.68	16.68 / 11.25 / 7.12	17.51 / 10.21 / 6.71	12 / 18 / 27	64.1 / 39.1 / 22.8	24.3 / 48.7 / 96.0	73.0 / 110.1 / 181.8
5092 Petroleum products (72)	3.50 / 2.12 / 1.55	3.63 / 2.06 / 0.86	14.13 / 8.31 / 5.33	5.97 / 4.16 / 2.69	22 / 32 / 52	28.1 / 17.6 / 11.4	17.3 / 36.9 / 68.3	39.1 / 75.7 / 142.0

Reproduced by permission of Dun and Bradstreet, Inc., from "Key Business Ratios in 125 Firms — 1964."

* Not computed.

(1) *How the Ratios Are Figured.* In the ratio tables each group of ratios in each industry carries three sets of figures. The top figure is the upper quartile, the center figure is the median, and the bottom figure is the lower quartile. They are calculated as follows: Year-end financial statements are selected from a sampling of corporations whose tangible net worth, with few exceptions, exceed $35,000. The financial statements are those appearing in the Dun & Bradstreet credit reports on these businesses. Statement copies are referred to statisticians who compute each of the "14 Ratios" on each of the concerns. The ratios are then punched on data processing cards, and arranged into industry groups. After this, ratio figures are arranged so that the best ratio figure is at the top, and the weakest at the bottom. The figure which falls just in the middle of this series becomes the median for that ratio in that line of business. The figure halfway between the median and the highest term of the series is the upper quartile; and the term halfway between the median and the bottom of the series is the lower quartile. The purpose of these interquartile ranges is to show an upper and lower limit area without reflecting the extremes either at the top or the bottom of the series. After the first of the "14 Ratios" has been compiled for a particular industry, the identical process is followed for the remaining 13 ratios in this industry group, and then for remaining industry groups.

(2) *Current Assets to Current Debt.* Current assets are divided by total current debt. Current assets are the sum of cash, notes, and accounts receivable (less reserves for bad debt), advances on merchandise, merchandise inventories, and listed, federal, state, and municipal securities not in excess of market value; current debt is the total of all liabilities falling due within 1 year. This is one test of solvency.

Financial Analysis and Control 155

Table 25 — Continued

	(2)	(3)	(4)	(5)	(6)	(7)	(8)	(9)
Line of business (and number of concerns reporting)	Current assets to current debts, times	Net profits on net sales, %	Net profits on tangible net worth, %	Net sales to tangible net worth, times	Collection period, days	Net sales to inventory, times	Current debt to tangible net worth, %	Total debt to tangible net worth, %

Manufacturing & Construction

3522 Agricultural implements & machinery (66)	4.25 / 2.53 / 1.96	5.87 / 4.01 / 1.96	17.48 / 11.78 / 8.34	4.34 / 3.07 / 2.26	28 / 34 / 54	7.2 / 4.1 / 3.2	22.2 / 44.6 / 60.0	49.5 / 78.2 / 100.0
3714 Automobile parts & accessories (91)	4.10 / 2.57 / 2.09	5.87 / 4.01 / 2.62	15.92 / 12.50 / 7.70	3.56 / 2.88 / 2.20	34 / 41 / 47	8.1 / 5.8 / 4.4	22.6 / 39.2 / 56.0	40.8 / 66.9 / 93.4
287 Chemicals, agricultural (35)	3.48 / 2.07 / 1.56	4.10 / 2.04 / 0.76	10.74 / 6.25 / 2.36	3.86 / 2.69 / 1.80	25 / 47 / 123	12.8 / 6.6 / 4.9	21.1 / 49.2 / 79.1	63.6 / 84.8 / 151.8
2211 Cotton cloth mills (43)	5.88 / 3.88 / 2.69	6.76 / 4.55 / 2.55	10.81 / 8.12 / 6.13	2.35 / 1.92 / 1.30	29 / 47 / 62	8.4 / 5.4 / 4.2	12.2 / 18.9 / 19.6	19.2 / 33.8 / 58.8
202 Dairy products (118)	2.25 / 1.65 / 1.25	3.04 / 1.69 / 1.02	12.52 / 8.69 / 5.94	7.48 / 5.25 / 3.49	16 / 22 / 29	50.9 / 30.9 / 20.8	24.5 / 39.7 / 67.3	42.8 / 72.0 / 120.7
203 Fruits & vegetables, canners (56)	3.35 / 1.88 / 1.51	4.64 / 2.68 / 1.54	13.13 / 8.11 / 5.22	4.79 / 3.19 / 2.02	14 / 22 / 37	8.7 / 5.9 / 3.0	19.2 / 56.0 / 88.3	42.7 / 92.9 / 128.4
204 Grain mill products (58)	3.96 / 2.50 / 1.49	3.94 / 1.91 / 0.86	12.45 / 8.74 / 3.04	5.72 / 4.03 / 2.61	20 / 31 / 47	18.1 / 11.2 / 8.8	18.3 / 30.3 / 49.8	38.0 / 67.3 / 109.1
2011 Meats & provisions, packers (107)	3.46 / 2.28 / 1.65	1.79 / 1.09 / 0.53	15.73 / 9.81 / 5.23	12.54 / 8.40 / 6.30	9 / 11 / 15	44.7 / 27.6 / 19.4	19.3 / 32.3 / 55.0	44.0 / 75.2 / 99.6
2911 Petroleum refining (54)	2.49 / 1.47 / 1.00	7.17 / 4.14 / 2.01	12.81 / 7.79 / 5.07	3.14 / 1.53 / 1.07	26 / 41 / 50	17.6 / 9.9 / 7.2	12.9 / 21.1 / 45.4	9.9 / 33.4 / 85.0

(3) *Net Profits on Net Sales.* Obtained by dividing the net earnings of the business, after taxes, by net sales (the dollar volume less returns, allowances, and cash discounts). This important yardstick in measuring profitability should be related to the ratio which follows.

(4) *Net Profits on Tangible Net Worth.* Tangible net worth is the equity of stockholders in the business, as obtained by subtracting total liabilities from total assets, and then deducting intangibles. The ratio is obtained by dividing net profits after taxes by tangible net worth. Tendency is to look increasingly to this ratio as a final criterion of profitability. Generally, a relationship of at least 10 percent is regarded as a desirable objective for providing dividends plus funds for future growth.

(5) *Net Sales to Tangible Net Worth.* Net sales are divided by tangible net worth. This gives a measure of relative turnover of invested capital.

(6) *Collection Period.* Annual net sales are divided by 365 days to obtain average daily credit sales and then the average daily credit sales are divided into notes and accounts receivable, including any discounted. This ratio is helpful in analyzing the collectibility of receivables. Many feel the collection period should not exceed the net maturity indicated by selling terms by more than 10–15 days. When comparing the collection period of one concern with that of another, allowances should be made for possible variations in selling terms.

(7) *Net Sales to Inventory.* Dividing annual net sales by merchandise inventory as carried on the balance sheet. This quotient does not yield an actual physical turnover. It provides a yardstick for comparing stock-to-sales ratios of one concern with another or with those for the industry.

(8) *Current Debt to Tangible Net Worth.* Derived by dividing current debt by tangible net worth. Ordinarily, a business begins to pile up trouble when this relationship exceeds 80 percent.

(9) *Total Debt to Tangible Net Worth.* Obtained by dividing total current plus long-term debts by tangible net worth. When this relationship exceeds 100 percent, the equity of creditors in the assets of the business exceeds that of owners.

sanct about any of them — and indeed, that any one would exactly fit the needs of a particular firm would be pure accident. But they do give the manager some idea of other firms' experience and may stimulate him to investigate his own situation.

Liquidity Ratios

A second set of ratios has been developed as an indicator of a firm's ability to meet its current obligations. Conceivably, a firm could have a very strong net worth position in relation to total assets, and still be so starved for working capital that it is unable to take advantage of quantity discounts, to meet emergencies, or even to pay current bills.

We suggested in chapter 3 that a common measure of net working capital is arrived at simply by subtracting current liabilities from current assets. Many managers and analysts prefer to look at a firm's current position in these terms. But there are several ratios which measure a firm's liquidity that are also frequently used.

Probably the most popular is the current ratio — total current assets ÷ total current liabilities. Current assets include those which can be converted into cash within a year. A common criticism of this ratio is that, even though it may suggest a strong liquid position, money tied up in inventories and the like may not be readily convertible into cash. Further, rapid liquidation of inventories, accounts receivable, marketable securities, etc. could sharply reduce their value. To get around some of these problems, a modification — the acid-test ratio (cash + marketable securities + accounts receivable ÷ total current liabilities) — is frequently used. It is not uncommon to further modify the acid-test ratio by excluding receivables that exceed a certain age, and in some extreme cases they are excluded altogether.

As far as Lauderdale is concerned its current ratio is as follows:

$$\text{Current ratio} = \frac{\text{current assets}}{\text{current liabilities}}$$

$$= \frac{\$669{,}920}{\$450{,}900}$$

$$= 1.49$$

What this says is that for each dollar of current liabilities, there is $1.49 of current assets. In spite of a historic rule of thumb that recommends that the current ratios should be at least 2:1, the Lauderdale Company, in view of the kind of business it is in, would be considered reasonably liquid. The large inventory it holds (mostly grain) could rather quickly be converted into cash. In this case one might be more concerned with the age of accounts receivable than inventory holdings as far as their impacts on liquidity are concerned. In view of this, developing acid test ratios for Lauderdale could be an idle exercise. On the other hand, if a large portion of Lauderdale's business was in farm supplies, which typically move much slower than grain and which can present a greater accounts receivable problem, development of an acid-test ratio would probably be in order.

Which liquidity ratio or ratios a firm should choose must be governed by the composition of the firm's current assets and the volume and timing of claims against them. The ratio that best reflects the ability of the firm to meet its short-term obligations on time is the appropriate one. This also suggests that outsiders must be careful as they attempt to interpret or apply ratio analysis with reference to firms about which they know very little. General rules of thumb can lead to erroneous diagnosis if they are used without *particular knowledge* about the operations of a *particular firm*, in a *particular industry*.

Solvency Ratios

Solvency ratios deal primarily with a firm's ability to meet long-run claims. In one way or another they reflect the portion of a business's capital requirements which is being supplied by the owners. From a lender's point of view, solvency measures indicate the kinds of problems they would have in recovering their money in the event of failure, and these ratios, therefore, can have considerable impact on the availability of outside capital to the business. Such measures can also lead to questions as to who is controlling the firm; as creditors supply more and more capital and thereby assume more risk, they can and usually do impose restrictive covenants on managerial independence. On the other hand, solvency ratios may indicate that the firm should consider borrowing more, with a consequent opportunity of increasing return on investment.

Three solvency ratios are illustrated by using data from the Lauderdale Company:

$$\text{Solvency} = \frac{\text{total debt}}{\text{net worth}}$$

$$= \frac{\$450,900 + \$ 61,000}{\$100,000 + \$161,035}$$

$$= 2.0$$

$$\text{Solvency} = \frac{\text{net worth}}{\text{total net assets *}}$$

$$= \frac{\$100,000 + \$161,035}{\$669,920 - \$450,900 + \$103,015}$$

$$= 82\%$$

* Net working capital + net fixed assets.

$$\text{Solvency} = \frac{\text{long-term debt}}{\text{capitalization}}$$

$$= \frac{\$61,000}{\$61,000 + \$100,000 + \$161,035}$$

$$= 18.9\%$$

The total debt/net worth ratio at face value would seem to appear unfavorable. But in the case of Lauderdale this is probably not the best measure of solvency because of the heavy proportion of assets that are in very liquid grain inventory, a situation that is typical of firms of its type.

If we look at the net worth/total net asset ratio we see that the owners are contributing 82 percent of the capital required to support total net assets, which by most standards is an acceptable situation. Or looking at long-term debt/capitalization, we see that "lenders" are contributing slightly under 19 percent of total permanent capital, which under normal circumstances is not considered excessive. Once again, the application and interpretation of these ratios as far as Lauderdale is concerned emphasizes the need for "tailor making" measures suited to the peculiar requirements of the firm.

Efficiency Ratios

Several commonly used ratios which do not fit neatly into the categories discussed previously, will be referred to as efficiency ratios. In these, we include measures of accounts receivable and inventory turnover as well as some measures of plant, selling, and administrative expense.

Let's look at inventory turnover first. A number of alternative combinations of balance sheet and operating statement data can be utilized in developing such a measure. One common one, again using Lauderdale data, is as follows:

$$\text{Inventory turnover} = \frac{\text{cost of sales}}{\text{ending inventory}}$$

$$= \frac{\$1,254,000 + \$60,766 + \$42,355}{\$463,000}$$

$$= 2.9$$

According to this measure, Lauderdale's inventory turned over almost three times in the year. This particular formulation used ending inventory in the denominator, which may or may not have been typical of the situation throughout the year. Had another day of the year been chosen, Lauderdale might have had an inventory only one-half or one-third as large as that shown on its balance sheet and, of course, the turnover ratio would have been much higher. Some analysts use an average of the beginning and ending inventories, but there is no particular merit in this approach either, since the beginning inventory is simply a reading on one day of the year also. Another modification of this ratio uses sales in the numerator instead of the cost of sales.

The concern with inventory turnover puts focus on how well working capital is being managed. Turnover ratios that are low relative to an appropriately developed standard suggest that working capital that might be used more productively elsewhere in the firm is tied up in merchandise. On the other hand, extremely high ratio values may go hand in hand with items being out of stock, which means a loss of sales.

Another measure of how well working capital is being managed is the average collection period of accounts receivable. Longer than planned collection periods result in reduced profit for each dollar of sales because of additional costs of collection, bad debt losses, and the costs of the extra funds required to support such accounts. Conversely, an extremely short collection period might indicate that the firm is losing sales due to overly strict credit policies.

A commonly used measure of days in accounts receivable is as follows:

$$\frac{\text{receivables}}{\text{total sales} \div 360} = \text{days sales in receivables}$$

Using Lauderdale once again, we have:

$$\frac{\$130,500}{\$1,425,000 \div 360} = 33 \text{ days}$$

As in the case of other indicators, how good or bad an average collection period of 33 days is depends primarily on the firm's own credit policy as well as the direction or trend in the indicator.

We remind the reader that this measure also employs a balance sheet figure, accounts receivable, that holds only on the day in the year in which it is recorded. It is therefore subject to all of the pitfalls that this implies. Modifications which would give a particular firm a better picture of its receivables situation are completely in order. Separation of sales into cash and/or credit, developing readings for shorter time periods, as well as determining the actual number of days or weeks that specific accounts are outstanding, all improve management's view on how well it is handling its credit policies.

In addition to these two turnover ratios, it is useful to have measures of cost in relation to sales as indicators of operating efficiency. A typical one is as follows:

$$\frac{\text{plant expense}}{\text{total sales}} = \frac{\$60,766 + \$42,355}{\$1,425,000}$$

$$= 7.2\%$$

Viewed in relation to some pre-established standard as well as previous readings, this measure would give us an indication of how operating costs were moving in relation to total sales.

One may wish to focus on some particular cost item in relation to sales. For most agricultural marketing and supply firms, labor is an important component of overall operating costs. There is much evidence to suggest that profitable firms typically utilize their labor input more effectively than less profitable ones. Frequent readings on a ratio such as the one below may assist management in keeping its labor costs in line with those necessary for efficient operations:

$$\frac{\text{labor cost}}{\text{total sales}} = \frac{\$60,766}{\$1,425,000}$$

$$= 4.2\%$$

We emphasize, however, that keeping tabs on this ratio does not relieve management of its obligation to seek new and better ways of doing whatever job needs to be done.

Finally, management would be well advised to keep careful watch over the trends in the relationship of administrative and selling expenses to sales. Administrative "dead wood" can sap the strength and profitability of any firm. A disproportionately heavy load of administrative expense may sound a warning of the need for an administrative overhaul. Similarly, selling expenses that appear out of line with trends in sales volume may call for a reexamination of the cost and impact of the sales effort.

Common Size Statements

Common size statements are another useful form of ratio analysis. These are balance sheets and operating statements which show their component accounts as a percent of some base. Total assets are used as the base for balance sheets, and total sales are normally used as the base for operating statements. Common size statements for Lauderdale are illustrated in table 26.

Table 26. Common size statements for Lauderdale Farm Marketing Company, December 31, 1976

Income statement	%	Balance sheet	%
Sales	100.0	**Current assets**	
Cost of goods sold	88.0	Cash	9.9
Gross margin	12.0	Accounts receivable	16.9
Plant expense		Inventory	59.9
Labor	4.3		86.7
Other	3.0	Net fixed assets	13.3
Selling expense	.1	Total assets	100.0
Administrative expense	1.9	**Current liabilities**	
Operating income	2.7	Accounts payable	54.3
Interest expense	.4	Notes payable	.6
Income before tax	2.3	Accruals	3.4
Income tax	.2		58.3
Income after tax	2.1	Long-term debt	7.9
Dividend paid	.4	Equity	12.9
Retained earnings	1.7	Retained earnings	20.9
			100.0

Such statements are useful in comparing present operations with those in previous periods or with budgeted expectations (see chapter 6). They are also widely used in comparing one firm's operations with another's. Because, in final form, common size statements mask total sales volume there is some danger that interfirm comparisons might be meaningless. For example, a firm with annual sales of $50 million might have a common size statement similar to one with $100,000 volume, but have little else in common. Such a comparison could lead to a completely erroneous conclusion as to the overall economic health of either firm. Common size statements are best used to supplement comparisons of regular statements in which actual dollar volumes are available.

Summary of Ratio Analysis

In developing ratios, management must first determine what it wants to measure. Then it selects the most appropriate ratio or ratios for that use. Next, it develops standards both internal and external to the firm to use as benchmarks in evaluating results. No ratio should be considered immutable; as conditions change or the value of certain accounts change they must be reflected in revised ratios. The review process should be continuous.

At best, ratios are useful approximations. They fail to reflect cash flows, uncertainty, and the time value of money. Using them constantly and uncritically may slow improvements in estimation procedures. On the other hand, when personnel, time, or research funds are limited, or when ratios prove to be an understandable language for nonfinancial personnel and other interested parties, they can be helpful in the decision process.

In this text we are limited as to how much detail we can include with respect to systems of analysis and control for particular kinds of marketing and supply firms. In the appendix to this chapter we include an example of a system that was developed for farm supply firms. Much of the material discussed could be modified to suit the needs of other types of firms.

APPENDIX[52] Chapter 7
An Example Financial Control System for a Farm Supply Firm

One of the major problems confronting the manager of any small business, since he usually must function in several capacities, is time pressure. Many managers, when confronted with masses of data associated with financial analysis, find it easy to convince themselves that they simply don't have the time to deal with the problem. As a consequence, they do what they have to do and no more.

The control system described in the following sections was developed in recognition of the tremendous time pressures under which the managers of local farm supply firms operate.

Essentials of a Control System

There are three essential steps in any control process: (1) Setting standards at strategic points, (2) checking and reporting on performance, and (3) taking corrective action.[53]

In developing a control system to meet the needs of farm supply firms, the assumption was made that firms using it would have enough accounting data available to make up simple balance sheet and income statements. Development of the system itself was a seven-step process as follows:

1. Identifying profitability centers.
2. Establishing budgets for each profitability center.
3. Selecting the most important control points.
4. Establishing operating standards.
5. Making use of the management-by-exception principle.
6. Developing a method to facilitate information flow.
7. Presenting data in such a way as to aid the decision-making process.

The system is designed to move step by step from basic general ledger information, through simple calculations, to a two-page graphic summary of the major control points in the operation. In selecting the control points, the following questions were considered:

1. Is the measure important and meaningful from a farm supply firm manager's point of view as opposed to an investor or lender viewpoint?
2. Does it present the condition of an important factor in a farm supply business in understandable fashion?
3. Does it have real meaning on a monthly basis?
4. Is the measure "action oriented?"

By judging each potential control point against these criteria, several commonly used ratios were rejected (e.g., current ratio, return on total assets) because of their lack of clear meaning or their lack of applicability to monthly use in the farm supply industry. The control points ultimately selected were:

[52] This Appendix draws heavily on Robert J. Moeller and Frank J. Smith, Jr., *Financial Analysis and Control of the Farm Supply Business*, Special Report 17, Agricultural Extension Service, University of Minnesota, September, 1965.
[53] William H. Neuman, *Administrative Action*, Englewood Cliffs, N.J.; Prentice-Hall, Inc., 1961, p. 240.

164   The Financial Management of Agribusiness Firms

1. A measure of liquidity — an acid-test ratio consisting of cash, marketable securities, notes receivable, and accounts receivable of less than 60 days ÷ current liabilities.

2. Measures of efficiency as indicated by inventory turnover, the average collection period of accounts receivable, and sales per dollar of merchandising wage expense.

3. Measures of growth and profitability as indicated by sales volume, gross margins, and net operating margin.

Developing Associated Materials

After the selection of control points, development of coordinated materials to permit computation of the control points was undertaken. The complete system, including computational instructions to the bookkeeper, is presented in the next section.

One feature of the system is a method of coding designed to aid the users in completing the necessary bookwork with the maximum simplicity. In addition, operating standards and the principle of management by exception have been incorporated into it. It provides:

1. A form for a departmentalized breakdown of sales, inventories, cost of goods sold, gross margins, and merchandising expenses, leaving as a final figure the amount of money available for the payment of fixed expenses. This form is valuable in assessing the profitability of each department.

2. A form for determining the monthly rate of depreciation and the total accumulated depreciation.

3. A comparative operating statement.

4. A comparative balance sheet.

5. A worksheet for accumulating and summarizing all of the data needed for the development of two control charts.

6. Two control charts which present the control variables graphically.

Figure 10 is an illustration of one of the graphs presented in the control charts. This one relates to inventory turnover. Several features are readily apparent:

1. It permits easy analysis of an important facet of the business, in this case inventory turnover, on a monthly basis.

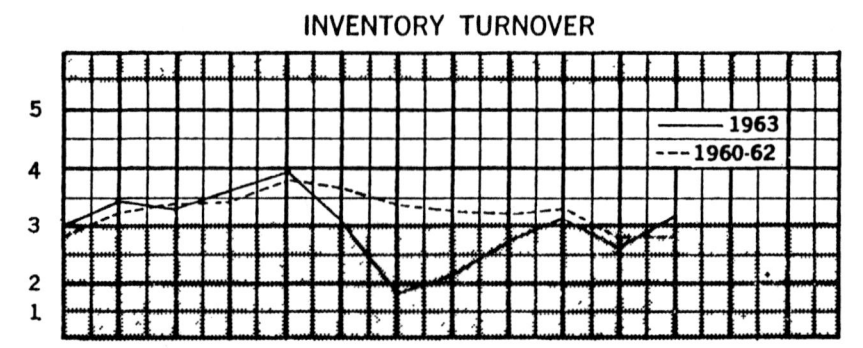

Figure 10. Inventory turnover control chart illustration.

Financial Analysis and Control 165

2. It encourages planning and budgeting by the use of operating standards, and management by exception techniques. As can be seen, the graph has two shaded areas on it. If the manager of a feed and seed firm has set upper and lower limits of 6 and 3, respectively, on inventory turnover, should it fall outside these limits in 1 month his attention is immediately called to it. Action is called for. If, on the other hand, it never goes beyond these two limits, by using the principle of management by exception the time spent in the analysis of this factor is reduced.

The operating standard boundaries are straight. In an industry where seasonality is such a strong factor, the effectiveness of a fixed standard is reduced. It would be extremely difficult, however, to design a form for general use that would have a variable boundary line; to compensate for this it is suggested that in addition to the fixed standards, an average of the past 2 or 3 years' performance be plotted on the same graph. This would provide a basis for comparison that takes seasonality into account.

Problems of Implementation

To arrive at accurate cost of goods sold figures or accurate ending inventory figures, a monthly inventory is needed. Some managers may resist the idea of taking a monthly physical inventory. Two alternatives to this exist. One is the use of a perpetual inventory system with a quarterly physical inventory. The other is to estimate the cost of goods sold (which in this industry usually means the amount of inventory used) by multiplying their average gross margin times the monthly sales volume. Where departmentalization exists, more specific gross margins can be used. A quarterly physical inventory is recommended when using this system of determining inventory levels also. In cases where a few items make up most of the sales, a combination of the two could be used — keeping a perpetual inventory of the few important items sold and estimating the inventory level of the goods sold less frequently.

Another problem is that adjusting entries are necessary for a completely accurate statement. Insofar as managers do not take the trouble and time to make the necessary adjusting entries, they may get a distorted picture of the several facets of the business.

On the other hand, the material is developed in such a way that any reasonably competent bookkeeper, following step-by-step instructions, can make all of the calculations necessary and develop the graphic presentation. If, in fact, a major reason for the lack of interest in controls is the time consumed studying large volumes of data from many sources, then this system may prove attractive to managers.

The manager's role with this system, at least in terms of time, is relatively minor. Initially, of course, he must establish the upper and lower limits (operating standards) between which a particular control point could fluctuate without causing alarm. Only he can do this. This requires looking over past performance, and where possible, comparing it with performance enjoyed by similar firms. On the basis of this, the critical upper and lower limits are set.

Once the standards have been set, the manager's contribution is largely completed. From then on, the bookkeeper makes the monthly calculations and supplies the easy-to-read graphs which show him where he stands relative to his pre-

166   The Financial Management of Agribusiness Firms

viously established goals. From time to time, of course, he needs readings on other aspects of the business as we outlined them in the beginning of this chapter.

Instructions for the Bookkeeper

This system is designed to use the monthly totals of sales, expenses, purchases, inventories, etc. in developing important business control measurements on two summary charts.

It consists of the following forms and graphs:

(a) Two summary control charts.
(b) An operating statement (form *A*).
(c) A balance sheet (form *B*).
(d) A sales and inventory breakdown form (form *C*).
(e) A depreciation form (form *D*).
(f) A worksheet for calculating the ratios (form *E*).
(g) A worksheet for calculating inventory figures (form *F*).

The forms are coordinated through the use of a coding system. This permits easy transfer of numbers from one form to another. Further, a worksheet is included to aid in calculating the values to be plotted on the graphs.

Before examining the individual forms and graphs, some general items will be discussed:

1. A cutoff date should be established for each month of the year. Consistent use of this cutoff date will permit accurate monthly comparisons from year to year. (A period in the month when inventory is low and most bills have been received is normally recommended.)

2. The coding system designed to coordinate the forms works as follows:

(a) Each form has an identifying letter (*A*, *B*, *C*, *D*, *E*, or *F*) at the top.
(b) Each major financial figure blank on the forms has an *identifying code* which is composed of a number and a letter (C1, B8, E23, etc.).

(1) If the letter on *top* of the page is *different* from the letter *before the number*, the code indicates the page and location where the information can be found. (For example, if form *A* is being worked on and a financial entry *on that page* is labeled (C1), refer to form *C* and locate (C1). Transfer the indicated amount back to (C1) on form *A*.)

(2) If the code letter is the *same* as the letter on *top of the form*, the figure must either be transferred from the monthly total in general ledger or be calculated from the figures on the same form.[54] (For example, if the form letter is *A* and the code is (A4), then you know you must either calculate the figure from information *on that form* or transfer the figure from your monthly totals in the general ledger.)

3. A physical inventory should be taken on a *monthly* basis. This will permit an accurate measurement of inventory control and profitability. If for some reason an actual inventory cannot be taken in a certain month, an alternative method

[54] The total figures for the month's operation are normally recorded in a general ledger. If you do not use this approach, then transfer the total figures from the point where they are totaled.

can be used to estimate the inventory figures. It should be emphasized, however, that a monthly inventory should be taken whenever possible and that, at the absolute minimum, a physical inventory should be taken every third month. There are two important points in estimating inventory:

    (a) The more accurately the estimated gross margin reflects the products that were sold, the more accurate this method will be. Therefore, if a separate inventory figure is estimated for each main product group the accuracy of the final figure will be greatly increased.

    (b) As the period between actual inventories becomes longer, the error in the inventory figures will greatly multiply.

The actual method of estimating the inventory will be discussed later under the instruction for form *F.*

4. The following things should be done each month on the date designated as the cutoff day.

    (a) Take a physical inventory.
    (b) Total up all your ledger accounts.
    (c) Total up all accounts payable at this date.
    (d) Total up the bank and check balances at this date.
    (e) Total up the sales for each product line.
    (f) Total purchases for each line.
    (g) Age the accounts receivable. This is done by determining the amount of each month's sales that are still on account. Normally the following classifications are used:

        (1) Accounts receivable under 30 days old.
        (2) Accounts receivable 30-60 days old.
        (3) Accounts receivable 60-90 days old.
        (4) Accounts receivable over 90 days old.

    For example, if the cutoff date was January 31, 1965, and $18,000 of January credit sales were outstanding, the figure for accounts receivable under 30 days would be $18,000. If $6,000 of December sales were still outstanding, the figure for accounts receivable 30-60 days old would be $6,000. If $2,500 of November sales remained on the books, the accounts receivable 60- to 90-day figure would be $2,500. Any older accounts would be classified as over 90 days old.

The information above applies to the system in general. The discussion following will describe the forms and the method of using them and is written directly to the bookkeeper.

Form *C*—Sales, Cost of Goods Sold, and Gross Margin Composition

You will begin using this system by completing form *C.* In looking at this form, you will note a letter enclosed by parentheses above each column heading. These letters are designed to aid you in making calculations on this form. For example, the gross margin figure (V) is calculated by subtracting the cost of goods sold figure from the sales figure. This action is indicated by the symbols (R) — (U), which simply means to subtract this figure in column (U) (cost of goods sold) from this figure in column (R) (sales).

168   The Financial Management of Agribusiness Firms

Refer to the section of form *C* completed in the table below. Hypothetical figures have been used to show the way the form should be completed. You will see in the classification "Hog Feed" that sales (R) = $100 and the cost of goods sold (U) = $85. Therefore, (R) − (U) = $100 − $85 = $15, which is the gross margin (V).

Sales, cost of goods sold, and gross margin composition
For period beginning January 1, 1965 and ending January 31, 1965

	(R) Sales	(S) Beg. inv. ($) + pur. ($)	(T) End. inv. ($)	(U) Cost of goods sold ($) = (S) − (T)	(V) Gross margin ($) = (R) − (U)	(W) % of sales (%) = (V)/(R)	(X) Cash merch. expenses ($)	(Y) Contr. to fixed expense, overhead, and profit ($) = (V) − (X)	(Z) % of sales
FEED									
Hog	100.00	135.00	50.00	85.00	15.00	15	5.00	10.00	8.0
Poultry	75.00	110.00	47.00	63.00	12.00	16	4.25	7.75	9.0
Dairy cattle	125.00	180.00	80.00	100.00	25.00	20	5.75	19.25	13.0
Beef cattle	50.00	90.00	50.00	40.00	10.00	20	3.50	6.50	13.0
Other	50.00	85.00	43.50	41.50	8.50	17	3.50	5.00	10.0
Overhead	—	—	—	—	—	—	6.50	—	—
TOTAL FEED	400.00	600.00	270.50	329.50	70.50	17.5	28.00	42.50	10.5

Completing the Form

1. Referring to your total monthly sales record, fill in the sales for each major product line in column (R).

2. For each major product line, take the beginning inventory and add to that figure purchases that were made during the month. Put the sum of those two figures in column (S).

3. Take the ending inventory figure determined by taking a physical inventory at the cutoff date and insert it in column (T). If no physical inventory is taken, refer to form *F*, No. 2, and calculate for each product line the estimated ending inventory. Again, it should be stressed here that a physical inventory should be taken whenever possible (refer to the instructions for form *F* on page 171).

4. Determine the cost of goods sold by subtracting the ending inventory, shown in column (P), from the total of the beginning inventory plus purchases, shown in column (S).

5. Determine the dollar gross margin for each product line by subtracting the cost of goods sold, shown in column (U), from the total sales figure, shown in column (R).

6. Divide the gross margin figure, shown in column (V), by total sales, shown in column (R). This gives you the percentage of gross margin for each product line.

7. Try to determine the amount of merchandising expenses incurred in selling each line of goods. Only those cash wage, truck, advertising, and other selling costs directly associated with a particular item are included in column (X) after the item. Cash costs that clearly arise in a particular department (e.g., feed) but are not directly associated with a particular item are charged to overhead in that

Financial Analysis and Control 169

department. Cash expenses not clearly chargeable to a department are carried in general overhead.

8. Subtract the merchandising expenses, as shown in column (X), from the gross margin, as shown in column (V), and place the remainder in column (Y), the figure which indicates the funds available to pay fixed expenses, contribute to overhead, and to provide profit.

9. Divide this contribution to fixed expenses, overhead, and profit, as shown in column (Y), by the total sales figure in column (R). The figure is the percentage of the sales dollar that remains to pay fixed expenses and overhead and to provide profitability to the firm from this particular product line.

When all of these columns have been completed for all the product lines and services performed in your organization, enter totals at the bottom. Note that separate spaces are left for grain sales and mixing and grinding revenue.

After completing form *C* go next to *D*.

Form *D*—Worksheet for Determining Depreciation Costs

1. Begin by filling in the upper three blanks concerning the report dates. This form is fairly self-explanatory and involves determining the depreciation costs for the month. By using the income tax returns for the previous year, you should be able to determine the book value of your fixed assets at the end of the last fiscal year, column (B), and the annual rate of depreciation for these assets, column (C). Divide the annual depreciation rate by 12 to develop a monthly depreciation rate, column (D).

2. Next, if you have purchased any new assets during the year, enter their value in column (E). Determine an annual rate of depreciation for these new assets, column (F), and determine a monthly rate by dividing the figure by 12, column (G). Add columns (D) and (G) to determine the depreciation rate for the month.

3. Room is provided to determine the accumulated depreciation on the products which will be used later in form *A*. Note the code numbers on the bottom of the form; they will be referred to in forms *A*, *B*, and *E*.

Form *A*—Operating Statement

1. Notice that there is room for two sets of figures. When data from the past year are available, it is desirable to fill in the monthly figures for the present year and the monthly figure for the same month of the previous year. This will allow valuable comparisons between years. The abbreviations behind certain of the main items will be useful later in the system.

2. For the current year's operation, record sales, cost of goods sold, and the gross margin figures from the bottom of form *C* as indicated by the codes (C1), (C2), and (C3).

3. Complete the rest of the operating statement by using the total figures from the monthly ledger.

4. When you come to the depreciation cost figure, refer to (D5) on form *D*.

5. Add the total merchandising expense figure, the total administrative expense figure, and the total general expense figure. Put the sum of these three in the total operating expense category.

170   *The Financial Management of Agribusiness Firms*

6. Subtract the total operating expense figure from the gross margin figure (C3) and put it in the net operating margin location (A6).

7. Now add any nonoperating revenues such as interest earned, dividends, or gain on fixed assets and place that total under nonoperating revenue.

8. Subtract any nonoperating expenses such as interest paid, bad debt expense, and cash discounts.

9. Adjust the net operating figure by the balance of the nonoperating revenue and expense figure and put the remaining figure in the net income column (A7).

10. If there are any patronage refunds or federal income tax figures, place them in the proper column and determine your retained income for the period (A8).

This completes form *A*.

Form *B*—Balance Sheet

As in the case of the operating statement, room is provided for data for the comparable period of the previous year.

Asset Section

1. Fill in from your ledger records the totals for the following accounts: cash, which includes both checking and savings accounts, marketable securities, notes receivable, and net accounts receivable, taking into consideration allowance for doubtful accounts.

2. For the inventory on hand, refer to form *C* and fill in the inventory section, listing first the dollar total volume of each inventory category and then determining what percentage of the total inventory each separate category contributes. To do this, divide the individual amounts by the total amount and place that number in the percent of total column. The total inventory figure should correspond to the figure in (C13).

3. Add any prepaid expenses or other current assets that you may have. Total all the figures in space (B14).

4. Determine the value of fixed assets by adding (D20) and (D21). Subtract from that figure the total accumulated depreciation, which is found in (D22). This will give you your total fixed asset figure, which should be placed in (B15).

5. If you have any investment credits from regional cooperative suppliers, place that figure on the next line.

6. Total up the figures in (B14) and (B15), add the investment figure, and place the sum in (B16). This figure should represent all the assets of the firm.

Liability Section

7. Record all bills payable by your firm within the 1-year period, including notes payable, wages payable, taxes payable, and all accounts payable. Mortgages are covered under the long-term liability section.

8. The total of the current liabilities, as shown in (B17), plus all long-term liabilities (such as mortgages and long-term notes) should be added together and placed in (B18).

Net Worth Section

The final section of the balance sheets is the net worth section. This indicates the amount of assets that are owned by the business.

9. In the owner-invested capital space fill in the amount of original capital raised by the owners and subsequent capital contributions they have made.

Financial Analysis and Control 171

10. Under retained earnings fill in the amount of retained earnings that have been and are now present in the firm. Complete the Statement of Retained Earnings on form *E*.

11. Insert the total of all figures in the net worth section at (B19).

12. The total of (B18) and (B19) should be placed under total liabilities and net worth. This figure should be exactly the same as the figure in (B16), total assets. If they are not equal, the work should be reexamined to determine why this difference exists.

Form *E*—Worksheet for Control Point Calculations

1. This form is self-explanatory. Note, however, in steps 3 and 4, that abbreviations are used in several places. These abbreviations refer to the appropriate items on forms *A* and *B* and should aid you in making the calculations.

2. Simply fill in the blanks as indicated and do the division and multiplication as indicated. For example, in step 4, the following data are found:

$$\text{ACID TEST RATIO} = \frac{E25}{B17} = \frac{QA}{CL}$$

The numbers are obtained from the coded locations, which in this case are quick assets divided by the current liabilities, which is the acid-test ratio.

3. After computing the various ratios, the next step is to plot them on control charts 1 and 2 for the month indicated on the chart.

Statement of Retained Earnings

4. This statement of retained earnings is useful in understanding the changes in the retained earnings account. To begin, refer to your last fiscal period report and transfer the retained earnings figure from that report to the "Beginning Retained Earnings Balance" spot on the form. After this has been done once, the ending balance (E26) for one period will be the beginning balance for the next period.

5. Refer to (A8) on the operating statement. Transfer that amount to the appropriate spot on form *F*, depending upon whether a profit or a loss was realized.

6. If dividends were paid, subtract them from the balance.

7. Place the final balance in the (E26) space and also transfer it to (E26) on the balance sheet (retained earnings location).

Form *F*—Worksheet for Inventory Calculations

1. If a physical inventory has been taken, part 1 of this form simply aids you in making the necessary calculations.

2. If a physical inventory was not taken, refer to part 2 of this form. One of the most important requisites for useful estimations is an accurate knowledge of the gross margin generated by each product line. If this is known accurately, the estimation method becomes much more reliable.

3. The form is self-explanatory. However, an example should help clear up questions. Assume the following to be true:

- Hog feed inventory on hand January 1, 1965 = $35.
- Normal hog feed gross margin for this firm = 15 percent.

172 The Financial Management of Agribusiness Firms

- Hog feed purchases during the month of January = $100.
- Hog feed sales for the month of January = $80.

Given this information and using part 2 on form *F* we will estimate the cost of goods sold, the ending inventory, and the gross margin generated through this month's hog feed sales.

4. If physical inventory is not taken at the end of period:

Inventory of product line at beginning of period — January 1, 1965	(A)	$ 35
Purchases of product during period	(B)	$100
Total inventory and purchases (A) + (B)	(S)	$135
Sale of product line for period	(R)	$ 80
Estimated gross margin (%) for product line	(W)	15%
Estimated $ gross margin (R) × (W)	(V)	$ 12
Estimated cost of goods sold during period (R) − (V)	(U)	$ 68
Estimated inventory remaining at end of period (S) − (U)	(T)	$ 67

5. While this estimation technique can be quite accurate if used the month after the physical inventory has been taken, it loses accuracy quickly when used for more than 2 consecutive months without a physical inventory.

This completes the instructions for this system. Although it may seem long and complex at first, it will quickly become routine and the amount of time needed to complete the system will drop sharply.

Forms and Charts for the Control System

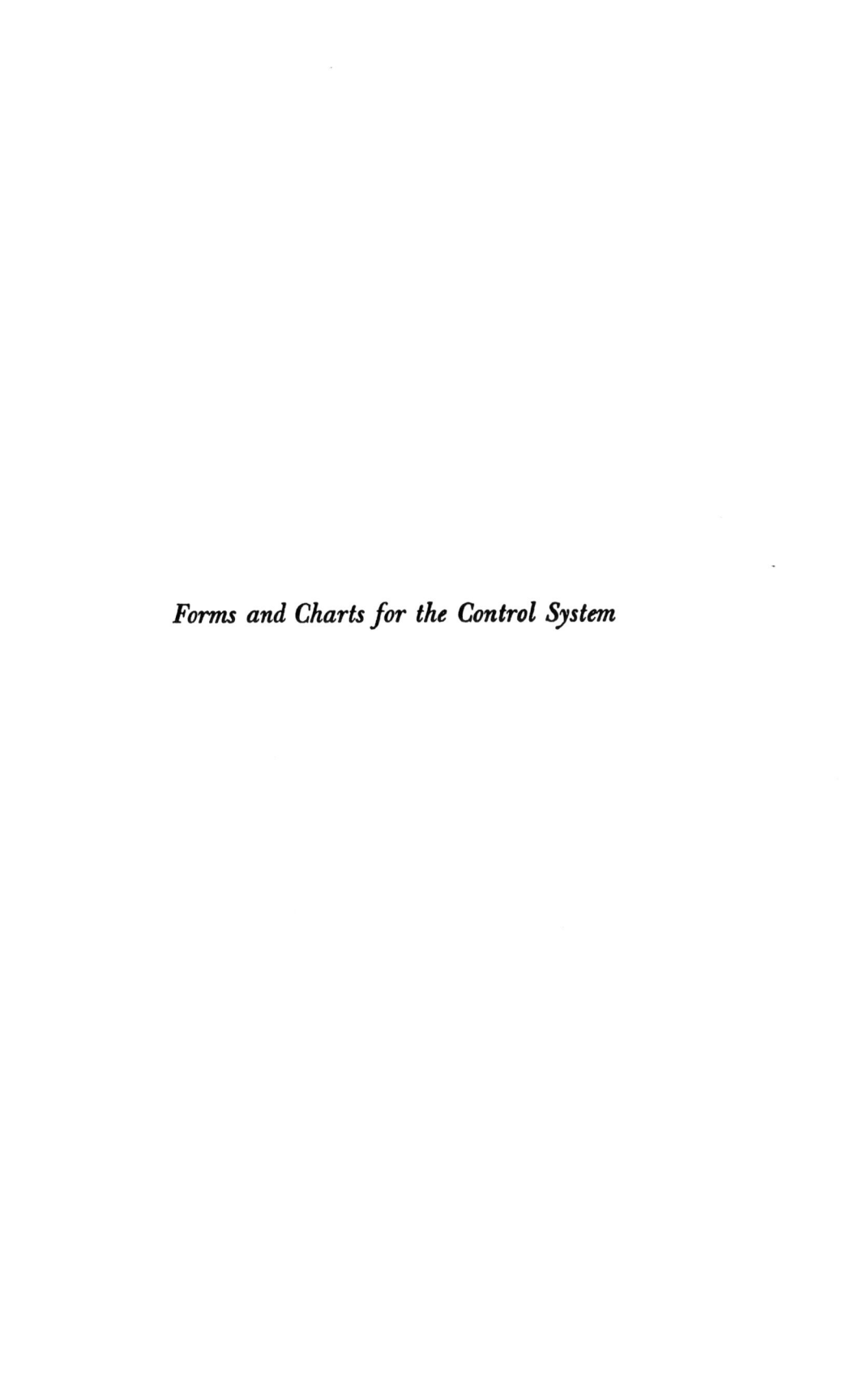

Form *A* OPERATING STATEMENT

For periods beginning_____
          and_____
And ending_____
          and_____

		19___		19___	
		$	%	$	%
SALES	(C1)				
Less: COST OF GOODS SOLD (CGS)	(C2)				
GROSS MARGIN (GM)	(C3)				
OPERATING EXPENSE SECTION					
MERCHANDISING EXPENSES					
Merchandising wages (MW)	(A4)				
Commissions					
Truck expenses					
Supplies					
Advertising					
TOTAL MERCHANDISING EXPENSES					
ADMINISTRATIVE EXPENSES					
Auditing fees and expenses					
Directors' fees and expenses					
Manager's (owner's) salary					
Office wages					
Office supplies and postage					
Telephone and telegraph					
Travel expenses					
TOTAL ADMINISTRATIVE EXPENSES					
GENERAL EXPENSES					
Depreciation	(D5)				
Insurance					
Rent					
Repair and supplies					
Fuel, water, heat, light					
Property taxes					
Payroll taxes					
Employee benefit expenses					
Dues and subscriptions					
Miscellaneous expenses					
TOTAL GENERAL EXPENSES					
TOTAL OPERATING EXPENSES					
NET OPERATING MARGIN (NOM)	(A6)				
Plus: Interest and dividends earned					
gain on fixed assets					
TOTAL NONOPERATING REVENUE					
Less: Interest paid					
Bad debt expense					
Cash discounts					
TOTAL NONOPERATING EXPENSES					
NET INCOME (NI)	(A7)				
Plus: Patronage refunds					
Less: Dividends and refunds to patrons					
Less: Federal and state income tax					
RETAINED INCOME FOR PERIOD	(A8)				

Form * B *
BALANCE SHEET

Financial position as of _____, 19_____ and _____, 19_____

Asset Section

Total cash	(B9)	
Marketable securities	(B10)	
Notes receivable	(B11)	
Accounts receivable		
Less: Allowance for doubtful accounts		
Net accounts receivable (A/R)	(B12)	
Inventory on hand $	(% of total)	
Feed		
Seed		
Fertilizer		
Petroleum		
Farm supplies		
Grain		
Other		
Total inventory (INV)	(C13)	
Prepaid expenses		
Other		
TOTAL CURRENT ASSETS (CA)	(B14)	
Book value of fixed assets (D20) + (D21) _____		
Less: Accumulated depreciation (D22)		
TOTAL FIXED ASSETS (FA)	(B 15)	
Investments		
TOTAL ASSETS (TA)	(B 16)	

Liability Section

Accounts payable		
Notes payable		
Taxes payable		
Wages payable		
TOTAL CURRENT LIABILITIES (CL)	(B17)	
Mortgage		
TOTAL LIABILITIES (TL)	(B18)	

Net Worth Section

Owner invested capital		
Retained earnings (E26)		
TOTAL NET WORTH (NW)	(B 19)	
TOTAL LIABILITIES AND NET WORTH		

Form * C *
SALES, COST OF GOODS SOLD, AND GROSS MARGIN COMPOSITION

For period beginning_____ and ending_____

	(R) Sales	(S) Beg. Inv. + Purch.	(T) End Inv.	(U) Cost of Goods Sold (S)-(T)	(V) Gross Margin (R)-(U)	(W) % of Sales (V)/(R)	(X) Cash Merch. Expenses	(Y) Contr. to Fixed Exp., Overhead, & Profit (V)-(X)	(Z) % of Sales (Y)/(R)
FEED									
Hog									
Poultry									
Dairy cattle									
Beef cattle									
Other									
Overhead	--	--	--	--	--	--		--	--
TOTAL FEED									
SEED									
Barley									
Beans									
Corn									
Oats									
Rye									
Other									
Overhead	--	--	--	--	--	--		--	--
TOTAL SEED									
FERTILIZER									
Bag									
Bulk									
Overhead	--	--	--	--	--	--		--	--
TOTAL FERTILIZER									
PETROLEUM									
Gas-bulk									
Gas-station									
Fuel oil									
Motor oil									
TBA									
Other									
Overhead	--	--	--	--	--	--		--	--
TOTAL PETROLEUM									
FARM SUPPLY									
Insecticides									
Chemicals									
Hardware									
Other									
Overhead	--	--	--	--	--	--		--	--
TOTAL FARM SUPPLY									
SUBTOTAL									
TOTAL GRAIN									
MIX-GRIND REVENUE									
GENERAL OVERHEAD	--	--	--	--	--	--		--	--
TOTAL									

(C1)   (C13)   (C2)   (C3)

Financial Analysis and Control 177

Form * D *
WORKSHEET FOR DETERMINING DEPRECIATION COSTS

The present fiscal year began:_____

This report covers the period beginning:_____ and ending:_____

The number of months that have elapsed during this fiscal year: (A)_____

	(B) Book value, end of fiscal year	(C) Annual rate of depr. ($)	(D) Monthly rate = (C) ÷ 12	(E) Book value of new assets purch. this fiscal year	(F) Annual rate of depr. on new assets	(G) Monthly rate = (F) ÷ 12	(H) Present monthly depr. rate = (D) + (G)	(J) Accum. depr. at end of fiscal year	(K) Accum. depr. on old assets from 1st of new fiscal year to present (A) × (D)	(M) Accum. depr. on new assets = no. mos. in use × (G)	(N) Total accum. depr. = (J) + (K) + (M)
Land											
Buildings											
Trucks											
Mach. & equip.											
Other											
TOTALS											
	D20		D21		D5						D22

178   The Financial Management of Agribusiness Firms

Form * E *
WORKSHEET FOR CONTROL POINT CALCULATIONS

Step 1. Using the data from the BALANCE SHEET, fill in the following blanks.

(B9) TOTAL CASH_____

(B10) MARKETABLE SECURITIES_____

(B11) NOTES RECEIVABLE_____

   TOTAL (E23)_____

Step 2. After aging the ACCOUNTS RECEIVABLE, add all A/R 60 days old or less together and write the total here:

   (E24)_____

Step 3. To compute TOTAL QUICK ASSETS (QA), add (E23) + (E24) from above.

   QUICK ASSETS (E25)_____

Step 4. Using the data from the BALANCE SHEET, OPERATING STATEMENT, and this worksheet, fill in the blanks below, and calculate the indicated ratios.

ACID TEST RATIO
$$\frac{(E25)}{(B17)} = \frac{(QA)}{(CL)} = \underline{\qquad}$$

INVENTORY TURNOVER
$$\frac{(C2)}{(C13)} = \frac{(CGS)}{(INV)} = \underline{\qquad}$$

AVERAGE COLLECTION PERIOD
$$\frac{(B11)}{(C1)} = \frac{(A/R)}{(SALES)} \times 30 \text{ days} = \underline{\qquad}$$

$ SALES PER MERCH. WAGE DOLLAR
$$\frac{(C1)}{(A4)} = \frac{(SALES)}{(MW)} = \underline{\qquad}$$

% NET MARGIN
$$\frac{(A6)}{(C1)} = \frac{(NOM)}{(SALES)} \times 100 = \underline{\qquad}$$

% GROSS MARGIN
$$\frac{(C3)}{(C1)} = \frac{(GM)}{(SALES)} \times 100 = \underline{\qquad}$$

Step 5. Plot sales and the above calculated values on Control Graphs 1 and 2.

STATEMENT OF RETAINED EARNINGS

BEGINNING RETAINED EARNINGS BALANCE
   Date_____ $_____

ADDITIONS:
   RETAINED EARNINGS FOR PERIOD   (A8)_____

DEDUCTIONS:
   LOST FROM OPERATIONS   (A8)_____

DIVIDENDS OR PATRON REFUNDS PAID_____

ENDING RETAINED EARNINGS
   Date_____(E26) $_____

Form * F *
WORKSHEET FOR INVENTORY CALCULATIONS

1. If physical inventory is taken at end of period:

        Inventory at beginning of period   _____

  plus: Purchases during period   _____

        Total inventory and purchases   _____

  less: Inventory at end of period   _____

        Cost of goods sold during period   _____

        Sales for period   _____

  less: Cost of goods sold during period   _____

        Gross margin   _____

$$\frac{\text{Gross margin}}{\text{Sales}} = \text{\% Gross margin}$$ _____

2. If physical inventory is not taken at end of period:

Inventory of product line at beginning of period	(A)	$_____
Purchases of product during period	(B)	$_____
Total inventory and purchases (A) + (B)	(S)	$_____
Sale of product line for period	(R)	$_____
Estimated gross margin (%) for product line	(W)	_____ %
Estimated $ gross margin (R) × (W)	(V)	$_____
Estimated cost of goods sold during period (R) − (V)	(U)	$_____
Estimated inventory remaining at end of period (S) - (U)	(T)	$_____

Chart 1 — Control points

ACID TEST RATIO

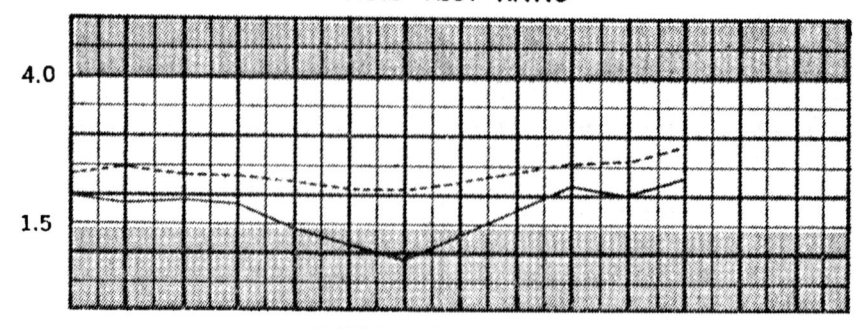

INVENTORY TURNOVER

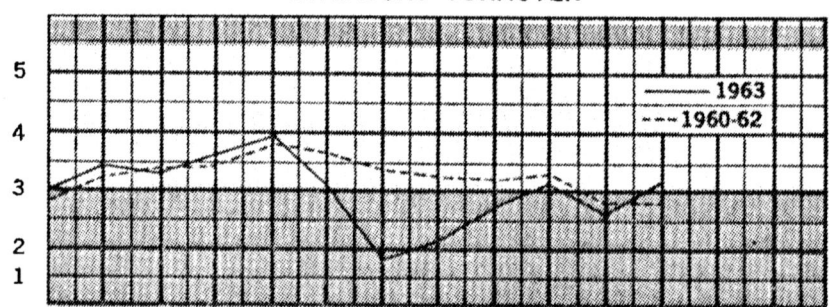

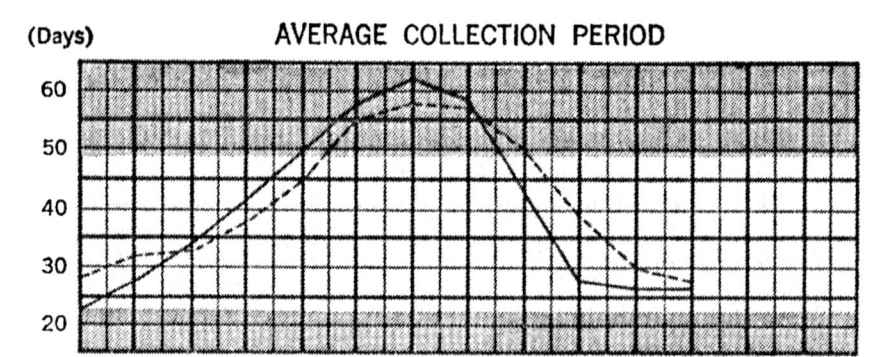

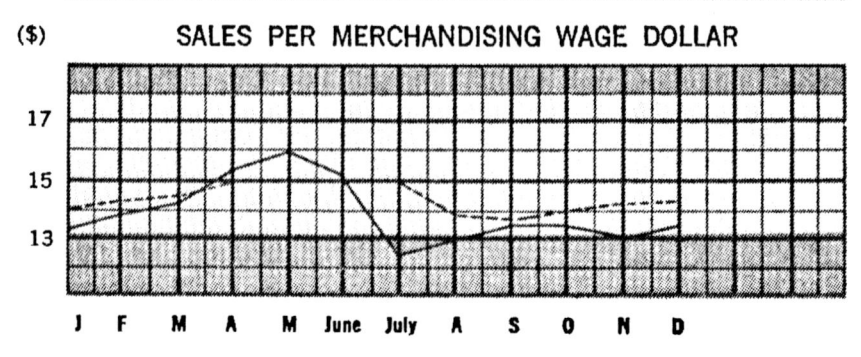

―――― 1963
- - - - 1960-62

AVERAGE COLLECTION PERIOD (Days)

SALES PER MERCHANDISING WAGE DOLLAR ($)

J F M A M June July A S O N D

Chart 2 — Control points

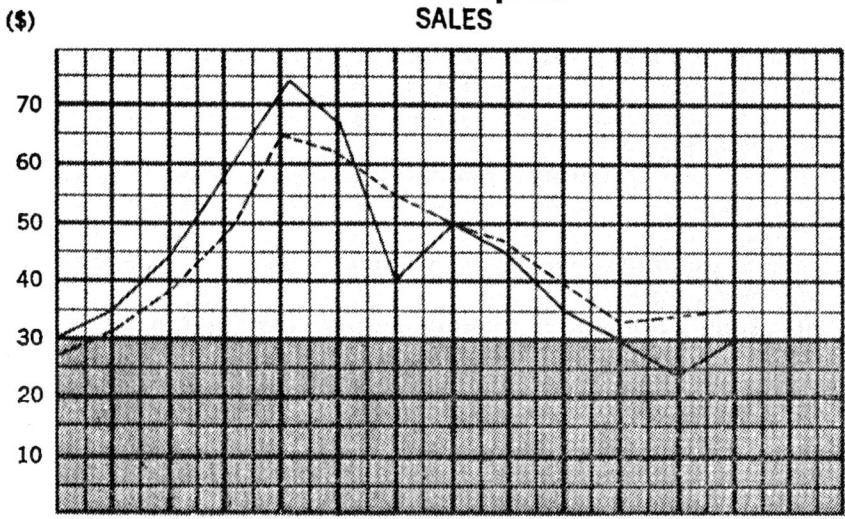

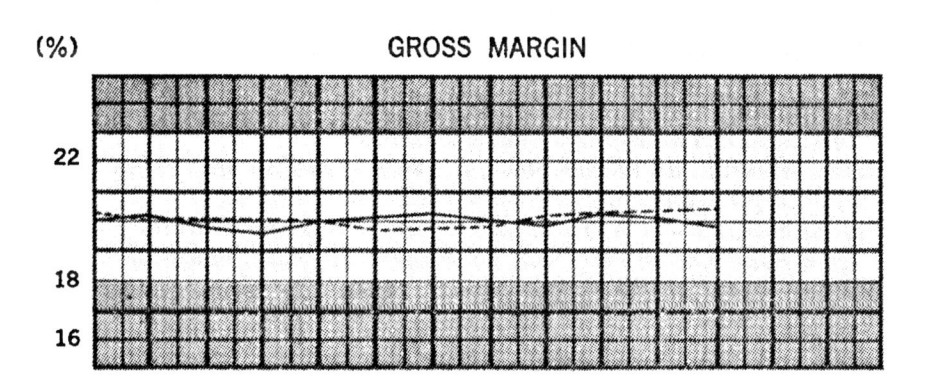

SALES
($)

GROSS MARGIN
(%)

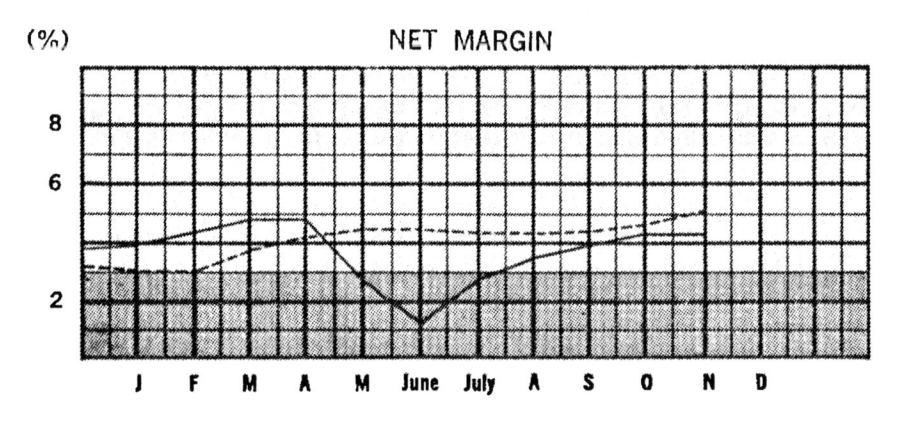

NET MARGIN
(%)

Suggested Readings

Burkes, Marshall R., and George F. Henning. *Ratio Analysis Used to Measure Financial Strengths of Agricultural Business Corporations.* Wooster, Ohio: Ohio Agricultural Experiment Station, A.E. 340, 1963.

Costs of Doing Business in 185 Lines — Corporations. New York: Dun and Bradstreet, Inc., 1965.

Davis, T. C. "How the DuPont Organization Appraises Its Performance," American Management Association — Financial Management Series No. 94, 1950, p. 1–24.

Executive Committee Control Charts. Wilmington, Del.: E. I. DuPont de Nemours and Company, 1959.

Helfert, Erich. *Techniques of Financial Analysis,* revised edition. Homewood, Ill.: Richard D. Irwin, Inc., 1967, p. 55–73.

Hunt, Pearson, Charles M. Williams, and Gordon Donaldson. *Basic Business Finance,* third edition. Homewood, Ill.: Richard D. Irwin, Inc., 1966, p. 141–151.

Johnson, Robert W. *Financial Management,* third edition. Boston: Allyn and Bacon, Inc., 1966, p. 69–93.

Lewis, Ralph L. *Management Uses of Accounting-Planning and Control for Profits.* New York: Harper & Bros., 1961.

Manuel, Milton. *Improving Management of Farmer Cooperatives.* Washington, D.C.: Farmer Cooperative Service, U.S. Department of Agriculture, 1964.

Miller, Donald E. *The Meaningful Interpretation of Financial Statements.* New York: American Management Association, 1966.

Moeller, Robert J., and Frank J. Smith, Jr. *Financial Analysis and Control of the Farm Supply Business.* University of Minnesota Special Report 17, 1965.

Schermerhorn, Richard W. *Financial Statement Analysis for Agricultural Marketing Firms.* College Park, Md.: University of Maryland Agricultural Information Series No. 24, 1964.

Weston, J. Fred, and Eugene F. Brigham. *Managerial Finance,* second edition. New York: Holt, Rinehart, and Winston, Inc., 1966, p. 67–92.

Willson, R. A., and Frank J. Smith, Jr. *Managing the Farm Supply Business — 10 Areas.* Agricultural Extension Special Report 16, University of Minnesota, September 1965, p. 91–99.

Additional suggested readings listing texts, manuals and pamphlets relating to specific agricultural marketing and farm supply industries, follow chapter 8. Many of these selections have ratio analysis discussions on specific types of firms.

PROBLEM SET
Ratio Analysis

Below are the balance sheet and income statements for the Slama Farm Supply Company.

Year-End Balance Sheet		
Current assets		
Cash		$23,800
Marketable securities		650
Accounts receivable		13,000
Merchandise inventories		137,013
Other current assets		2,235
Total current assets		$176,698
Investment in other firms		$254,976
Fixed assets (net)		146,316
Total assets		$577,990
Current liabilities		$ 93,672
Long-term debt		100
Net worth		484,218
Total liabilities and net worth		$577,990

Annual Income Statement	
Sales	$569,993
Cost of goods sold	436,386
Gross margin	$133,607
Selling and adm. expenses	$112,437
Net operating margin	$ 21,170

Problems:
1. Prepare a common size statement from each of the above statements.
2. Calculate each of the following financial ratios for the firm:
   (a) Current
   (b) Acid test*
   (c) Net worth total assets
   (d) Cost of goods sold/inventory
   (e) Average collection period†
   (f) Net margin/total assets
3. Comment on the financial status of Slama. To assist you in your analysis, example ratio and common size statement data for 28 firms handling feed, seed, fertilizer, and petroleum products in Slama's market area are presented on page 184.

* For this problem include cash, marketable securities, and accounts receivable.
† For this problem measure as follows: accounts receivable × 300 ÷ sales.

Seven average ratios of 28 farm supply firms

	Most profitable (14 companies)	Least profitable (14 companies)
Current ratio	4.3	2.5
Acid test ratio *	2.3	1.3
Net worth/total assets	.9	.76
Cost of goods sold/inventory	6.8	5.4
Average collection period (days)†	25.4	29.9
Net operating margin/net worth	.0999	.0440
Net operating margin/total assets	.0889	.0334

* Cash, marketable securities, accounts receivable ÷ current liabilities.
† Accounts receivable × 300 ÷ sales.

Average common size income statement of 28 farm supply firms

Sales	100.00
Cost of goods sold	79.00
Gross margin	21.00
Selling and administration expenses	17.25
Net operating margin	3.75

Average year-end common size balance sheet of 28 farm supply firms

Current assets		Liabilities	
Cash and marketable securities	10.4%	Current liabilities	27.2%
Net receivable	20.6	Noncurrent liabilities	8.5
Inventories	20.8	Net worth	64.3
Other	.5	Total liabilities and net worth	100.0
Investment in other firms	21.8		
Fixed assets	25.9		
Total assets	100.0		

CHAPTER 8
Financial Problems in the Growing Firm

Growth is a dominant theme in any discussion of agriculturally related businesses. To many, the notion of "not growing" is tantamount to impending failure. On the other hand, there is substantial evidence which indicates that not all firms that grow, rapidly or otherwise, are necessarily profitable or invulnerable to failure. In fact, it is precisely in a rapid growth situation that a firm may be most vulnerable. Such firms may be operating at the limit of their managerial and financial capacity, and an unexpected technical, market, or random breakdown can very quickly remove such a firm from orbit.

In a text such as this, our coverage of the growth process must be limited. In fact, as the title to this chapter suggests, our focus is on financial problems associated with growth. Thus, we will not concern ourselves with the implications that growth has for such important matters as market development, facilities planning, personnel recruitment and training, or management staffing. Each of these areas presents problems in its own right which must be considered concurrently with those associated with finance. In not treating them, we are in no way inferring that they are subsidiary to finance.

In what follows, we will look first at a brief resumé of the economic reasons for growth; second, at the methods of growing and the related financial considerations; and third, at a case of a rapidly growing agricultural marketing firm.

Why Grow?

We don't see firm growth as an end in itself. Not all firms should grow; indeed, there are some firms whose best interests would be served if they became smaller; and there are many more firms who, by virtue of location, markets, managerial capacity, and other factors, will be unable to continue in business at all. Having said this, we are quick to point out that the "typical" healthy agricultural marketing or supply firm will undoubtedly be growing. The reason it will be growing is simply that it finds it more profitable to do so than not to grow. If profitability is not increased by growth, there is no economic reason for a firm to grow. There may be other reasons — pride, prestige, ignorance,

186   The Financial Management of Agribusiness Firms

etc.; if the discipline imposed by the firm's particular market is lax, survival may be possible. But the bankruptcy courts frequently settle the affairs of firms that grew without economic justification.

What economic motives underlie the growth process of agriculturally related firms? Mueller has suggested five:[55]

1. Economies of scale.
2. Decreasing procurement and field service costs.
3. Vertical integration.
4. Diversification of product lines.
5. Achievement of market power.

The existence and exploitation of scale economies has probably been the largest single factor underlying the growth of agricultural marketing and supply firms. Most studies by agricultural economists of plant operations suggest the existence of scale economies for nearly all processing and handling operations. In fact, most studies of *plant* costs suggest that they decrease continuously, at least within the ranges observed. This is not to say that *firm* costs, which may involve multiple plants and centralized management, may not at some point increase as scale increases. But as a practical matter, it is common as far as agricultural marketing and supply firms are concerned for plant and firm to be synonymous. In any case, the existence of scale economies is a fundamental and legitimate reason for growth.

Decreasing procurement and field service costs are, of course, not unrelated to the exploitation of scale economies. Assembly and distribution activities typically carry a fairly heavy load of fixed labor and/or equipment costs. A fieldman or salesman is paid a full day's wages whether he contacts 10 customer-patrons or 20. Research studies have shown that procurement or distribution costs are reduced as density of volume in an area increases, or, conversely, that overlapping routes served by a number of firms increase these costs.[56] It is also true, for example, that a 40,000-pound milk tank truck does not cost twice as much as a 20,000-pound one does, but to operate the larger one efficiently requires a volume in line with its capacity. Thus, there are legitimate economic pressures for growth on the procurement and distribution side of the business.

The argument for a firm growing vertically, that is, taking on additional functions that move it closer to the consumer or to the producer,

[55] Willard F. Mueller, "The Role of Mergers in the Growth of Agricultural Cooperatives," California Agricultural Experiment Station Bulletin 777, February 1961, pp. 23-25.
[56] Mueller, *op cit.*, p. 24.

hinges on the competitiveness of these vertically related markets as well as their capacity to produce qualities and quantities of goods and services which satisfy the firm's particular requirements. If vertically related firms are unable to exercise major market power and produce satisfactory products or services, there is little to be gained through vertical integration. On the other hand, if prices are above or below competitive levels on the procurement or market sides, respectively, or if a firm cannot obtain the kinds of products or services it requires, revenues may be increased if it assumes the function involved.

Diversification of product lines may perform four functions. First, it may allow a firm to keep its funds invested in higher return activities than would be possible if it continued to invest in a single product line. Second, diversification may reduce variability of total profits, which in turn can have a favorable effect on the cost of capital. Third, complementarity of products and/or services may result in higher profits for the diversified firm than for the highly specialized one. Fourth, diversification may yield higher returns through fuller use of capacity.

There are arguments on the other side of the diversification coin. These are built primarily on the relationship of the stockholder and the firm. The argument goes that when the stockholder-investor is free to buy and sell securities he can develop a portfolio that is in line with his personal risk preferences. If, therefore, a firm cannot reinvest its funds at acceptable profit rates in its own internal specialized operation, it should return the surplus to the stockholder for his personal use. There is a good deal of merit to this position and in fact many stockholders do invest in specialized firms which are in tune with their own risk preferences. But few will argue that, from the point of view of the firm and its capacity for survival, diversification may well be profitable.

Market power, of course, relates to the capacity of a firm to manipulate or otherwise influence the prices it receives for products or pays for inputs. A small firm competing with a large number of other small firms in the sale of relatively homogeneous products typically regards itself as a "price taker" as far as sales or purchasing transactions are concerned. A large part of what happens to the firm, particularly in respect to revenue, is beyond its control under these conditions. Insofar as growth does permit the firm to achieve some power to affect price or other trading conditions, either because it captures enough of the total market to be able to do so, or because its size permits it to provide services or volume that would otherwise differentiate it from its competitors, profitability may be enhanced. Growth to achieve market power is clearly sensible.

Underlying the discussion in the remainder of this chapter is the basic assumption that growth is undertaken to achieve increased profitability. Any one, or all five, of the factors we have just discussed can play a role in the growth decision process. In the next section we will focus briefly on alternative methods of growth and then discuss the associated financial problems.

Methods and Problems of Growth

There are two major means by which firms can grow. They can either expand internally by adding new plants, machinery, equipment, and personnel to what they already have, or they can expand through various forms of combinations with other existing firms — through mergers, consolidations, or acquisitions.

The matter of internal growth is simply an extension of the concept of capital budgeting that we discussed in chapters 4 and 5. We don't have much to add to that discussion in this chapter except to repeat some warnings sounded earlier, as we will in the next section.

In recent years, various forms of business combinations have accounted for a high proportion of the growth in agricultural marketing and supply firms. Business combinations are frequently referred to as mergers even though the latter term has a distinct legal meaning. In a strict legal sense, merger means bringing the assets of two firms together with only one of the two retaining its identity. Consolidation involves bringing the assets of two firms together to form an entirely new corporation. Acquisition refers to the outright purchase of all or part of the assets of one firm by another. Our concern is not with legal details but rather with the financial problems associated with bringing together the assets of two or more business firms into a single firm. In what follows, we will use the term merger in a generic sense to include all types of business combinations.

Why have agricultural marketing and supply firms relied so heavily on merger rather than internal expansion for growth? Mueller offers several reasons:[57]

1. Competitive considerations.
2. Cheaper to buy than to build.
3. To get technical and management know-how.
4. Financial considerations.[58]

[57] Mueller, *op. cit.*, p. 26–28.
[58] He also suggested that World War II played an important part in the spurt in merger activity that took place in that period.

Competitive considerations have played a major role in the choice of merger over internal expansion for agriculturally related business firms. In many markets, for one firm to expand its volume may require that one or more other firms suffer volume decreases. Since volume decreases not only affect the revenue side of the profit equation but also have important impacts on costs, firms are justifiably reluctant to retreat from their market share under competitive attack. Various retaliatory tactics are usually undertaken, including price cutting or offers of various nonprice benefits. The end result of these various countervailing activities may be that no competitor increases his volume but that all may suffer substantial reductions in profits, or, at the extreme, failure. On the other hand, when firms merge, all or a large part of the volume of each is part of the merger package and, therefore, costly competitive maneuvering is avoided.

Acquiring facilities that already exist may be *cheaper than expanding old facilities or building new ones* assuming that those acquired are appropriate for the intended use. Existing facilities have had some depreciation and if the value of certain "intangibles" associated with a going concern are not high, cost savings to the acquiring firm may be substantial. It may also be true that even though the value of intangibles is high, the income benefits to both parties of a merger may be such that the value of facilities will be brought into the agreement at a price below new costs.

Technical and management personnel talent may well be the scarce factor in the expanding firm. To train people internally for greater responsibilities can be a time-consuming process, however worthwhile. To lure persons with specialized capabilities away from other firms who may also be aware of their talents can be costly. When growth takes place through merger, acquiring appropriately trained personnel need not be a problem. It is possible that certain key people may choose not to stay with the merged organization and in some cases there may be redundancies in certain positions in the merged organizations. These may be considered to be the cost of acquiring desired management and technical personnel in a reasonably short period of time.

Growth through merger may also offer *considerable advantage from the financial point of view*. When one going concern merges with or otherwise acquires the assets, personnel, and markets of another going concern, much of the uncertainty about income flows common to internal expansion is avoided or is greatly reduced. Previously developed markets are ready for exploitation; experienced management and personnel are in control; where scale economies exist they can be taken advantage of immediately. These conditions greatly reduce the risks of the lender and/or investor, which in turn affects their willingness to supply adequate volumes of capital to meet the firm's needs at favorable rates.

To the above four motives for growth by merger we would add a fifth, namely, speed. To generate sufficient funds internally to permit growth may take considerable time under the best of circumstances. If the rate at which a firm is growing in an industry is lower than that of its competitors, assuming that such growth is justified by increased profits, it may find itself at a serious disadvantage in the competition for survival. Markets for certain commodities can level off and if a firm has not achieved optimum size by the time this happens, it may never achieve that size. Merger tends to remove the time barrier.

Other reasons for growth through merger could probably be given but the above are probably the major ones. With this brief review on why and how firms grow, we now turn to a consideration of the financial problems associated with growth and their causes.

Financial Problems

Haphazard planning methods and in some cases the total lack of planning are probably the major causes of financial problems in a rapid growth situation. For many firms, growth, whether by internal expansion or merger, just happens — the result of a series of individual and not necessarily integrated decisions which were shaped by opportunities and environmental conditions that existed at a single point in time. It would be safe to say that this is how most growth in agricultural marketing and supply firms has taken place; and this is precisely why many of these firms find themselves strapped for working capital (see chapters 3 and 4), with a debt/equity structure that is seriously out of balance, with an inappropriate combination of fixed assets to achieve efficient cost levels, with badly located facilities, and management and labor capabilities not in line with firm needs. The number and magnitude of financial and other problems that could arise under these conditions is virtually infinite. We won't, therefore, attempt to enumerate them here. But in earlier chapters we did examine methods of analyzing short- and long-term capital needs and of planning and controlling the firm's operations, which, if used, would reduce the problems of managing growth to reasonable proportions.

At a minimum, from a financial point of view, sound growth requires the anticipation and adequate provisions for working capital needs, and the development of a capital structure that will give the growing organization "reserve strength" so that it can withstand unexpected economic, technical, and random shocks. This will not happen automatically. Nor is it likely that persons or institutions who finance growth are going to be willing to do so without a pretty clear blueprint of how the growth is going to take place. A firm that has "a problem" of financing growth may simply be the victim of its own unwillingness to plan.

The Valuation Problem. Assuming that adequate planning takes place, a major problem in bringing two or more organizations together through merger or other means is establishing the value of the assets involved. In a merger between firm A and firm B, for example, how much should the owners of the respective firms receive for the assets they supply to the newly combined organization? Their stake in this determination is evident and is typically the central issue in the negotiation process. Is there any "sure-fire" way of settling this problem? The answer is "No." In a bargaining situation, and this is what merger negotiations really are, the outcome will be determined in part by the relative bargaining strength of the respective parties. But it will also depend on how well each of the respective parties does his homework in regard to discovering and defining the economic boundaries within which the bargaining process will take place. In what follows we will examine various ways of looking at the value of firms.

Book Value — One common way of looking at the value of a firm is on the basis of that recorded in its own accounting records. At practically any point in time, an accountant can render a precise measure of his firm's value — based on "sound" accounting principles and techniques. But what does "book value" really mean?

Suppose that a firm avails itself of accelerated depreciation privileges, as we suggested was desirable in an earlier chapter. Does the real value of assets so depreciated fall as rapidly as the book value might suggest? For example, is the value of the assets of two essentially identical grain elevators, organized at the same point in time and managed with the same degree of proficiency, really different because one uses accelerated depreciation and the other does not? Are book values of inventories, typically arrived at by arbitrary accounting rule, always reflections of what they are really worth? How much is a processing plant worth, however new, when its intended use ceases to exist? The countryside is dotted with creameries and other agricultural marketing and supply installations whose supply areas or markets have evaporated. What does book value mean in these cases? On the other side of the coin, could a building erected 5 years ago at a cost of $100,000 be replaced for that amount under present labor and material cost conditions?

Finally, and perhaps most importantly, would the owners of a going concern be willing to part with their assets at book value? The answer to most of these questions is probably "No," or "Not very much." But does this rule out book value as being useful in the evaluation process? Again the answer is "No." Parties to any bargaining situation would want to pay close attention to their own book valuations as well as to those of the others involved. These are data that clearly have a role in the bargaining process; they may not be the final determinants of the agreement reached, but they do give the bargainers one point from which to establish a bearing.

Replacement Value — The replacement cost approach to valuation recognizes that labor, power, material, and other costs change over time and that it is highly unlikely that we can produce an identical building or piece of equipment today for what it cost us last year or 5 years ago. This approach involves estimating the costs of reproducing whatever assets are involved under present conditions. A major problem is the estimation of these costs. Over time, designs change, one material is substituted for another, efficiency of machinery and equipment is improved, and proportions of various input combinations may change. These factors all complicate the estimation process but certainly don't preclude making a reasonably satisfactory estimate.

If we were to offer replacement costs, appropriately depreciated, plus an additional amount for the intangible values of a going concern, the owners might be more receptive than if we offered book value plus an allowance for intangibles. But if we are talking in terms of replacement value, the natural question is why not simply construct our own new facilities? Clearly, if a firm thinks that the intangible values of another firm are limited, it would be at the margin of indifference when the bargaining process reached that level. As in the case of book value, we might look at replacement value as another point from which a bearing can be taken.

Liquidation Value — If a firm has little value as a going concern, it could dispose of its assets, singly or in combination, to other firms in the same industry or to firms in different industries at whatever the market would bear. Certain highly specialized assets might be sold at no better than scrap value while other less specialized ones might be disposed of at the going "second-hand" price. Clearly, no one would sell his assets for less than their liquidation value, so this in a sense establishes a floor to the total bargaining process. Thus, this concept may provide another point which will eventually establish the bargaining arena.

Market Value — Many will argue that the true value of anything is best determined by the impersonal workings of the market. And indeed if a market is composed of a reasonably large number of expert buyers and sellers continuously and simultaneously alert to changes in factors that affect price, then market price may in fact be the best estimate of the value of a given set of assets. But these conditions are seldom met, even in the case of corporations whose stocks are widely traded on the open market.

Frequently, purchases and sales of stock represent only a small portion of the total available. So we are not always sure how "representative" sales price really is. The problem of establishing the market value of the firm whose stocks are not widely traded — as is typically the case with agricultural marketing and supply firms — is even more difficult. At any one point in time, the total number of creameries, grain elevators, or farm supply firms that are for sale in the United States may be quite large. But if we look at a particular county or town we may find few or none at all for sale; and buyers may be just as scarce. Since these facilities are largely immobile the fact that trading is brisk somewhere else in the country will have no impact on the local market scene. Thus, the market price does not necessarily reflect the interaction of a fairly large number of highly informed buyers and sellers but may simply reflect a bargain reached between two individuals, dealing in isolation with extremely limited knowledge. Such a transaction does result in some price being agreed upon, but whether or not someone else would be willing to look at that price as an estimate of the value of his own assets is highly questionable. Certainly, bargainers would not want to ignore such transactions, but they may not want to use them as the final criteria on which agreement is based.

Capitalized Earnings Approach — How much assets are really worth is, in the final analysis, dependent on how much they can earn. In chapters 4 and 5 we treated the capital budgeting problem at length. In large part, what we said in those chapters relates to the problem at hand. We are clearly concerned with estimating income flows over time as well as an appropriate discount rate to apply to those flows. Certain conventions and slightly different terminology have developed for use in evaluation of whole firms. We treat these briefly below.

When we discussed the investment decision process in chapter 4, our focus was on the evaluation of a particular asset with a particular economic life. An investment in a truck might be expected to have an economic life of 4 years, or that of a building, 30 years. But when we are concerned with the value of a whole business, we normally have an expectation that its existence will be continuous. There are exceptions, of course. Some might acquire the assets of a firm simply to liquidate them. But typically this is not the case. Thus, normally we are dealing with an income stream that we expect will last indefinitely.

Recall that the income stream we focused on in chapter 4 was the net cash flow after taxes that resulted from the particular investment. This flow included anticipated changes in revenues and costs over the life of the asset. Depreciation was not deducted to arrive at net cash flow. Whole firms are conventionally evaluated in much the same way, except that depreciation is normally deducted from net cash flow so that we are dealing with a firm's net profit flow before interest over time. The argument is advanced that depreciation is a sort of proxy for necessary outlays on fixed assets that would be required to keep the business in operation continuously; that is, machines and equipment and buildings wear out over time and depreciation is an approximation of the outlays necessary for replacement. For reasons that we have suggested earlier in this chapter, such an assumption may not be entirely justified; accounting conventions or changes in price level and technology may lead to depreciation rates that do not reflect replacement costs. Where there is evidence to suggest that this might be true, appropriate adjustments for outlays on fixed assets must be made.

It has become more or less conventional to treat the income flow from a firm as though it were constant from year to year in the evaluation process. This has the obvious advantage of simplifying the computational procedure. But we are not interested in simplicity for its own sake. Indeed, only if income is constant is it appropriate to treat it in this way. On the other hand, if there is evidence of upward or downward trends, these must be built into the estimate. Or, if the pattern of income is expected to be irregular, appropriate adjustments must be made. Blind acceptance of convention can lead to costly errors.

Assuming that an appropriate estimate of the income flow has been made, the next problem relates to the choice of the discount rate to be applied to arrive at net present value. In the case of whole firm valuation, this is commonly called the capitalization rate. The same kinds of considerations enter the determination of the capitalization rate that we discussed in connection with the cost of capital in chapter 5. The capitalization rate is shaped by the alternative investment opportunities facing the firm as well as by the level of risks associated with the particular investment in question. High-risk businesses typically carry relatively high capitalization rates; the opposite is true in the case of low-risk ventures. Since attitudes toward risk vary from individual to individual and from firm to firm, there is no one approach to evaluating it that will satisfy everyone. In chapter 4 we suggested ways in which individual subjective probabilities could be plugged into a risk evaluation problem. Individuals may develop other techniques that suit them better. In any case, the capitalization rate chosen is going to have an important impact upon the value placed on a firm.

For example, two individuals looking at the same firm (which promises an annual income of $10,000 a year) but who see the risks involved in a different light will employ different capitalization rates. In one individual's eyes, the risks associated with the business may be such that he would be satisfied with a 10 percent rate of return on capital, in which case he would be willing to pay $10,000/0.10, or $100,000, for it. The other individual might feel somewhat less certain about the associated risks and demand a 15 percent return, in which case he will be willing to pay only $10,000/0.15, or $66,667. How right the individuals are in their evaluation of risk is known only after time has tested the decision. Those who consistently demand high rates of return may find it difficult to purchase the assets at a price they are willing to pay. If this evaluation is excessively pessimistic, they may thereby deny themselves substantial income opportunities. On the other hand, the individuals who are less sensitive to risk situations will find it easy to procure assets but may run the risk of substantial losses.

Is the capitalized earnings approach the final answer to the evaluation of the problem? The answer, as in the case of other methods of evaluation, is "No!" It does provide another way of looking at evaluation and has the advantage of putting focus on the income flow which, under ideal circumstances, is really the best measure of what assets are really worth. But circumstances are seldom ideal. Difficulties in estimating income flows and problems associated with the choice of appropriate capitalization rates can lead to badly biased estimates of value.

It appears then that there is no single "best" way of going about the evaluation process. As we suggested earlier in this section, the merger process is essentially a bargaining situation whose outcome will be determined in part by the relative power positions of the respective organizations as well as by their knowledge about the value of the assets involved. The various methods of evaluation that we discussed above will help establish the economic boundaries within which the negotiation process should take place. A discussion of bargaining strategies is beyond the scope of this text.[59] Under any circumstances, it must be kept in mind that the merger process is not an end in itself. It is simply one method of growing, and, as we suggested earlier in this chapter, the only justification for growth is increased profitability. If, in the final analysis, the profit picture cannot be improved, growth through merger or other means is not justified.

[59] For a rather extensive discussion of the negotiation process as far as cooperative organizations are concerned, see Eric Thor, Miriam Revzan, Adrian O. Hutchens, *A Guide to Procedures Leading to the Consolidation of Agricultural Marketing Cooperatives*, Giannini Foundation of Agricultural Economics, Information Series in Agricultural Economics No. 67-1, March 1967, 67 pages. Also see *Appraising the Problems and Opportunities of Merger*, Northeast Extension Marketing Publication No. 1, University of Maryland, Cooperative Extension Service Bulletin 203, College Park, Md., April 1965.

Emblem Dairy Corporation Case

In 1953, the Emblem Dairy Corporation was in the hands of the receivers. A cooperative organization, it was serving 42 milk producers and had an annual output of 400,000 pounds of butter. The firm also had a small bottling business. In its headquarters town it had two plants — one received whole milk and packaged fluid products; the other received cream and manufactured butter.

The board of directors of the organization, all of whom were farmers and patrons, were determined to identify the underlying cause of the cooperative's predicament. They engaged a reputable management consulting firm, whose fee they guaranteed by their individual personal notes, to study the situation. The diagnosis was that the two plants, each with its own manager, were essentially out of communication with one another; the resultant lack of coordination precluded efficient operations. The consulting firm recommended that a single manager be placed in charge of both operations.

A search for a new general manager for Emblem was initiated. It was successful. Francis X. McNulty, who had recently liquidated his own small bottling plant in another state and was casting about for a new opportunity in the dairy industry, agreed to take over management of the organization on a temporary basis. He was a graduate of a midwestern agricultural college with an academic background in dairy manufacturing and agricultural economics to go along with his practical experience in the bottling business.

After he had had an opportunity to study Emblem's operations, McNulty's diagnosis of the underlying problems was somewhat at variance with that of the consulting firm. While it was true that there was much to be desired in coordinating the two then-existing plants, he discovered that the primary problem could be pinned down to high-cost, low-volume operations. For example, he found that the bottling business, with a total daily output of only 400 quarts, employed three men in the plant plus two drivers. Similarly, the butter plant, which was small even by then-existing standards, was overstaffed with five full-time workers.

McNulty spent most of 1954 and part of 1955 in establishing sound internal operations. He was able to increase the number of producers supplying milk for bottling purposes from 4 to 28; Emblem became a supplier of milk to other bottlers in the trade territory. Because of high churning costs, he temporarily ceased churning operations in 1954 and switched to selling whole milk to other manufacturers in the area.

By 1955, McNulty began to feel that he was in control of the situation at Emblem. The job that he had accepted on a temporary basis less than 2 years before had become such a challenge that he dropped the idea of leaving. His thoughts turned to expansion. He began looking for firms which were experiencing financial difficulties as potential acquisitions.

In 1955, Emblem acquired the assets of Dana Creamery, with a 60,000-pound-per-day milk volume and annual sales of $250,000, by assuming an $11,000 debt. Dana's processing operations were halted and it became a receiving station. In the following year, Emblem acquired the Hand Creamery, which had an annual sales volume of approximately $400,000, for $20,000 cash. In both cases the acquired organizations were cooperatives which had equities in larger regional marketing associations. Trusteeships were established so that members of the respective acquired organizations received the full benefit of their equities in regional organizations when they were "revolved."

In 1956, Emblem made a $200,000 capital expenditure on a 250,000-pound-per-day capacity milk-drying plant in its headquarters town. Half of this expenditure was financed with debt capital and the other half with an issue of preferred stock sold locally.

It was in 1956 that McNulty introduced evidence to his board of directors that the traditional use of cans in assembling milk resulted in higher costs than would be the case with the use of bulk tanks. The adoption of bulk tanks became all the more desirable when the government raised the quality standards on milk powder. The use of cans made achievement of these standards extremely difficult. The board of directors decided that Emblem should convert to a 100 percent bulk handling operation. By 1957, the shift to bulk tanks was completed. When the changeover began, Emblem was serving 450 producers; when the shift was completed, only 225 remained. During the period of the transition, Emblem paid a premium on bulk milk which reflected the savings in handling and processing costs. The producer applied this premium to defray his investment costs in the bulk tank and associated equipment. Emblem had worked out an arrangement to have the tanks financed through local Production Credit Associations.

Between 1958 and 1960, attention was focused primarily on consolidating earlier gains and soliciting new producers. No acquisitions were made and the Dana and Hand receiving stations were closed when Emblem opened a new one, intermediate between them, at Clayton.

In 1961, Emblem acquired use of the assets of the nearly bankrupt Stone River Creamery (annual sales of $400,000) through a rental arrangement in which it agreed to pay $700 a month for Stone River's plant. Stone River was used strictly as a receiving station. In 1962, Emblem purchased the assets of Bow Lodge Creamery, with annual sales of $500,000, for $25,000 in cash. As in the cases of Dana and Hand, Bow Lodge's equities in the regional organization to which it belonged were returned to its own members.

The years 1963 and 1964 were devoted to internal consolidation.

The year 1965 was marked by four additional acquisitions. Included was the largest single acquisition ever made by Emblem — Bell Town Creamery — which had an annual volume of $4.5 million. It was purchased with a $325,000 bank loan. The other three creameries acquired had a total dollar volume of approximately $1,650,000 and cost Emblem approximately $84,000 in cash.

In 1966, Emblem acquired the assets of Blue Stream Creamery, with an annual volume of about $1 million, by assuming $14,000 of debt obligations (which it paid in cash) as well as agreeing to pay out $35,000 of accumulated equities to Blue Stream members over a 12-year period. It also opened a new receiving station in a border town of a neighboring state. Buildings and equipment were financed by the municipality and Emblem has the use of them on a rental basis.

A capital improvement program involving approximately $1.4 million was also undertaken in 1966. The expenditures were divided about evenly between a new butter manufacturing setup in Emblem's headquarters town and a new dryer and evaporator in the Bell Town plant. These expenditures were financed by internally generated cash and a large bank loan.

By the end of 1966, Emblem's processing operations were concentrated in its headquarters town (butter and powder manufacturing) and in the Bell Town plant (powder manufacturing). It operated seven other facilities as receiving stations.

In 1967, McNulty devoted considerable time to reviewing his earlier growth strategies and in developing a new growth policy for the firm. Figure 11 illustrates the growth pattern of sales and assets. To a large extent, growth had been financed by internally generated funds and debt capital. Only in 1956 was preferred stock used in any significant way. Acquisitions of other firms accounted for a high proportion of the overall expansion. While the Bell Town plant and one or two other Emblem acquisitions were going concerns, most of its acquisitions were firms in serious financial difficulties whose alternative was liquidation. McNulty's interest was not in their assets as such, but rather in the volume of milk that these organizations represented. In a sense, he was "buying volume." Some acquisitions were for strategic competitive purposes. For example, while McNulty feels that several of the present receiving facilities are too far away from the main manufacturing plants from an efficient assembly cost point of view, he is convinced that this dis-

Figure 11. Trends in sales volume and total assets for Emblem Dairy Corporation.

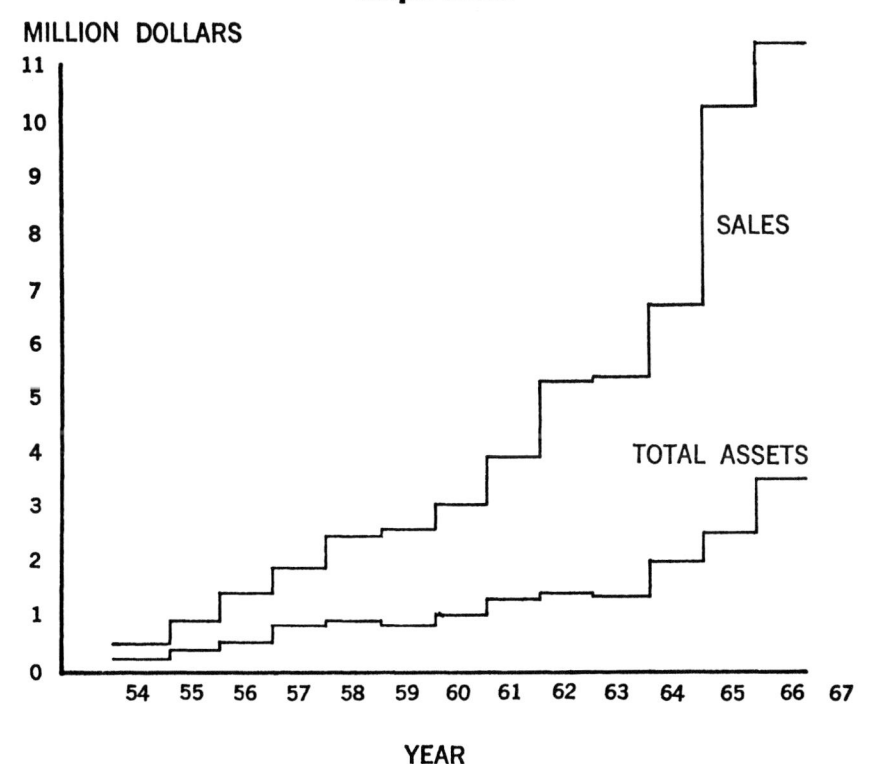

advantage will be more than offset by reduced costs of entry into outlying supply areas at some future point in time.

McNulty has come to believe that the benefits to be enjoyed by acquiring nearly defunct organizations have about run their course. On the other hand, he feels that Emblem must more than double its 1966 size to achieve critical marketing economies. He has the feeling that future mergers ought to be between firms of a size comparable to Emblem.

As he thought about further growth, McNulty was bothered by some recent developments in his supply area. Because other area dairy organizations are "volume conscious" also, competition for milk supplies has become intense; as a consequence, net margins are being squeezed. Because McNulty is relying heavily on internally generated cash to finance Emblem's growth, a continued squeeze on margins could create critical financial problems.

A second factor causing McNulty concern is the activity of a farmer bargaining organization, which appears to be gaining strength in his part of the country. Emblem was not unsympathetic to the farm organization's objective of raising farmer incomes and, therefore, had come to terms with it. Not all dairy manufacturing firms in the area are of like mind on this matter, nor are all the farmers in the supply area members. McNulty is concerned that any attempt by the farm organization to reduce supplies which results in a substantial reduction in volume processed through Emblem's plants without an offsetting increase in price could result in substantial losses for it, while at the same time benefitting its uncommitted competitors.

McNulty is also concerned about the management organization of Emblem. When he took over, the organization was small and he could comfortably "wear many hats," ranging from technician to decision maker, without great difficulty. But Emblem has grown at an average rate of 20 percent per year in terms of total dollar volume, and in the hectic process of engineering this accomplishment McNulty did not give much thought to establishing a line of management succession. He has recently brought in Joe Green and intends to groom him as his second man. Green has been with the firm only a short time but has a sound background in the technical aspects of dairy manufacturing. While he shows promise, it is too early to judge how he would handle major management responsibilities.

Assume that you were invited by McNulty to advise him on the development of his growth policy. What factors would you take into account in your analysis? To provide you with a data base, we present annual balance sheets and operating statements for Emblem for the years 1954 through 1966 in tables 27 and 28.

*Balance Sheets and Operating Statements for
Emblem Dairy Corporation*

Table 27. Balance sheets for Emblem Dairy Corporation, 1954-1966

	1954	1955	1956	1957	1958
ASSETS					
Current Assets					
Cash on hand and in banks	$481.99	$1,702.61	$41,276.40	$237.00	$830.05
Accounts receivable	26,306.28	53,259.24	65,933.61	71,009.81	155,940.74
Trust funds, patrons overdrafts, etc.	6.88	538.78	156.31	939.52	1,094.84
Notes and other receivables	..	..	5,716.56	13,388.03	11,592.90
Inventories	15,175.88	50,347.56	35,939.73	134,537.27	130,572.49
Prepaid insurance	718.14	589.60	2,381.84	2,669.28	3,323.85
Total Current Assets	42,689.17	106,437.79	151,404.45	222,780.91	303,354.87
Long-Term Investments					
Stocks	14,467.80	15,288.13	15,525.56	15,742.18	19,440.44
Prepaid Assets				1,485.43	2,330.19
Total Long-Term Investments	14,467.80	15,288.13	15,525.56	17,227.61	21,770.63
Fixed Assets					
Land and buildings	105,457.71	104,483.05	106,865.57	211,322.99	244,455.67
Equipment	90,063.51	99,251.70	186,766.82	259,728.41	252,664.13
Trucks and tanks	10,549.12	23,293.41	38,402.60	39,324.46	32,521.21
Subtotal	206,070.34	227,028.16	332,034.99	510,375.86	529,641.01
Less: Accumulated depreciation	61,176.97	69,272.21	55,563.66	71,371.85	87,829.68
Total Fixed Assets	144,893.37	157,755.95	276,471.33	439,004.01	441,811.33
Goodwill	..	2,077.00	2,077.00	2,077.00	2,077.00
Total Assets	202,050.34	281,558.87	445,478.34	681,089.53	769,013.83
LIABILITIES					
Current Liabilities					
Total	52,040.81	110,784.54	133,577.92	166,834.98	203,042.31
Other Liabilities					
Total	..	..	..	6,822.58	7,077.87
Long-Term Liabilities					
Notes payable	13,100.00	15,926.86	50,715.74	161,923.70	136,671.70
Reserve for outstanding checks	587.61	587.61	610.14	610.14	31,620.12
Total Long-Term Liabilities	13,687.61	16,514.47	51,325.88	162,533.84	168,291.82
NET WORTH					
General reserve	20,544.17	20,349.27	20,349.27	20,349.27	20,349.27
Common stock	4,452.13	3,820.00	3,310.00	5,980.00	7,200.00
Preferred stock	75,100.00	75,100.00	155,034.00	181,600.00	181,600.00
Patron equities	36,225.62	54,990.59	81,881.27	136,968.86	181,452.56
Total Net Worth	136,321.92	154,259.86	260,574.54	344,898.13	390,601.83
TOTAL LIABILITIES AND NET WORTH	202,050.34	281,558.87	445,478.34	681,089.53	769,013.83

Table 28. Operating statements for Emblem Dairy Corporation, 1954-1966

	1954	1955	1956	1957	1958
SALES					
Dairy Products					
Returns from butter	$62,405.79	$116,945.94	$165,246.32	$834,682.49	$1,412,659.47
Returns from powder				577,617.75	652,516.42
Grade A milk				234,501.47	332,971.03
Other milk and cream sales	280,304.88	643,654.59	1,126,268.66	195,062.03	622,301.00
Total Sales	342,710.67	760,600.53	1,291,514.98	1,841,863.74	2,460,377.02
Cost of Milk Purchased	302,047.21	654,782.34	1,138,908.77	1,521,662.80	2,063,672.61
Gross margin on dairy products	40,663.46	105,818.19	152,606.21	320,200.94	396,704.41
Other Income	1,838.61	5,521.75	33,663.72	40,719.14	10,827.63
Gross Margin on Operations	42,502.07	111,339.94	186,269.93	360,920.08	407,532.04
EXPENSES					
Manufacturing	26,016.93	63,108.57	108,759.50	181,737.90	245,547.64
General and Administrative	11,416.37	27,206.40	47,631.95	114,840.41	110,935.84
NET MARGIN	5,068.77	21,024.97	29,878.48	64,341.77	51,048.56

Financial Problems in the Growing Firm 203

Table 27 — Continued

1959	1960	1961	1962	1963	1964	1965	1966
$8,718.70	$13,584.09	$10,049.67	$2,027.77	$61,829.11	$251,053.35	$180,293.24	$120,312.75
145,301.88	92,157.16	191,185.62	237,660.68	281,124.74	319,952.55	520,182.78	438,336.83
62,099.77	32,606.36	18,529.99	15,613.69	5,419.43	27,077.92	6,055.30	..
3,034.05	14,581.05	18,984.33	42,515.12	20,128.40	9,851.61	2,718.74	3,877.24
87,704.32	154,949.36	248,057.14	289,681.42	184,640.73	455,518.28	451,547.61	881,710.76
3,026.10	3,455.62	3,214.00	3,383.24	3,761.30	8,317.87	3,650.43	6,642.35
309,884.82	311,333.64	490,020.75	590,881.92	556,903.71	1,071,771.58	1,164,448.10	1,450,879.93
21,324.73	24,300.04	23,733.74	17,410.03	11,625.15	12,019.85	36,490.76	82,732.38
3,692.15	5,064.18	7,334.61	10,255.33	12,492.54	14,726.10	..	7,000.00
25,016.88	29,364.22	31,068.35	27,665.36	24,117.69	26,745.95	36,490.76	89,732.38
244,291.07	244,291.07	279,387.62	307,070.91	315,419.15	392,101.33	452,020.98	726,541.03
246,720.19	330,473.22	443,159.24	432,821.51	437,944.63	654,016.88	1,097,994.30	1,508,787.88
20,660.78	18,559.36	18,559.36	13,940.80	35,552.37	123,176.38	181,453.59	244,126.77
511,672.04	593,323.65	741,106.22	753,833.22	788,916.15	1,169,294.59	1,731,468.87	2,479,455.68
94,139.15	121,173.81	152,190.93	161,271.74	208,206.37	281,816.00	395,345.11	496,825.93
417,532.89	472,149.84	588,915.29	592,561.48	580,709.78	887,478.59	1,336,123.76	1,982,629.75
752,434.59	812,847.70	1,110,004.39	1,211,108.76	1,161,731.18	1,985,996.12	2,537,062.62	3,523,242.06
156,528.67	201,820.53	370,370.57	477,192.04	390,395.00	900,859.65	975,724.86	1,405,579.42
11,355.44	13,189.31	..	..	..	..	..	..
116,800.00	93,892.00	132,932.00	45,375.00	2,195.00	254,695.00	654,795.00	1,026,095.00
25,966.41	1,220.28	1,256.28	1,420.96	1,420.96	1,420.96	1,952.53	2,376.24
142,766.41	95,112.28	134,188.28	46,795.96	3,615.96	256,115.96	656,747.53	1,028,471.24
20,349.27	20,349.27	20,349.27	25,842.40	25,842.40	25,842.40	26,977.87	26,977.87
4,860.00	4,990.00	4,530.00	6,360.00	6,680.00	6,040.00	9,620.00	11,520.00
181,400.00	166,500.00	199,800.00	202,500.00	196,500.00	167,800.00	201,400.00	204,500.00
235,174.80	310,886.31	380,766.27	452,418.36	538,697.82	629,338.11	666,592.36	846,193.53
441,784.07	502,725.58	605,445.54	687,120.76	767,720.22	829,020.51	904,590.23	1,089,191.40
752,434.59	812,847.70	1,110,004.39	1,211,108.76	1,161,731.18	1,985,996.12	2,537,062.62	3,523,242.06

Table 28 — Continued

1959	1960	1961	1962	1963	1964	1965	1966
$1,434,519.33	$1,633,616.93	$2,238,343.37	$3,232,602.48	$3,418,501.30	$4,129,934.41	$6,803,190.52	$7,641,251.24
720,670.82	843,108.48	1,235,188.44	1,676,609.75	1,576,949.73	1,928,608.98	3,093,313.10	3,577,585.17
328,169.61	331,321.12	356,598.19	302,220.08	223,949.73	223,198.96	205,084.65	188,498.06
47,333.77	204,777.40	76,517.98	69,940.00	78,881.36	341,959.87	169,109.94	102,318.65
2,530,693.53	3,012,823.93	3,906,647.98	5,281,372.31	5,298,282.12	6,623,702.22	10,270,698.21	11,509,653.12
2,183,712.19	2,665,638.76	3,445,655.74	4,714,016.52	4,695,251.20	5,934,301.89	9,225,235.23	10,224,210.41
346,981.34	347,185.17	460,992.24	567,355.79	603,030.92	689,400.33	1,045,462.98	1,285,442.71
37,794.58	40,734.86	19,734.53	31,348.91	11,905.60	25,528.80	50,144.00	82,614.96
384,775.92	387,920.03	480,726.77	598,704.70	614,936.52	714,929.13	1,095,606.98	1,368,057.67
235,882.68	211,519.70	289,263.42	357,922.76	361,035.32	442,998.20	733,414.96	854,767.24
86,968.53	78,790.21	100,767.43	144,581.14	145,403.93	164,592.04	275,623.23	320,196.38
61,924.71	97,610.12	90,695.92	96,200.80	108,497.27	107,338.89	86,568.79	193,094.05

Suggested Readings

Hunt, Pearson, Charles M. Williams, and Gordon Donaldson. *Basic Business Finance*, third edition. Homewood, Ill.: Richard D. Irwin, Inc., 1966, p. 588–606.

Johnson, Robert W. *Financial Management*, third edition. Boston: Allyn and Bacon, Inc., 1966, p. 651–665.

Moeller, Robert J., and Frank J. Smith, Jr. *Financial Analysis and Control of the Farm Supply Business*. Agricultural Extension Service, University of Minnesota, Special Report 17, September 1965.

Mueller, Willard F. *The Role of Mergers in the Growth of Agricultural Cooperatives*. California Agricultural Experiment Station Bulletin 777, February 1961, p. 23–25.

Neuman, William H. *Administrative Action*. Englewood Cliffs, N.J.: Prentice-Hall, Inc., 1961, p. 240.

Northeast Extension Marketing Association. *Appraising the Problems and Opportunities of Mergers*. College Park, Md.: University of Maryland Extension Service, April 1965.

Segall, Joel, and William W. Alberts. *The Corporate Merger*. Chicago: University of Chicago Press, 1966.

Thor, Eric, Miriam Revzan, and Adrian O. Hutchens. *A Guide to Procedures Leading to the Consolidation of Agricultural Marketing Cooperatives*. Berkeley, Calif.: Agricultural Extension Service, 1967, p. 58–60.

Weston, J. Fred, and Eugene Brigham. *Managerial Finance*, revised edition. New York: Holt, Rinehart, and Winston, 1966, p. 632–642, 659–692, 790–802.

Wyatt, Arthur R. *A Critical Study of Accounting for Business Combination*. New York: American Institute of Certified Public Accountants, 1963.

Additional Suggested Readings

An Analysis of Environmental and Managerial Factors in the Success or Failure of Small Manufacturing Enterprise. Small Business Management Research Reports, 1963.

Andersen, R. Clifton, and Charles M. Hewitt. *Management and Financial Control for Oil Jobbers.* Small Business Management Research Report, 1961.

Childress, Russell L. *Fiscal Control in Food Retailing.* Small Business Management Research Report A-32, 1964.

Dickens, Robert L. *Management Accounting for Frozen Food Locker and Related Plants.* Washington, D.C.: U.S. Department of Agriculture, Farmer Cooperative Service, 1961.

Engberg, Russell C. *Financing Farmer Cooperatives.* Bank for Cooperatives, 1965.

Gardner, Kelsey B., and Anne L. Gessner. *Trends in Growth of Farmer Cooperatives, 1950-60.* U.S. Department of Agriculture, Farmer Cooperative Service General Report 110, 1963.

Gessner, Anne L. *Statistics of Farmer Cooperatives, 1961-1962.* U.S. Department of Agriculture, Farmer Cooperative Service General Report 119, 1964.

Glass, Max R., and Albert J. Ortego, Jr. *An Analysis of Financial Statements of Virginia's Retail Farm Equipment Business.* Blacksburg, Va.: Virginia Polytechnic Institute, Virginia Agricultural Experiment Station, Technical Bulletin 168, 1964.

Griffin, Nelda. *Financial Structure of Regional Farm Supply Cooperatives.* U.S. Department of Agriculture, Farmer Cooperative Service General Report 124, 1965.

Grimes, Glenn, and Charles Cramer. *Missouri Livestock Auction Markets Operating Costs and Returns.* University of Missouri Extension Division, C-833/2, 665/m, 1966.

———. *Operating Costs and Returns.* Missouri Livestock Auction Markets, 1966.

Handbook on Major Regional Cooperatives Handling Supplies, 1962-1963. U.S. Department of Agriculture, Farmer Cooperative Service General Report 125, 1965.

Improved Methods of Financing Dairy Cooperatives. Washington, D.C.: Ernst & Ernst.

Managerial Controls for More Profit. Proceedings of the 1964 Grain and Feed Management Conference, Kansas State University, 1964.

Mather, J. Warren. *Major Regional Cooperatives Handling Supplies, 1962-1963.* U.S. Department of Agriculture, Farmer Cooperative Service General Report 125, 1965.

McKeever, John L. *A Study of the Problems of Small Retailers in Wyoming.* Small Business Management Research Reports, 1960.

Mitton, W. E. "An Economic Analysis of Sidelines in Country Grain Elevators." Unpublished Master's Thesis, Department of Agricultural Economics, University of Minnesota, 1960, 112 pages.

Moeller, Robert J., and Frank J. Smith, Jr. *Financial Analysis and Control of the Farm Supply Business.* University of Minnesota Special Report 17, 1965.

Operating Cost Ratio Report. Washington, D.C.: Ernst & Ernst.

Rosenberger, Stanley E. *Operational Analysis of Independent Florida Garden Supply Businesses, 1964.* University of Florida Economic Series 65-7, 1965.

Roy, E. P., and B. E. Williamson. *The Retail Farm Supply Business in Louisiana.* Washington, D.C.: Louisiana State University in Cooperation with the Small Business Administration, Department of Agricultural Economics and Agribusiness, Bulletin No. 570, 1963.

Smith, Frank J., Jr., and James Gresham. *Budgeting for the Farm Supply Business.* University of Minnesota Special Report 18, 1965.

Storey, D. A., and R. A. Gillfillan. *Illinois Country Grain Elevator Financial Organization and Operation.* University of Illinois Agricultural Experiment Station Bulletin 702, 1964.

Summary of Comparative Costs of Operations and Balance Sheet Ratios. Cooperative Auditing Service, Inc., Vol. 3, second series.

Summary of Comparative Costs of Operations, Marketing Returns and Balance Sheet Ratios. Cooperative Auditing Service, Inc., Vol. 4, second series.

The Structure and Economic Significance of the Canning Industry. Division of Statistics and Economics, 1963.

Traylor, Harlon D., and Bernis E. Williamson. *The Local Grain Elevator Business in Louisiana.* Louisiana State University Bulletin 573, 1963.

Wallace, William H. *Use of Financial Records in Small Food Stores.* University of Rhode Island Circular 149–4.

Westerhold, R. W., and D. I. Padberg. *Trends in Size, Specialization and Profitability of Elevators in Western Ohio.* Ohio Agricultural Research and Development Center Research Bulletin 978, 1966.

INDEX

Accounts payable, 29
  discount terms, 29

Accounts receivable:
  analyzing impacts on sales and profits, 34, 40–42
  as a competitive device, 33
  collection of, 44–45
  convenience aspects of, 33
  trade credit analysis, 39–45
  trade credit to whom, 42–44

Accrued liabilities:
  defined, 28
  management of, 28–29

Acid test ratio, 156

Amortized loan:
  effective cost of, 90
  illustration of, 89–90

Analyzing investment proposals, 50
  new, 61–64
  replacement, 64–69
  service, 69

Assets:
  debt holder claims on, 86
  preferred holder claims on, 87
  residual claims on, 87
  turnover, 149–150, 151

Balance sheet:
  approach to source and use analysis, 9-20
    identifying changes in capital composition, 10–13
    identifying working capital position, 15, 17
    projecting financial needs, 13–15
  pro forma, 140–143
  ways of changing composition of, 16

Bibliography; see suggested readings.
  Additional readings, 205–206

Bierman and Smidt, 66, 77

Bonds:
  debenture, 86
  mortgage, 86
  sinking funds for, 85

Book value, 191

Break-even analysis, 127–136
  appraisal of, 135–136
  operating leverage illustrated, 132–135
  profit planning, 130–132

Budgeting:
  capital, 49–107
    maximizing returns on, 49–80
    minimizing cost of, 83–107
  cash, 137–140
  cost, 123–125
  profit, 122–127, 126

Call feature, 86

Capital:
  cost of, 83–107
  effect of financial leverage on cost of, 101–104
  structure, 83, 100, 101, 103

Capital gains:
  impact on capital costs, 95–96

Case problem, 197–203

Cash:
  budget, 137–140
  management of, 34–36

Cash flow; see fund flows

Collection procedures, 44–45

Compound interest:
  computation of, 53–54

Contribution margin:
  defined, 120, 131
  illustrated, 119–120

Control, financial analysis and, 147–181

207

Control system:
  control points, 147–148, 164, 180–181
  essentials of, 163
  example of, 163–181
  problems of implementation, 165–166
Cost of capital, 83–107
  leverage impacts on, 101–104
  methods of measuring, 89–101
  preferred stock, 90–91
  quality considerations, 84–89
  residual equity, 91–96
  term loans, 89–90
Costs:
  accounting, 117
  allocation of overhead, 118, 121, 124
  analysis of, 117
  concepts of, 117
  direct, 121
  fixed, 119
  opportunity, 118–119, 52
  variable, 119
Credit:
  as sales device, 33
  collection of receivables, 44–45
  convenience aspects of, 33
  discounts, 29–30
  impacts on sales and profits illustrated, 34, 40–42
  to whom granted, 42–44
Cumulative rights, 86
Current ratio, 156
Dean, Joel, 118
Debt; see also fixed payment obligations
  cost of, 89–90
  effect on cost of capital, 89, 90, 100
  incidence of risk, 85, 86
  short- and long-term defined, 85
Depreciation:
  as a source of funds, 19–20
  defined, 19
  impact on taxes, 62–63
Dilution, 85, 88, 93
Discounted cash flow:
  background and mechanics, 52–61

Discounted internal rate of return:
  computation of, 57–61
Discounts:
  as an inducement for early payment, 29
  calculation of savings from, 30
Dividends:
  impact on capital costs, 94
Dun and Bradstreet:
  key business ratios, 154–155
DuPont chart: relationship of factors affecting return on investment, 151
Earnings:
  capitalized, 193–196
  debt holder claims on, 86
  impact on capital costs, 93–94
  on assets, 151, 152
  on equity capital, 101, 103, 152
  on sales, 152
  preferred holder claims on, 86
  residual claims on, 86
Economic value and time:
  concept of, 52
  mechanics of, 52–61
  present value, 52–57
  rate of return, discounted internal, 57–61
Equity capital:
  cost of in cooperatives, 97–99
  cost of in proprietary corporations, 92–97
    common stock, 93–94
    preferred stock, 90–91
    retained earnings, 95–96
External investment opportunities:
  as a measure of cost of retained earnings, 96
Finance function:
  defined, 2
  performed by, 3
Financial leverage:
  favorable, 101–103
  unfavorable, 103–104
Financial objectives, 3–4
Financial structure, 83, 100, 101, 103

Fixed payment obligations:
  effective cost of, 89–91
Forecasting:
  balance sheets, pro forma, 140–143
  cash budgets, 137–140
  profits, 122–127
  sales, 113–117
Fund flows:
  balance sheet approach to, 9–19
  concept of sources and uses, 7–9
  management of long-term, 49–80, 83–107
  managing short-term, 23–45
Fund statement:
  examples of, 11, 12, 13, 17
Garoian and Haseley, 1, 85
Gross margin:
  measurement of, 153, 167–168
Growth:
  financial problems of, 190–196
  methods of, 188–190
Growth model, 94
Helfert, Erich, 68
Income; see earnings
Income statement; see operating statements
Interest:
  compound interest computation, 56
  daily interest calculation, 25
  effective rate of, 89–90
  simple interest computation, 52–53
  tax deductability advantage of, 87, 89, 90, 102
Inventory management, 31–33
  economic order quantity, 32
Investment analysis:
  objectives of, 50
  new, 61–64
  replacement, 64–69
  service, 69
Investment cutoff point; see cost of capital
Johnson, Robert W., 3, 8

Leasing:
  as a source of funds, 105–107
  lease or buy illustrations, 106–107
Leverage:
  financial, 101–104
  operating, 132–135
Levin and Kirkpatrick, 31
Liquidation value, 192
Liquidity, 155
  defined, 155
  ratios, 155
Management of long-term funds:
  maximizing returns, 49–80
  minimizing the cost of capital, 83–107
Managing short-term funds:
  elements of efficient liquidity, 23–28
  optimizing working capital sectors, 28–36
  short-term uses from long-term sources, 36–37
Market value, 193
Moeller and Smith, 163
Mueller, William F., 186, 188
Net earnings; see profit forecasting
Net investment:
  defined, 50–51
Net present value:
  illustrated, 62, 64–65, 67
Net working capital:
  defined, 16, 23
New equity:
  cost of, 93–94
New investment decision:
  illustrated, 61–62
Newman, William H., 163
Noncash expenses as a source of funds, 105
Operating statement:
  profit forecast, 122–127

210 The Financial Management of Agribusiness Firms

Opportunity costs:
defined, 118–119, 52

Optimizing working capital sectors, 28–36

Overall cost of capital, 100–101

Payback approach:
limitations of, 69–70

Personal opportunity cost approach to estimating cost of retained earnings, 95

Planning, profit, 111–112

Preemptive rights, 85, 87–88

Present value:
concept of, 52–57
discount factors, 75–76

Present-value tables, 55, 60

Price policy, profit-volume analysis, 130–132

Pro forma balance sheet, 140–143

Probability considerations in forecasting, 73–74

Problem sets, 21–22, 47–48, 81, 109, 145–146, 183–184

Product mix analysis, 120–122

Profit forecast, 122–127

Profit objectives in focus, 3–4
adaptation to cooperatives, 4

Profit planning, 111–112
benefits from, 112–113

Profitability:
measures of, 149–155

Ranking investment proposals, 76–78

Rate of return:
discounted internal, 57–61
simple, 70–71

Ratio analysis, 148–162
common size statements, 160–161
commonly used ratios, 149–162
efficiency ratios, 158–160
liquidity ratios, 155–157

profitability ratios, 149–155
solvency ratios, 157–158

Receivables; see accounts receivable

Replacement investment decisions:
illustrated, 64–69

Replacement value, 192

Residual equity:
proprietary corporations, 92–97
cooperatives, 97–99

Retained earnings:
cost of, 95–99

Return, minimum rate of; see cost of capital

Return, rate of:
discounted internal, 57–61
simple, 70–71

Risk:
acceptable level of, 76
related to financial leverage, 103–104
related to operating leverage, 132–135

Sales volume forecasting, 113–117

Securities, quality features, 85, 84–89

Seiden, Martin H., 39

Simple interest, 52–53

Sinking fund, 85

Solomon, Ezra, 94, 96

Solomon, Martin B., 68, 69

Solvency:
defined, 157
ratios, 157

Sources and uses of funds:
balance sheet approach to, 9–19
concept of, 7–9

Stock:
cost of new common, 94
cost of old common, 93
cost of preferred, 90–91

Subordinated claims, 86

Suggested readings, 6, 20, 45–46, 80, 107–108, 143–144, 182, 204

Sunk costs:
in relation to replacement investment decisions, 51, 67

Target rate; see cost of capital

Taxes:
impact of depreciation on, 62–63
interest deductibility feature of debt, 89–90, 102

Terborgh, George, 68

Term loans:
effective interest cost of, 89–90

Thor, Revzan, Hutchens, 196

Time value of money; see relation of economic value and time

Trade accounts payable:
savings from discounts, 30

Trade credit:
analysis of, 39–45

Turnover of assets, 149, 150, 151

Turnover of inventory, 158

Uncertainty problem:
dealing with, 71
probability of outcomes, 74

Valuation, methods of, 191
book value, 191
capitalized earnings, 193
liquidation value, 192
market value, 192
problems of in merger, 191
replacement value, 192

Volkin and Neely, 92

Voting rights, 87

Weston and Brigham, 94

Willson and Smith, 147

Working capital accounts identified, 23

Working capital, net:
defined, 15, 23
illustration, 17

Working capital sectors, optimizing, 28–36

Printed in the United States
22891LVS00003B/199